MW01049757

Phoenix Claws and Jade Trees

Phoenix Claws and Jade Trees

Essential Techniques of Authentic Chinese Cooking

———

Kian Lam Kho

PHOTOGRAPHS BY JODY HORTON

CLARKSON POTTER/PUBLISHERS
NEW YORK

To Warren
for believing in me and
supporting me ceaselessly

Published in the United States by
Clarkson Potter/Publishers, an
imprint of the Crown Publishing
Group, a division of Penguin
Random House LLC, New York.
www.crownpublishing.com
www.clarksonpotter.com

CLARKSON POTTER is a
trademark and POTTER with
colophon is a registered trademark
of Penguin Random House LLC.

Library of Congress Cataloging-in-
Publication Data
Kho, Kian Lam.
   Phoenix claws and jade trees :
essential techniques of authentic
Chinese cooking / Kian Lam Kho ;
photographs by Jody Horton. —
First edition.
      pages cm
   Includes bibliographical
references and index.
   1. Cooking, Chinese. I. Title.
   TX724.5.C5K485 2015
   641.5951—dc23

2014046694

ISBN 978-0-385-34468-5
eBook ISBN 978-0-385-34469-2

Printed in Dubai

Book design by Jan Derevjanik
Cover design by Jan Derevjanik
Cover photographs by Jody Horton
Prop styling by Johanna Lowe
Food styling by Suzanne Lenzer

10 9 8 7 6 5 4

First Edition

CONTENTS

INTRODUCTION

Phoenix claws and jade trees are poetic metonyms, or metaphorical substitutions, you'll find on many Chinese restaurant menus. "Phoenix claw" (鳳爪) is a synonym for chicken feet, and "jade tree" (玉樹) is used for *gailan*, or Chinese broccoli. To most Chinese diners, this is familiar terminology, and I grew up learning it naturally at daily meals. But for many Westerners, authentic Chinese cuisine remains just out of reach linguistically and geographically. Yet with so many ingredients readily available and a wok just one click away online, it's time to extend these thrilling and transportive flavors to eager home cooks everywhere.

In this book I demystify Chinese cooking by taking a unique approach. I believe that the cuisine is easiest to learn by technique. A dry stir-fry is no more difficult to prepare than a moist one; the key is to know which technique to use for which ingredient and for which final result. Armed with this knowledge, you can not only re-create dishes from all over China and many East Asian countries, but you can cook almost any ingredient in any fashion you'd like. If you discover you love dry stir-fry with leeks and you are wild about duck, you can combine the two to make a successful Chinese dish all your own.

As China opens up to the world, her emigrants bring many regional cooking traditions to their adopted countries. They introduce new ingredients and open restaurants to satisfy their longing for food from home. At the same time, Western expatriates flock to China as companies from all over the world scramble to do business there. After short stints in China they return home, yearning to re-create the incredible array of food they experienced abroad.

This confluence of immigration and business travel creates new demands and sets higher standards for authentic Chinese food outside China. No longer are we satisfied with Beef with Broccoli and General Tso's Chicken. We now demand Xinjiang Lamb Burgers and Lan Zhou Pulled Noodles. From New York to Melbourne, people are curious about authentic Chinese food.

My own experience of cooking Chinese food in America parallels the narrative of these new Chinese immigrants. Arriving in America from Singapore in the 1970s to attend university in Boston, I longed for the abundance of wonderful food from home. At that time most restaurants in town were still serving up chop suey and other substandard Cantonese fare. My only defense against bad Chinese food was to cook at home. Unable to find a good Chinese cookbook, I resorted to writing home to my aunts and other relatives for instructions and recipes.

Over the years I mastered techniques and developed recipes that helped me in my kitchen. I found that by taking one technique and switching up the ingredients, I could make an entirely new dish typical of a different region. Once I had the many methods under my belt, I could make almost anything. I hope this book will help illuminate fundamental Chinese cooking methods for the Western cook and make this fascinating cuisine practical to prepare at home.

Thus, the chapters here are organized according to cooking methods rather than the usual division by ingredients or region. Some techniques are defined by heat sources. Cooking with oil, for example, is divided into five techniques: light frying, deep-frying, oil steeping, yin-yang frying, and pan-frying. The procedures are different but all use oil as the heat medium. This approach can greatly facilitate the learning of a cuisine by identifying similarities and differences among related techniques.

Although the preparation methods outlined in this book are based on a comprehensive set of Chinese

SHARING A MEAL

Sharing a meal is still considered the ultimate sign of pride and respect in Chinese families. Special celebrations, such as major birthdays and weddings, are elaborate and can consist of ten to twelve courses accompanied by the best rice wine and the most expensive tea. Truly extravagant banquets are regularly hosted by the upper echelon of Chinese government officials and industry tycoons.

The main components of a Chinese meal are set by a long-standing tradition. The Chinese term for aliment, or food, is *yinshi* (飲食), which literally translates as "drink" and "food." The *yin* (飲) refers to all sorts of drinks including tea, wine, and brewed herbs, whereas the *shi* (食) consists of *fan* (飯) and *shan* (饍). *Fan* represents a group of foods made from grain, and *shan* comprises all the wonderful dishes made from meat and vegetables. A Chinese meal is almost always made up of these three components of *yinshi*. This sense of balance continues into our modern era and is reflected in both daily family meals and gala banquets.

The grain food in a Chinese meal covers a wide assortment of dishes, from steamed white rice and fried rice to steamed bread, noodles, and dumplings.

(Noodles, dumplings, steamed cakes, and pancakes are primarily considered snack foods and form a distinct branch of Chinese cooking known as *dianxin* [點心] in Mandarin or as *dimsum* in Cantonese. An entire separate realm of cooking with specific techniques and dining rituals has evolved around them and currently exists in all regions of China. As such, these dishes are beyond the scope of this book.)

Traditionally, there will be one dish per person at a meal and all the dishes are shared. For a basic meal for two, the menu usually consists of a meat (or other protein) dish and a vegetable dish served with a simple starch. For a family of four, the menu would be expanded to four dishes with the inclusion of a soup or a cold dish. Banquet menus often feature more dishes than diners—but with smaller portions.

A distinct difference between traditional Chinese and Western eating habits is the concept of dessert. This end-of-meal indulgence is not part of the Chinese tradition. Still, this doesn't mean that Chinese people do not enjoy sweet dishes, which are often served with savory dishes to balance them. It is, however, common to end a meal with fresh fruit.

cooking techniques, I have kept the home cook in mind and have thus omitted some seldom-used ones. Many of these omitted techniques simply put too fine a point on a general method. For example, pan-frying in Chinese can be minutely defined in three ways: *jian* (煎), *tie* (貼), and *ta* (塌), depending on whether the ingredient is fried whole, cut into pieces, or covered in batter. Since the technique is fundamentally the same, I combine them into pan-frying.

The recipes include many classic home-style and restaurant dishes, appropriate for everyday family meals as well as elaborate banquets. They illustrate the cooking techniques rather than a specific regional cuisine, though the region where each recipe originated is identified when appropriate.

A fundamental Chinese cookbook would not be complete without references to history and culture. You'll find a discussion of regional flavors as well as sections on dining customs, pantry ingredients, and kitchen tools. I also include common ingredient preparation and knife techniques. If you are already familiar with Chinese food, you may choose to skip these sections. They can, however, be entertaining reading while you wait for your braised chicken to cook.

Be adventurous with the techniques and ingredients you'll find in these pages. Don't be daunted by the technical details. They are there to help you to understand the theory and allow you to be creative. Above all, have fun learning the world of classic Chinese cooking.

CHAPTER ONE

The Essence of Chinese Food

VERY FEW PEOPLE THINK OF EUROPEAN CUISINE AS A SINGLE ENTITY. When one thinks of French cooking, the first thing that comes to mind is complex sauces enveloping delicately prepared ingredients. With Italian cooking it may be pasta topped with fresh and bright flavors, conjuring up images of leisurely al fresco dining along the Mediterranean coast. Think Scandinavia and think of pickled herring. China is as geographically expansive and culturally diverse as Europe. Regional cuisines abound, and every part of the country has its own unique culinary traditions and customs. To understand Chinese cooking, you need to understand the history and diversity of its different regions.

Throughout its long history, Chinese culinary culture has been molded by many different factors other than its vast geography. Many Westerners have an image of China as insular, but in reality it has been greatly affected by foreign imports. Chinese food is cosmopolitan by nature because of the nation's thriving trade with many foreign lands. Arab traders along the Silk Road imported exotic ingredients like the pomegranate and cooking methods such as meat grilling. Chinese seafaring traders brought back highly prized seafood such as sea cucumber and shark fin from the warm waters of Southeast Asia and the Indian Ocean. Portuguese merchants introduced peanuts, chiles, and potatoes from South America. Many of these imports are now so integral to regional Chinese cooking that we almost forget that they are in fact not native to that part of the world.

Religion also played a big part in shaping Chinese cuisine. Buddhism, the predominant religion in China, developed a separate school of vegetarian cooking over the years. Vegetarian meals are served in Buddhist temples and consumed by observant believers at home. To appeal to laypeople, special ingredients like tofu skin were created to imitate meat products.

REGIONAL CHINESE CUISINE

During the mid-19th century, Chinese culinary scholars identified eight regional cuisines as the most important. Among them Guangdong (or Cantonese 廣東), Sichuan (四川), and Hunan (湖南) are the ones most familiar outside of China. The other less-known cuisines include Fujian (福建), Shandong (山東), Anhui (安徽), Jiangsu (江蘇), and Zhejiang (浙江).

But these culinary scholars included only the cuisine of the majority Han people and ignored that of China's hundreds of minority peoples, who are widely scattered around the western and southwestern fringes of the country. The cooking in Tibet (西藏), Lanzhou (蘭州), Yunnan (雲南), and Xinjiang (新疆) is still not familiar to most Han Chinese today.

The Birth of China's Culinary Culture

Smack in the middle of China, located mostly in present Henan (河南) province in the fertile Yellow River basin, also known as the Central Plain (中原), is the cradle of the Chinese civilization, which developed during the Stone Age. It was here that the earliest Chinese dynasties built their government seats and where archeologists found the first evidence of cooking. Over time, after the Ming Dynasty and the Central Plain declined in importance, the political and commercial centers shifted toward the coastal regions. But culinary historians cite the cuisine of the Central Plain as the mother of all Chinese cooking.

Known as Yu (豫) cuisine in Chinese, it developed over more than three thousand years, from the earliest known Chinese dynasty. Large quantities of steaming and boiling vessels have been found in many archeological sites, indicating that these cooking techniques were developed in this area. Excavated tomb records also show a wide array of meats, vegetables, fruits, and grains used as ingredients.

Additionally, some contemporary culinary scholars consider the cooking of Beijing and Shanghai to be unique cuisines. To a degree this makes sense, since each of these metropolises absorbed many neighboring regions' cooking customs to make something new. What is evident, though, is that Chinese cooking defies stereotyping and that its underlying unity amid such diversity makes it one of the most fascinating foods in the world.

GUANGDONG CUISINE | 粤 YUE OR CANTONESE

When Westerners think of Chinese food, the first regional cuisine that comes to mind is Cantonese cooking, which Chinese immigrants, a majority of whom were originally from Guangdong province, brought to their adopted countries during the 19th century.

Cantonese cooking is one of the most refined and celebrated cuisines in China. A popular refrain pronounces that a good life is to "be born in Suzhou, dress in Hangzhou, dine in Guangzhou, and die in Liuzhou," referring to the many beauties in Suzhou, brilliant silk in Hangzhou, sumptuous food in Guangzhou, and durable camphor wood for coffins in Liuzhou.

Like all southern coastal Chinese cooking, Guangdong cuisine takes advantage of abundant fresh local ingredients, which make it possible to create simple dishes that highlight their natural essence. As a result, Guangdong dishes are often not very spicy. Steaming, quick stir-frying, barbecuing, braising, and soup making are several signature techniques of Guangdong cuisine.

Yet Guangdong cuisine is not just simply traditional Chinese. The Pearl River Delta area of the province, anchored by Guangzhou (廣州 Canton), was the first region sanctioned by the Qing Dynasty imperial court, during the late 17th century, to

THE BANQUET

In 1972 President Richard M. Nixon made a historic visit to China. Americans watched intently on television as President Nixon attended a state banquet at The Great Hall of the People in Beijing. The sumptuous scene was alluring in spite of the fact that the meal, in comparison to modern celebratory banquets, was rather proletarian. Still, it was a great representation of how the Chinese show hospitality to their guests.

The structure of a formal Chinese banquet has changed very little since the early Han Dynasty during the second century BCE.

1. Wine is served to welcome the guests.

2. Geng (羹), which historians believe was a large pot of braised meat, is served after all the guests are seated.

3. Other dishes such as grilled, steamed, and pickled foods follow.

4. Some kind of grain dish such as bread, rice, or porridge is served next.

5. Fruit is served to end the formal meal.

6. After-dinner drinks can be offered, accompanied by dried and cured meat or fish.

A modern banquet follows this general outline, but with some adaptations. It usually starts with an assortment of cold dishes, followed by a series of main dishes that balance meats and vegetables. There's always a good variety of poultry, pork or beef, seafood, and vegetable courses. An elegant banquet will be sure to include sea cucumber, abalone, lobster, or turtle, while the truly extravagant banquet will use exotic ingredients such as camel hump or bird's nest. One of the main courses is usually a soup. A whole fish is always welcome and is traditionally served just before the grain course. If a dessert is served, it is usually offered with the fruit and is not considered a separate course. The number of courses in a banquet depends on the preferences of the host, but the number must always be even, with ten or twelve courses being the standard.

Planning the seating arrangement at a Chinese banquet is as important as planning the menu itself. The first recorded description of seating at a Chinese banquet appeared in the *Book of Han* (漢書), penned around the 1st century CE. Known as the Feast at Hong Gate (鴻門宴), this meal took place near modern Xi'an (西安) and involved two battling warlords fighting for supremacy of China during the interregnum period between the Qin and Han dynasties. Xiang Yu (項羽), the head of the Chu Kingdom (楚), hosted a banquet for Liu Bang (劉邦), the head of the Han Kingdom (漢), with the intention of assassinating him.

The seating arrangement was clearly described and gives us an insight into the importance rank played at banquets. Xiang Yu, the host, sat facing east, with the guest, Liu Bang, on his right facing north. Xiang Yu's advisor, Fan Zeng (范增), sat on the host's left facing south, and Liu Bang's advisor, Zhang Liang (張良), sat facing west. During the banquet Liu Bang distracted his hosts and managed to escape assassination. He went on to conquer the Chu Kingdom and establish the Han Dynasty, ushering in one of the greatest periods in Chinese history.

Seating arrangements in modern times follow the ancient example closely. Guests are seated according to their rank or importance. The host and the most important guest are usually seated at the head of the table, facing the main entrance of the dining hall, or, if no distinct entrance can be discerned, then facing east. The honored guest is always seated to the right of the host. Then to the left of the host, in descending order of importance, sit the second, fourth, and sixth most important guests. To the right of the honored guest the third, fifth, seventh most important guests are arranged. This pattern continues until all guests are seated. For family gatherings the order of importance is usually determined by the age of the guests. Nowadays, though, it is more common to seat the host and honored guest as in the traditional arrangement at the head spots and have the rest of the party sit wherever they choose.

be opened for trading with the outside world. As foreign traders arrived, they brought not only their merchandise but their culinary customs as well. Additionally, on the coastal edge of Guangdong province are two enclaves that were governed for many years by European colonial powers: Hong Kong, ruled by the British Empire, and Macao, administered by Portugal. Although they were returned to Chinese sovereignty during the waning years of the 20th century, the foodways of these two areas have been indelibly influenced by the foreign occupation.

In Hong Kong the Guangdong cooking traditions gradually absorbed Western ingredients and cooking methods. Examples include sweet-and-sour sauce that uses tomato ketchup, stir-fried sliced beefsteak flavored with steak sauce, and sweet custardy pastries. These dishes are found from the most formal banquet restaurants to the corner diner, or *cha chaan teng*.

Across the river in Macao, the Portuguese influence is even more dramatic. A distinct Macanese cuisine developed over three centuries, becoming a fusion of Portuguese, African, and Guangdong cooking. The use of tropical spices and ingredients such as turmeric, cinnamon, and coconut became part of everyday cooking. *Bacalhau* (salt cod) and cheeses were introduced into the regular diet. Many of these ingredients were brought from Portugal's far-flung colonies and from their trade in Africa, the Americas, and other parts of Asia. But the best known of Portuguese-influenced dishes would have to be the egg tart, now found at every dim sum restaurant all over the world. Few people realize that it is a version of the *pastéis de nata* that originated in Belém, outside of Lisbon.

FUJIAN CUISINE │ 閩 MIN

Although the people of Fujian province can trace their origins back to the Stone Age, the mass migrations of Han Chinese during the 4th and 10th centuries determined the cuisine of this region. The immigrants brought many condiments and cooking techniques from the highly developed cuisine of their native Central Plain. Adapting to the coastal environment, the Han started creating a distinct cuisine that is now known as Fujian, or Min, cooking.

Translated literally, *yuan zhi yuan wei* (原汁原味) means "original juice, original taste." As a common Chinese idiom it means "to cook plainly so as to retain the ingredient's original flavor." Fujian cooking is the poster child of this philosophy. Not widely known outside of Asia, Fujian cuisine is typical of the greater southern Chinese style of cooking and uses simple techniques and ingredients. Soup making and steaming are very common techniques in Fujian cooking, as they are terrific ways to prepare fresh ingredients while highlighting their natural flavors.

Across the southwest border between Fujian and Guangdong are two regions that claim a culinary culture more akin to Fujian than to their own province. One of them is Chaozhou (潮州), which is a coastal city abutting Fujian that has a distinct language and cultural tradition. It is thought that the Chaozhou area was established by settlers from southern Fujian who had originally migrated from the Central Plain. As the population grew, they developed their own distinct identity. Simple flavors and cooking techniques are also signatures of Chaozhou cooking, with steaming, braising, and stir-frying comprising the most common cooking methods. Chaozhou Flavor-Potted Goose (page 226) is an example of a fragrant braised dish. Steamed pompano, oyster omelets, and fish balls are common seafood preparations. A popular sweet dish made with mashed taro and lard, known as *yuni* (芋泥), is a favorite at many Chaozhou restaurants.

The second region covers a large swath north of Chaozhou that includes much of western Fujian, south of Jiangxi and the southeast corner of Hunan, where the Hakka (客家) people are scattered. Literally translated, *Hakka* means "guest people," a

China History Timeline

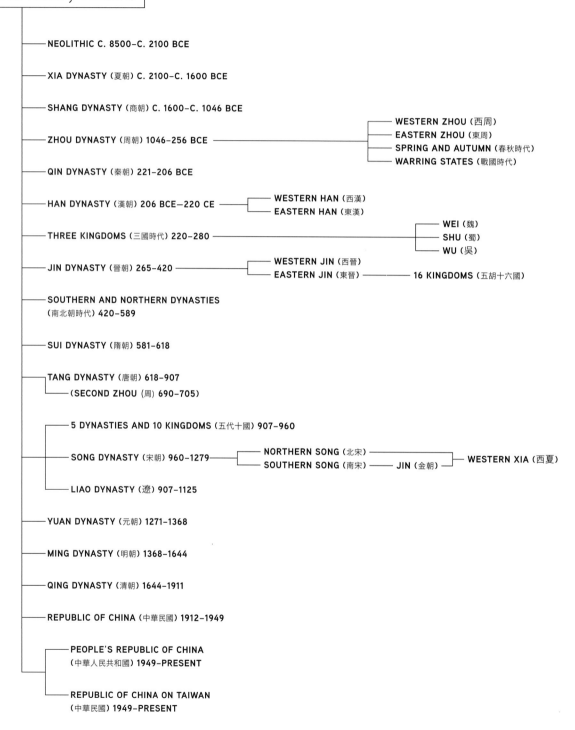

NEOLITHIC C. 8500–C. 2100 BCE

XIA DYNASTY (夏朝) C. 2100–C. 1600 BCE

SHANG DYNASTY (商朝) C. 1600–C. 1046 BCE

ZHOU DYNASTY (周朝) 1046–256 BCE
- WESTERN ZHOU (西周)
- EASTERN ZHOU (東周)
- SPRING AND AUTUMN (春秋時代)
- WARRING STATES (戰國時代)

QIN DYNASTY (秦朝) 221–206 BCE

HAN DYNASTY (漢朝) 206 BCE–220 CE
- WESTERN HAN (西漢)
- EASTERN HAN (東漢)

THREE KINGDOMS (三國時代) 220–280
- WEI (魏)
- SHU (蜀)
- WU (吳)

JIN DYNASTY (晉朝) 265–420
- WESTERN JIN (西晉)
- EASTERN JIN (東晉) — 16 KINGDOMS (五胡十六國)

SOUTHERN AND NORTHERN DYNASTIES (南北朝時代) 420–589

SUI DYNASTY (隋朝) 581–618

TANG DYNASTY (唐朝) 618–907
- (SECOND ZHOU (周) 690–705)

5 DYNASTIES AND 10 KINGDOMS (五代十國) 907–960

SONG DYNASTY (宋朝) 960–1279
- NORTHERN SONG (北宋)
- SOUTHERN SONG (南宋) — JIN (金朝) — WESTERN XIA (西夏)

LIAO DYNASTY (遼) 907–1125

YUAN DYNASTY (元朝) 1271–1368

MING DYNASTY (明朝) 1368–1644

QING DYNASTY (清朝) 1644–1911

REPUBLIC OF CHINA (中華民國) 1912–1949

PEOPLE'S REPUBLIC OF CHINA (中華人民共和國) 1949–PRESENT

REPUBLIC OF CHINA ON TAIWAN (中華民國) 1949–PRESENT

population that similarly migrated from the Central Plain to escape persecution but was never quite welcomed by the locals. The Hakka became nomads, only temporarily remaining in different towns and cities. Still, they were able to forge a unique cultural identity for themselves and created their own culinary tradition. As in the case of Chaozhou cooking, Hakka cuisine has been influenced by that of Fujian and similarly uses simple flavors and techniques. A signature dish of the Hakka is steam-braised pork belly with fermented dried mustard greens (page 267); it has become so popular that it can be found throughout southern China and in Hong Kong, Taiwan, and Southeast Asian countries. Other important culinary contributions by the Hakka include Steamed Stuffed Tofu (page 261), Salt-Baked Chicken (page 310), and Braised Chicken with Red Wine Lees (page 205).

Finally, on the island of Taiwan, the Fujian influence is even more noticeable. A large number of Han Chinese, who had been living in Fujian, began to settle the island at the height of the Qing Dynasty, around the 17th century, bringing the southern Fujian language, culture, and cuisine to the island. Modern Taiwanese cooking reflects the tumult of the 20th century. The culinary legacy of the Japanese occupation of Taiwan during the first half of the century includes grilling, rice balls, and other Japanese snacks. Separately, the removal of the Nationalist government from mainland China to Taiwan introduced a large population from all over the country, including Beijing, Shanghai, and the Sichuan, Hunan, and Shandong regions. Between the fall of the mainland to the Communists in 1949 and the economic reforms of the mid-1980s, Taiwan was the center of Chinese cuisine.

SICHUAN CUISINE ｜ 川 CHUAN

With its powerfully spicy ingredients, Sichuan cuisine is the total opposite of the cuisine of the southern coast of China. Introduced to the United States during the 1970s in New York City, the food's bold flavors found an immediate enthusiastic following. The spicy heat and the numbing sensation of Sichuan cuisine, known as *mala* (麻辣), can be utterly addictive.

During the Qin (秦) Dynasty, around the 2nd century BCE, the Central Plain's Han ruler annexed the region and the natives assimilated to the Han culture. Despite the two-thousand-year history of integration, Sichuan cooking is still influenced by the local minority's foodways: a diet tending toward spiciness thanks to the copious amount of subtropical spices of the region. These special tastes remain distinct from the rest of Chinese food even now.

The numbing and spicy hot flavors of Sichuan cooking come from Sichuan peppercorns and chiles. While Sichuan peppercorns are native to this region and have been used in the local cooking since the Western Han Dynasty, around the 2nd century BCE, chiles were not introduced until the Portuguese traders brought them to China from South America in the 17th century. The combination of these two spices is so compelling that it became the signature taste of Sichuan.

One of the best known dishes that uses this peppercorn-chile combination is Sichuan *mala* hot pot, whose deadly looking spicy red broth serves as the base for cooking all sorts of meats and vegetables. This dish, cooked in a fluted pot sitting on a small charcoal stove, has become so popular that it is now available everywhere in China; it is often served in a divided pot with the *mala* broth on one side and a mild chicken stock on the other. This double-broth hot pot is also known as the "Mandarin duck hot pot."

HUNAN CUISINE ｜ 湘 XIANG

Home of Mao Zedong and General Zuo Zhongtang (of General Tso's Chicken fame), Hunan is the source of one of the better-known Chinese cuisines in the United States and around the world. But in the West, Hunan cooking is often confused with Sichuan cooking. In China these two cuisines have very distinct characteristics. Whereas Sichuan is known for the hot and numbing sensation from dried chiles and Sichuan peppercorns, Hunan flavors are hot and sour from pickled chiles and pickled vegetables, made by letting brined fresh ingredients ferment naturally. This misperception has its roots in how the two cuisines were introduced to America.

During the 1940s a group of Chinese chefs trained in Hunan and Sichuan evacuated to Taiwan after the Communist takeover of mainland China. Some of these chefs prospered in Taiwan and sought opportunities in the United States during the 1970s. The dishes they introduced were adjusted to local tastes, resulting in an Americanized Sichuan/Hunan flavor consisting of spicy heat combined with strong fermented condiments.

One particular dish that's closely identified with Hunan restaurants of that era is General Tso's Chicken. It is now ubiquitous in takeout Chinese restaurants, but few people know that Chef Peng Chang-Kuei, who was the presidential palace chef of the Nationalist Government, invented this dish in Taiwan during the 1950s. Chef Peng was born in Hunan and had his culinary training there, so many of his dishes have a distinctive Hunan flavor (see page 173). Although the original General Tso's Chicken was close to the Hunan roots of spicy heat with tartness from black vinegar, the American version is considerably sweeter.

Hunan, along with many other southern regions of China, is known for producing excellent cured bacon and ham, two prized ingredients that also often characterize Hunan flavor.

JIANGSU CUISINE | 蘇 SU

The Yangtze River Delta region can trace its culinary history back to the Qin and Han Dynasties, more than three thousand years ago. Huai'an (淮安) and Yangzhou (揚州) were two prosperous cities during that time and had developed reputations as culinary centers. Combining the names of both cities,

the cuisine was referred to as *Huaiyang*. Huaiyang cooking is considered by many to be the primary heir of the original *Yu* cuisine, with ingredients and cooking techniques of the Central Plain civilization still discernable. Later this cuisine split into two branches: Jiangsu and Zhejiang. Current scholars are beginning to think of modern Shanghai cuisine as yet another branch.

Modern Jiangsu cuisine has been influenced by the introduction of many new ingredients, but it still retains much of its original traditions. Cooking techniques of steaming, braising, and saucing, *liu* (溜), are all part of Jiangsu customs. In addition to common meats such as pork, chicken, and duck, river fish is one of the main protein sources. The brackish tributaries and streams are home to a variety of crab that thrives in the mud: the hairy crab or mitten crab (大閘蟹).

Situated in some of the most fertile and productive farmlands of China, Jiangsu harvests a wealth of produce and livestock. Much of the local pork, lamb, duck, chicken, and fish is cured for consumption over the long, harsh winter. The town of Rugao (如皋) in northeast Jiangsu excels in curing ham and its product is considered one of China's top three. Many soup and vegetable recipes call for a small quantity of this ham to enhance the dish.

Jiangsu is also home to the town of Zhenjiang (鎮江), where the namesake black vinegar (also known as Chinkiang vinegar) is produced. Jiangsu specialties include black vinegar carp (鎮江香醋魚) and sweet-and-sour spare ribs (糖醋排骨). The vinegar is well known throughout China and is used all over the country for cooking and as a condiment.

ZHEJIANG CUISINE | 浙 ZHE

As one of the branches of Huaiyang cuisine, Zhejiang cooking is similar to Jiangsu and Shanghai cooking. As such braising and *liu* saucing are two common cooking techniques, and river fish are plentiful. However, there are subtle differences in the use of flavoring sauces and spices.

RUSSIA

KAZAKHSTAN

MONGOLIA

HEILONGJIANG

JILIN

KYRGYZSTAN

LIAONING

NORTH KOREA

XINJIANG

INNER MONGOLIA

• Beijing

GANSU

HEBEI

• Tianjin

Yellow Sea

SOUTH KOREA

QINGHAI

NINGXIA

SHANXI

SHANDONG

PAKISTAN

Yellow River

SHAANXI

HENAN

JIANGSU

Yangtze River

TIBET

SICHUAN

HUBEI

ANHUI

• Shanghai

Chongqing •

ZHEJIANG

East China Sea

NEPAL

BHUTAN

HUNAN

JIANGXI

INDIA

GUIZHOU

FUJIAN

BANGLADESH

YUNNAN

GUANGXI

GUANGDONG

TAIWAN

BURMA

VIETNAM

• • Hong Kong

Macau

© 2015 Meighan Cavanaugh

LAOS

HAINAN

South China Sea

THAILAND

The cuisine of Hangzhou, the capital of the province, dominates the region's cooking style. Many dishes, such as West Lake Beef Soup (page 276), Beggar's Chicken (page 314), and Stir-Fried Shrimp with Dragon Well tea, are specialties of Hangzhou. The tea produced in the village of Dragon Well or Longjing (龍井), north of Hangzhou, is widely used in local cooking. Fresh tea leaves are usually used in cooking, but many people overseas cook with the dried leaves instead.

Another famous Hangzhou specialty is Dongpo pork belly, a version of red-cooked pork that was purportedly created by the beloved Song Dynasty official and poet Su Dongpo, who was once the administrator of Hangzhou. But there is a lot of dispute about this legend because many Su Dongpo scholars assert that he was a vegetarian most of his adult life. Whether the story of the dish's origin is true or not, Su Dongpo's braised meat continues to bear his name and is absolutely delicious.

Shaoxing, another city in Zhejiang, produces some of the best yellow rice wine in China, and the

FOOD THERAPY

For thousands of years the Chinese have been diagnosing diseases and dispensing herbal medicine. As early as the 3rd or 2nd century BCE the Chinese chronicled traditional medicine in a book known as the *Inner Canon of Huangdi* (皇帝內經). One of the central tenets of this book is maintaining health through food therapy (食療), or living a healthy lifestyle by eating foods whose nutritional aspects maintain balance in the body.

To gain a deeper understanding of the concept, I spoke with my friend Peter D'Aquino, an acupuncturist and specialist in Asian herbal medicine. He explained the holistic thinking behind general well-being, which is affected by the innate condition of our body along with environmental and seasonal factors. Traditional Chinese medicine suggests that there are different aspects of vital energy in our bodies collectively known as *qi* (氣), and keeping them in harmony maintains fitness of body, mind, and spirit. One part of *qi*, energetic temperature, is closely associated with food and can be managed through food therapy. (While other therapeutic practices such as acupuncture, acupressure, and herbal medicine require special knowledge, the tenets of food therapy can be applied readily by everyone.)

According to Chinese philosophy everything (including people and food) contains complementary forces called *yin* and *yang*, which are constantly interacting. In humans, yin is seen as calming and relaxing while yang is energizing and vital. Foods with an abundance of yin are considered "cold" while those with yang are considered "hot." If, for example, your yin becomes too strong, you become ill, and eating foods strong in yang can heal you by restoring the lost balance. Many food preparations take these ideas into account, and many dishes have been created specifically to create a balance in one's daily diet.

Energetic temperature can be divided into cold, cool, neutral, warm, and hot. Each ingredient has a specific temperature classification based on ancient wisdom; impressively, recent scientific analyses of the chemical content in different foods have supported these classifications. When considering food's effect on a person, the body's innate characteristics play an important role. Some people tend to have a higher metabolism and are generally warm and dry, whereas others are cool and damp. So it is important that a warm person not overindulge in warm or hot foods, whereas cool or cold foods can be devastating for someone who is normally cool and weak. (Again, keep in mind that we're discussing the *energetic* temperature of foods and not the actual serving temperature.) At

local cooking takes advantage of it. Drunken chicken and drunken crab are some of the many well-known wine-flavored dishes here.

The cured ham produced in the town of Jinhua (金華) is the most famous of the top three hams of China. Widely sold in China and overseas, Jinhua ham is meaty and is excellent as a main ingredient or used as a flavoring accent.

ANHUI CUISINE | 徽 HUI

Anhui is situated directly to the west of Jiangsu and Zhejiang. Most northern Anhui cooking closely resembles that of these adjacent provinces.

Indeed, most culinary students consider it simply an extension of Huaiyang cooking. But southern Anhui, or Huizhou, cooking is of a completely different ilk.

Huizhou (徽州), or simply *Hui*, cuisine is influenced by the local ingredients. Situated in the foothills of the Yellow Mountain, the area's surrounding woods are sources of wild vegetation, wildlife, and river fish. Bamboo shoots of all kinds, fiddlehead ferns, wood ear mushrooms, and kudzu roots are examples of local vegetables commonly associated with Huizhou cuisine. Among these vegetables bamboo shoots stand out as the local specialty. With plentiful bamboo crops, a large the same time, hot food can warm up a person during the winter and vice versa for the summer. So seasonal considerations are just as important.

Fried or baked food and spices are considered hot and should be reduced during summer and for people who are warm, whereas cold foods such as vegetables and seafood are perfect under those circumstances. Aromatics such as ginger, garlic, and scallion are considered warm and are often used in cooking vegetables and seafood to bring the energetic temperature up.

Long before eating locally and seasonally became fashionable in the West, it was advocated in Chinese food therapy. Fresh vegetables in the summer keep our body cool, while the spices and cured meat used in braises and soups in the winter keep us warm. Additionally, moderate and equal proportions of meats, vegetables, grains, and fruits are considered essential in maintaining a balanced diet. Unlike the Western diet's fondness for huge chunks of meat, most Chinese meat dishes contain a small amount of it accompanied by vegetables. Food therapy also discourages overeating by suggesting that a complete meal should make one feel only about 70 percent full.

In addition to energetic temperature, traditional Chinese medicine also thinks of the flavor of food as being associated with its effect on the body. Five flavors are recognized and each is associated with one of the Earth's basic elements and a body part that it affects. Saltiness is related to water and the kidneys, sourness to wood and the liver, bitterness to fire and the heart, sweetness to earth and the spleen, and pungency to metal and the lungs. Note that the flavor associated with an ingredient refers to the ingredient in its natural state. For example, lemon is sour naturally; a vegetable that becomes sour after being pickled may not be considered a sour ingredient.

Efficiently digesting our food is another consideration that dictates how the Chinese eat. Cooking or preparing food is thought of as the first step in the digestive process. Therefore, only food that has been pickled, fermented, or cooked is consumed; traditionally, the Chinese don't eat raw food. Salads and other raw dishes found in modern Chinese cooking are in fact contemporary influences from foreign cuisines.

Although food therapy is itself a complete body of knowledge that's beyond the scope of this book, it is possible to understand its basic concepts and apply them in our daily life. We can use it as a way to become more aware of the state of our health and learn how it is affected by the seasons, what we eat, and how we cook.

proportion of the bamboo shoots are harvested and preserved by salting and drying. These cured bamboo shoots are later used for braising and soup making, producing some of the most flavorful dishes around.

A good complement to these vegetables is the local ham. Although not as well known as the other famous Chinese hams from Jinhua (金华), Xuanwei (宣威), and Rugao (如皋), this ham is equally appetizing. Dishes such as braised pork belly with dried bamboo shoots are enriched with small thin pieces of this ham.

The fish and shellfish from the waterways that crisscross Huizhou are a major part of the local diet. Mandarin fish in particular is a local favorite and is prepared in a unique way that lets the fish age and turn slightly sour before it is cooked. The process changes the texture of the meat and instills a subtle fermented taste, giving it the name "stinky Mandarin fish."

Another Huizhou specialty involving aging food is what the locals call "hairy tofu" (毛豆腐). In a process similar to allowing mold to grow on cheese, special mold spores are introduced to the surface of tofu blocks. The mold is then incubated and encouraged to grow until the tofu blocks are covered with white hair. The tofu is then fried and served with chiles and soy sauce, or braised and served in a brown sauce. There is no great change in the flavor, but the texture of the tofu becomes incredibly tender and has a custard-like consistency.

To wash down all these wonderful delicacies are teas grown on the slopes of the Yellow Mountain. The three main varieties produced in Huizhou include Keemun (祁門), Maofeng (毛峰), and Houkui (猴魁). Keemun, which is a black tea, was already being exported during the 19th century and is well known worldwide. The other two varieties are green teas and are widely consumed in China.

SHANDONG CUISINE | 魯 LU

Home to the vassal state of Lu during the Zhou Dynasty around the 1st century BCE, the province of Shandong is where Confucius was born. The area has a long political and cultural history as well as a rich culinary tradition. Confucius was himself a great epicure. In the Xiang Dang (鄉黨) chapter of his *Analects* (論語), he included a section devoted to the philosophy of cooking and dining. A phrase from that section has become an idiom to describe the appreciation of well-made food: "to winnow grains thoroughly and cut meat delicately" (食不厭精, 膾不厭細), indicating that meticulous preparation of food will produce the best delicacies.

Philosophy aside, Shandong cooking reflects the adaptation of Central Plain cooking customs to the northeast coastal environment, and has greatly influenced Dongbei (or the Northeast) region's cuisines after the assimilation of the Manchus in that region. A distinct characteristic of the northern diet is the type of grain consumed: Whereas rice is predominant in the south, wheat was the more prevalent grain in the north (at least until strains of rice from Southeast Asia, with shorter growing cycles, were introduced during the Song Dynasty). Wheat was most likely introduced to China from the ancient Mesopotamian civilization around 2000 BCE, and spread to the northeast as the Han Chinese expanded their territory. Over the years the regional wheat flour–based foods have grown to include

breads, noodles, pancakes, and dumplings. *Mantou* (饅頭), or steamed bread, is the quintessential starch food of northern Chinese cooking.

Jiaozi, or dumplings, are an iconic dish of northern China. Made exclusively with wheat flour, and stuffed with pork, beef, lamb, or seafood combined with all sorts of vegetables and herbs, these dumplings are most frequently boiled.

Lu cuisine is best known for its use of the abundant local seafood, which is often farmed these days. Fish, mollusks, and sea worms are all extensively consumed in the region.

Dongbei cuisine, prevalent in the Flushing area of Queens, New York, is similar to the cooking of the Shandong region.

BEIJING CUISINE | 京 JING

In 1644 the Manchu people crossed over the Great Wall, conquered the Han Chinese, and replaced the Ming Dynasty with the Qing Dynasty. They set up their capital in Beijing, which had also been the seat of the Ming Dynasty's government. They quickly adapted to Han customs, including their culinary ones.

The Manchu did not have a very sophisticated culinary background, so the imperial palace kitchen imported dishes from all over the Qing territories southern region and the Central Plain, as the dynasty expanded. Foreign ingredients were also adapted as trading with the West expanded during the 18th and 19th centuries. What resulted was some of the most cosmopolitan cooking of its time.

As imperial banquets became increasingly elaborate affairs, they started combining Han and Manchu dishes. The Man Han Quan Xi (滿漢全席), or Manchu Han Imperial Feast, is the most luxurious Chinese banquet ever recorded, spread over three days with a total of six meals, each meal consisting of thirty-six courses. Dishes included exotic items such as camel hump, bear paw, shark fin, sea cucumber, abalone, bird's nest, quail, swan, morel mushroom, and bamboo pith mushroom, to name but a few.

BUDDHIST VEGETARIAN COOKING

Most Chinese are not inclined toward vegetarianism in their daily life, even though Taoist and Buddhist vegetarianism has been practiced for millennia. Chinese Buddhism prohibits monks and nuns from eating meat, but there is no strict requirement for lay followers to practice vegetarianism. Still, it is common for believers to enjoy a delicious vegetarian meal for spiritual fulfillment after a visit to a temple. For this reason many temple dining halls, and for that matter commercial vegetarian restaurants, try to produce dishes that resemble meat so the food is more appealing to the casual vegetarian.

Meat imitation in Chinese cooking is highly developed and has its origin in two major food processing methods established in ancient China. One is making tofu from soybeans and the other is extracting gluten, or *seitan* as it is known in Japanese, from wheat flour.

Manufacture of soy products was first recorded during the Han Dynasty, around the 2nd century BCE, and has evolved into an industry that produces countless numbers of products. The process starts with the creation of soy milk, which is made by soaking dried soybeans, grinding the beans, and extracting the liquid. This soy milk is then boiled and the first product, tofu skin, is harvested from the top of the cooling milk.

Next, cooked soy milk curds are formed by adding a coagulant such as food-grade gypsum or nigari. The curds are then pressed to make tofu of different firmnesses for various applications. Tofu's added ability to be molded into various shapes is excellent for creating the texture of poultry meat, such as chicken and duck. Tofu skin is often used for adding a layer of mock skin over the mock poultry meat.

To imitate the texture of pork or beef, gluten is the choice. First produced during the Song Dynasty, around the 10th century, gluten is the elastic protein that forms after wheat flour is mixed with water. To extract the gluten, wheat flour is blended with water and the starch is washed away by repeated rinsing. Like tofu, gluten is flexible and can be molded into different shapes to imitate meat.

Mock meat is cooked just like real meat, using the same cooking techniques, herbs, and spices. In other words, mock beef can be braised with red-cooking soy sauce liquid and mock chicken can be fried with a five-spice coating.

In addition to tofu products and gluten, there is a curious technique that uses taro root mixed with starch and ammonia powder to imitate the flaky meat of fish. The leavening property of ammonia powder creates a fluffy texture and the result can be quite convincing.

Dining outside the Forbidden City, however, was a different proposition. Beijing cuisine is simply the folk dishes of the common people. Noodles, hot pot meals, braised pork, aspic, and sweet snacks are all enjoyed by the general population.

One exception to the everyday nature of Beijing cuisine is of course Peking Duck (page 297). This technique of roasting duck was perfected by the northern Chinese during the Qing Dynasty. Although similar techniques developed all over China, Peking duck remains a favorite and is distinct to the capital.

Modern Beijing still imports dishes from the provinces. A plethora of regional Chinese restaurants have sprung up since the economic liberalization of the 1980s. Beijingers now dine at many more regional restaurants than local ones.

SHANGHAI CUISINE | 滬 HU

Situated at the mouth of the Yangtze River, Shanghai has culturally always been similar to many of the surrounding regions. This is also true of its cuisine, an extension of Huaiyang cuisine that developed its own characteristics during the rapid development of the city after foreign concessions were established around the original old town during the 19th century. Shanghai cooking quickly became cosmopolitan and

distinct. It is characteristically mild and well-rounded but with a slight preference for a sweet taste. (No one has been able to ascertain how this predilection came about.)

Many dishes with roots in Huaiyang cooking have often been closely identified with Shanghai cuisine. One such example is lion's head (page 198). It originated in Yangzhou but now is served at family meals and at restaurants all over Shanghai. It is a savory and succulent dish with meatballs up to two or three inches in diameter; their huge size led diners to refer to them as "lions' heads." The meatballs can be braised in a red-cooked sauce or a clear broth.

On the other hand, soup dumplings were invented right within the Shanghai municipality. Created in Nanxiang (南翔), a suburban town just outside the urban core, these little dumplings contain an incredibly juicy pork filling wrapped within a very thin, chewy dough that's almost translucent.

HAINAN | 瓊 QIONG

Hainan cooking is not normally classified as one of the major regional Chinese cuisines because it has been so heavily influenced by the neighboring Cantonese and Fujian cuisines. It makes use of many of the same local ingredients, emphasizes natural flavors, and employs simple cooking techniques. But as the southernmost island of China, Hainan enjoys a more tropical climate, which produces plenty of local exotic ingredients; coconut, for example, is used in soups and sweet dishes.

Four important delicacies that have become synonymous with Hainan cuisine are chicken (文昌雞) from Wenchang County, duck (加積鴨) from Jiaji Village, goat (東山羊) from Dongshan Hill, and crab (和樂蟹) from Hele Village, along the east coast. Local preparations of all these ingredients are basic. The chicken and duck are usually steeped or boiled in hot water, the goat is stewed, and the crab is steamed.

Among these four delicacies the Wenchang chicken has become renowned throughout Asia as "Hainan chicken rice," and its popularity is gradually spreading to the United States and Australia by way of Singapore. A meal in itself consisting of steeped chicken served with the cooking broth and a rice cooked in the same broth, the dish was introduced to Singapore by a Hainan immigrant. It was a sensation and began to spread all over Southeast Asia.

YUNNAN | 滇 DIAN

As is the case with Hainan cuisine, the cooking of Yunnan Province is underappreciated and has been eclipsed by its northern neighbor, Sichuan. Like Sichuan, the food is spicy and complex. But unlike Sichuan, Yunnan cooking uses many Southeast Asian flavors borrowed from its southern neighbors.

Bordered by Vietnam, Laos, Myanmar, India, and Tibet, Yunnan is populated by large numbers of indigenous minority people, many of whom share their cultural roots with neighboring countries. In the hot and tropical lowlands of the south, fresh herbs such as ginger, lemongrass, Thai basil, mint, cilantro, culantro, jasmine flower, and chile dominate the flavors. In the northwest, on the other hand, the terrain rises to the frozen highland of the Tibetan plateau. Here the food reflects influences from Tibetan cuisine, with lots of cured meat and highland grains as the main ingredients. In the northeast region of Yunnan, though, the effects of the Han migration from Sichuan and other Chinese regions are evident. The food there is very close to the *mala*, or numbing and spicy hot, dishes found in Sichuan. The air-dried cured ham produced in Xuanwei, in northeastern Yunnan, is considered one of the top hams of China.

Yunnan cooking techniques are just as varied and sophisticated as the diverse cultural backgrounds of the population. Steaming, braising, and boiling are common in the northwest and central mountainous region, while grilling, stewing, and salads are typical in the southwestern tropical area.

But there is one uniquely Yunnan cooking method: Invented by a chef from Jianshui County (建水縣) in central Yunnan, it is known as "steam pot cooking." Chef Yang Li (楊瀝) was credited for creating a clay pot that is used to make soups by slowly condensing steam, which produces an intensely flavored broth that is indescribably delectable (see page 287).

Yunnan's tropical climate and sloping mountain regions create some of the best conditions for growing rice, making it one of the major rice production areas of China. Local cooks mash cooked rice into a smooth dough that can then be formed into rice cakes and rice noodles of all kinds.

Of all the Yunnan culinary specialties there is nothing more important than tea. Centered on Puer (普洱) in the southwestern part of the province, tea has been cultivated in Yunnan since ancient times. Tea leaves were exported to the rest of the world through a trading route known as the Ancient Tea Horse Road (also known as the Southern Silk Road). It is thought that Puer tea, a fermented tea, was the original Chinese export tea that popularized this beverage worldwide.

XINJIANG AND WESTERN REGION

Flushing is the New York City neighborhood with the largest concentration of recent Chinese immigrants. Since the 1990s many of the new arrivals have been coming from the interior parts of China rather than the east coast cities. As they bring their cooking traditions with them, this new wave of immigrants has attracted the attention of Chinese food enthusiasts who are discovering the delights of the cuisine of Xinjiang and China's western region.

They are discovering a cuisine that at times seems decidedly un-Chinese. This vast area is dominated by the Uighur people, who are not members of the Han majority and have their own foodways. The majority of the population in the west is Muslim and cooks with lamb and other halal ingredients as well as spices, often using cooking techniques imported from the Middle East. This is the only region in China where Han cooking is not the basis of the cuisine, but rather an overlay grafted on to a preexisting culinary tradition.

In Xinjiang, grilling on skewers and the use of cumin are evidence of Arab cuisine's influence, and the technique has become popular not just in Xinjiang but all over China. Grilled whole lamb is also a Xinjiang delicacy and is often served during celebratory feasts, when an entire lamb is roasted without being butchered and diners serve themselves by slicing meat off the carcass.

Along with large quantities of meat, the local population also consumes a wide variety of dairy products. Milk from both goats and cows is used to make yogurt and cheese. Very few vegetables are found in Xinjiang cooking, simply because produce is rare in the desert terrain of the province. A notable exception is the Hami melon (哈密瓜), an incredibly sweet melon that has a crunchy texture even when ripe. This special melon is the pride of Xinjiang and is beloved everywhere in China.

SLICING CLEAVER

何正岐刀刀正

CUTTING CLEAVER

CHOPPING CLEAVER

CHAPTER TWO

The Chinese Kitchen

NESTLED AMONG EIGHT GREEN HILLS ON
THE SOUTH SIDE OF HUANG SHAN (黃山),
OR YELLOW MOUNTAIN, in China's Anhui province sits an
ancient village called Chengkan (呈坎) that has preserved its appearance
since the Ming Dynasty. The history of the village, though, goes all the
way back to the Eastern Han Dynasty, more than 1,800 years ago. Built
according to the "eight diagram" rules (八卦), a principle of the universe
in Taoist cosmology, the entire village is a perfect example of the Chinese
philosophy of balance and harmony known as *feng shui* (風水). The village
layout was carefully considered and constructed to ensure stability,
prosperity, and good fortune. The village has escaped the relentless
development of modern China over the past few decades and has
preserved its rural way of life as if it were still in the dynastic era. Now
designated a UNESCO World Heritage Site, Chengkan welcomes visitors
to wander through its narrow streets and lanes lined with ancient houses
and mansions protected behind high walls.

While touring the village I stumbled upon a family cooking their early
evening meal in an open kitchen. After striking up a conversation with
the patriarch, I was invited to view their kitchen. Along the right side wall,
as I walked in, was a brick stove with two openings at the bottom where
firewood was burning. In the two round holes on top of the stove sat
two large blackened woks. The wok on the left was evidently set up as
a steamer; I saw steam streaming up around the edge of the cover. The
other wok sat empty with a spatula resting on it. Next to the stove, a

table was covered with cut-up vegetables, a fish, and some cured meat. It appeared that a stir-fry was in the making. At the back of the kitchen, a door opened onto a vegetable patch. Right next to the steps down to the garden there was a rusty charcoal stove with a pot of rice bubbling on top of it. That was the whole Chinese kitchen. I was struck by the sparseness and simplicity of it all.

Back in New York City I marveled at how our kitchens are stuffed full of all kinds of modern appliances and gadgets that we may use once for a special recipe and then forget about. Furnishing a modern kitchen to cook Chinese food is quite simple: a wok with a cover, a steamer, a few sharp knives or cleavers, and a cutting board are all that's needed.

CLEAVERS AND KNIVES

There are three basic types of cleavers used in the Chinese kitchen, each with a slightly different use. If you are just starting out in Chinese cooking and do not wish to invest in cleavers, a regular chef's knife will work just as well for preparing most ingredients. A paring knife is also useful.

There are two types of cleaver handles: metal molded together with the blade, and wooden fastened to the blade. The metal handle is generally more durable, but the wooden handle can be more comfortable to grip. The chopping cleaver usually has a wooden handle. Ultimately the choice of handle is up to the cook.

SLICING CLEAVER | 片刀

Lightest of the three types of cleavers, this is a utilitarian cleaver for basic ingredient preparation. The blade is rectangular, about 8 inches by 4 inches, and is usually thin. Its light weight makes it attractive for everyday use. The purpose of this cleaver is to cut slices, julienne strips, dice cubes, and make rolling cuts. It can also be used for mincing aromatics by crushing them with the flat side of the blade before chopping. This is an excellent choice for cutting vegetables and boneless meat.

It is not a good instrument, however, for mincing meat or for heavy-duty chopping. The blade is too thin for such tasks and could be damaged easily.

CUTTING CLEAVER | 切刀

Similar in shape and size to the slicing cleaver, the cutting cleaver is heavier and sturdier, making it a much better instrument for mincing meat. This cleaver can handle slicing, julienning, and dicing quite well, but its heavier weight can make it cumbersome when slicing delicate ingredients.

Cutting through joints of various meats is one of the other tasks this cleaver can handle very nicely. Still, I would discourage its use for chopping the bones themselves.

CHOPPING CLEAVER | 砍刀

Weighing more than half a pound, the chopping cleaver is the strongest of them all. The blade is larger and squarer than those of the other cleavers. It is about 8 inches by 5 inches and has a more pronounced curve on the blade's edge. Excellent for chopping and hacking meat with or without bones, this cleaver handles heavy-duty jobs. (As strong as these cleavers are, however, it is still not a good idea to hack into heavy bones, which should be sawed by a professional butcher.)

CUTTING BOARD

Along with a cleaver or knife, a cutting board is an important kitchen implement. I've used wood and resin cutting boards for years and they are equally suitable. Still, the heavier weight of a good thick wooden board does make it easier for heavier mincing and chopping. It offers a sturdier support for the work.

For those concerned with the health implications of using wood, a study conducted at the Food Safety Laboratory at the University of California at Davis showed that there is no advantage to using plastic. In fact, in some cases an old plastic cutting board is more difficult to sanitize than a wooden one. So just pick the type of cutting board that works better for you ergonomically.

A good size cutting board for Chinese cooking is probably about 18 inches by 12 inches. This is large enough to accommodate a whole fish or a whole chicken.

WOKS

In traditional Chinese kitchens, the stovetops are designed with a hole to accommodate a round-bottomed wok. Getting a Chinese wok and a modern Western stove to work together can take a little work. There are many types of woks, and understanding their different characteristics can help you decide which wok best fits your needs.

Most traditional woks are made of cast iron or carbon steel. They season well over time and perform better with use. A thin oil film forms as the wok is used, and this coating prevents ingredients from sticking.

Modern varieties include stainless steel, aluminum, and metal-clad woks, some of which are coated with nonstick Teflon. Although these modern woks can be easier to maintain, I do not recommend them. Stainless steel and aluminum woks do not prevent food from sticking at high temperatures, so a large amount of oil is needed to alleviate this problem. Teflon-coated woks, on the other hand, pose health risks because the coating compound starts to disintegrate at high temperatures, releasing carcinogens.

Given these considerations I recommend sticking with the traditional cast-iron or carbon steel wok. The cast-iron wok is much heavier and is more suitable with a stove designed to hold a wok as a permanent fixture. For American home kitchens, the carbon steel wok is lightweight and can be handled easily.

For the American cook, a flat-bottomed 14-inch carbon steel wok is probably the most appropriate choice. It will sit securely on the grate of a gas burner and receive direct heat from the flame, or on the flat surface of the heating element of an electric stove. (An electric stove is not recommended for stir-frying, though, because it is not capable of sustaining high temperatures during cooking, which in this case is essential.) The 14-inch size is small enough to use on a home stove without overcrowding the top, and large enough to accommodate the tossing and tumbling of the ingredients in the wok. A round-bottomed wok requires a ring to properly fit on a burner. Unfortunately, the ring raises the wok above the flame, making it difficult to heat the wok to a temperature high enough for proper stir-frying. If you can replace the burner grate on your stovetop with a special wok grate, allowing the flame to directly reach a round-bottomed wok, that would be ideal.

WOK LID

A wok lid is very important in stir-frying. It is used to steam ingredients, especially vegetables, that require even heat. Most lids are made of aluminum, and they come in two shapes: a round dome or a high

SEASONING A WOK

Seasoning a wok ensures that a layer of oil covers the inner surface; it often appears as a dark metallic patina. This greased surface is what makes a wok nonstick and imbues the food with a subtle glow of *wok hay* (鑊氣), a Cantonese term for the warm, fragrant bouquet that rises when a dish is served immediately after cooking.

Only carbon steel and cast-iron woks can be seasoned successfully with oil. Stainless steel or aluminum woks need to be washed thoroughly with soap and water after every use to keep the surface clean, and will never become nonstick. Do not attempt to season a wok made of anything other than carbon steel or cast iron.

In her wonderful book *Stir-Frying to the Sky's Edge*, Grace Young suggests two methods of seasoning a wok: on the stovetop and in the oven. The stovetop method is my favorite as it is easy and works very well.

If you've just purchased a brand-new wok, be sure to wash it with dishwashing detergent to remove most of the machine oil left over from the manufacturing process. (This is the one and only time that a carbon steel or cast-iron wok should be washed with soap.) Dry the wok with a paper towel, and then heat it over medium heat on the stovetop for about 15 minutes or until any remaining machine oil residue is burned off. By this time the wok will already be starting to darken and will be ready for the next step.

Add ¼ cup vegetable oil to the wok and heat it to just about 360°F. Meanwhile, cut about 6 ounces fresh ginger into ¼-inch-thick slices. Put the ginger slices in the wok and stir-fry for about 15 minutes. Press the ginger slices against the sides and slide them around in the wok. Be sure to cover the entire inside surface of the wok with the oil. Discard the ginger slices and wipe the inside surface of the wok with a paper towel, leaving a thin film of oil. (Grace suggests using both ginger and scallion, but I think ginger alone is sufficient.)

The second method is to coat the wok with a thin film of vegetable oil and then bake the wok in a 425°F oven for about 40 minutes. Let the wok cool for 20 minutes, and then coat the interior with another layer of oil before wiping it with a paper towel.

MAINTAINING A WOK

Wok maintenance is easy if the simple rule of "no soap" is followed. After every use the wok should be washed with a brush under hot running water. You can use a steel brush or steel wool to scrape off any food particles that are stuck to the surface.

It is important to remember that the surface should always be protected by a thin film of oil. If you've used the wok for boiling or stewing, the remaining oil may not be sufficient to coat the surface for the next use. To replace the finish, dry the wok with a paper towel and then rub the inside surface with a paper towel dipped in oil. Return the wok to the stovetop and heat it until the oil begins to smoke.

Store the wok on a piece of paper towel so the bottom will not stick to your shelf. If you do not use your wok very often, be sure to cover the entire wok with a plastic bag to prevent dust from adhering to the seasoned cooking surface.

---

flat-topped dome. Both work well, but the flat-topped dome is sometimes preferred because of its greater capacity.

STEAMING RACK

A metal or bamboo steaming rack is a very useful accessory that converts a wok into a steamer. Place a heat-resistant container with any food on top of the rack, pour water into the wok, cover it with the lid, and steam.

SPATULAS, LADLES, AND SKIMMERS FOR WOKS

Generally, cooking spoons and spatulas used at home can be used with a wok, but the traditional Chinese

STEAMERS

Steaming is an important technique in Chinese cooking. While it can often be accomplished over a steaming rack in a wok, a separate enclosed steamer is useful to have, especially if your wok is already in use. Steamers are also good for reheating food or making quick steamed side dishes.

BAMBOO STEAMER

This iconic steamer is an important and versatile implement in the Chinese kitchen. In addition to its standard use in making steamed buns and dumplings, it can be used for steaming rice, meat, and other ingredients. The bamboo actually infuses its fragrance into whatever food is steamed in it.

A 12-inch-diameter steamer fits perfectly in a 14-inch wok. Sold in a set, bamboo steamers usually include two layers of stacked steamers with a single cover. Do not use more than two layers at a time; otherwise the top level will not receive enough steam to cook the ingredients properly.

METAL STEAMER

Along with two steamers and cover, a metal steamer set includes a pot to hold boiling water and is a complete, self-sufficient steaming tool. It is indispensable when cooking a full multi-course Chinese meal at home. You can simultaneously cook food in the steamer while stir-frying in a wok. Additionally, the pot used to hold the boiling water is large enough for use on its own as a stockpot.

spatula and ladle are a lot more efficient for stir-frying. A wok spatula is a shovel-like utensil with a wide blade and a slightly curved bottom that is perfect for keeping ingredients in motion when stir-frying. It fits well with the sloping sides of the wok and has a wooden handle that keeps it from getting too hot to hold. Similarly, the Chinese ladle has a curved bottom to fit the shape of the wok. It often has a shallower bowl than Western ladles so that in addition to scooping stock, it can be used to stir-fry.

Another important tool is the skimmer or "spider." The Chinese version consists of a metal wire mesh tied to a metal ring and a bamboo handle. It is used for draining food after boiling or frying. For skimming scum off the surface of the liquid during parboiling, which is a common practice in Chinese cooking, a small fine-mesh skimmer about 4 inches in diameter is most helpful.

CLAY POTS

Go to a Chinese restaurant and you'll often find slow-braised dishes served in clay pots. Not only does the clay pot make a great presentation, but it is actually a perfect vessel for cooking over a long period of time. Clay pots transmit heat evenly and gently, allowing the food to cook gradually. A huge variety of Chinese clay pots are available, with the smaller, shallower ones normally used for braising and the larger, deeper types for making soup.

Regardless as to how they are used, special attention should be given to how they are heated. Chinese clay pots are designed for use on the stovetop, but it is still a good idea to use only gentle heat. If a recipe calls for browning aromatics or frying ingredients, this should be done separately in a metal pot or a wok. Clay pots generally need some liquid in the pot to work well, even if it is a very small amount. With proper care your clay pot can provide you many years of cooking pleasure.

UNGLAZED AND PARTIALLY GLAZED CLAY POTS

The most common of these rustic-looking vessels is the standard bowl shape, but they can also be tall and round or pot-bellied with a spout. The bowl-shaped pot is almost always used for braising, and the round one is more commonly used for making soup. Those with a spout are usually used for making herbal soup where only the broth is consumed; the spout allows the broth to be poured out separately, without disturbing the solid ingredients.

Both unglazed and partially glazed clay pots are prone to cracking when subjected to sudden changes in temperature. One precaution to help prevent this is to soak the clay pot for about 15 minutes in cold water before using it. Additionally, start cooking over low heat before gradually increasing the heat to the desired moderate level. These pots should never be used at a high temperature setting.

Unglazed and partially glazed pots are porous by nature, and will become seasoned with multiple use. The best way to clean them is to wipe them clean with a lightly soaped sponge and then rinse thoroughly. It is not a good idea to clean them in a dishwasher or even to soak them in soapy water.

GLAZED CLAY POTS

Glazed clay pots are more durable than unglazed ones, so they need less special care. Although they are not as vulnerable to sudden cracking from heat, the same attention to incremental changes in temperature is essential. Always start at a low heat setting at the beginning of cooking and only gradually increase to no more than medium heat. The glazing makes the pot nonporous, which means it is safe to wash in the dishwasher.

YUNNAN STEAM POT

Attributed to a Chef Yang Li (楊瀝), the Yunnan steam pot was invented in Jianshui County more than two hundred years ago. It is a curious-looking pot with a steam spout rising from the bottom up through the middle of the pot. The result is a round trough not dissimilar to a Chinese hot pot. It is covered and placed on top of another pot that is partially filled with boiling water. The steam from the boiling water rises up through the spout, condenses under the cover, drips down into the trough, and becomes the broth. This slow steaming action produces the most concentrated and clearest soup ever known. A recipe for cooking steam pot chicken soup can be found on page 288.

Most Yunnan steam pots are made of unglazed earthenware and should be used and maintained like any other unglazed clay pot. There is no issue with high temperature, however, since the pot always sits over boiling water.

FERMENTED DRIED MUSTARD GREENS

CHAPTER THREE

The Chinese Pantry

ALTHOUGH IT IS NOT POSSIBLE TO DESCRIBE EVERY INGREDIENT YOU'LL EVER NEED, THIS CHAPTER COVERS THE MOST COMMONLY USED PANTRY ITEMS IN CHINESE COOKING— many of which are now stocked in American grocery stores. Others may necessitate a trip to a local Chinatown, a visit to a specialty store, or some shopping on the Internet. Learning about these ingredients before you shop will make your excursion more enjoyable.

AROMATICS

Skim through Chinese recipes and you will find that ginger, garlic, and scallions appear everywhere. These are the three primary aromatic ingredients in Chinese cooking. But unlike Western cooking, where the trinity of celery, onion, and carrot frequently appears together, the three main Asian aromatics are often used in various combinations.

GINGER | 薑

Fresh ginger is no doubt the most important and distinctive aromatic in Chinese cooking. It possesses an intense spicy flavor that immediately identifies a dish as Asian. Unfortunately, it is often abused by many cooks. As an aromatic, ginger should be used sparingly, never overwhelming the other flavors in a dish. Its purpose is to complement the flavors of herbs, sauces, or condiments, not compete with them.

Ginger is a root-like rhizome that is covered in a brown skin that can be peeled off, exposing a juicy but sometimes fibrous interior. It can be used either raw or cooked. Minced or finely julienned raw ginger is often found in dipping sauces and in dressings for cold dishes. When using it as a condiment, look for tender young ginger.

Ginger is universally used to counter the gaminess of meat in Chinese cooking, so all types of meat are usually cooked with ginger, with one exception: Pork meat (but not pork innards or pork bones) is considered to have a "neutral" flavor, so it is rarely if ever prepared with ginger. Simple dishes using pork meat are usually flavored with garlic and scallions instead.

GARLIC | 蒜

Garlic is the next most important Chinese aromatic ingredient. And to a lesser extent, its flavor is also associated with Chinese food. As a member of the allium family, fresh garlic has a sharp, pungent, and spicy flavor.

When used raw, it contributes a definite piquant flavor that works well in cold dishes. Cooking sharply reduces the harsh garlic taste so it can act in a complementary role to enhance the flavors of spices and herbs. When minced and deep-fried until brown, garlic has an incredibly fragrant effect. Quite a few Chinese recipes call for smoky fried garlic as a garnish to elevate the flavor of a dish.

SCALLIONS | 蔥

Third in the trinity of Chinese aromatics, scallions have countless uses. The bottom white part of the scallion is usually the more pungent, so it is more often used for cooking. The milder top green portion is excellent for use as a garnish. Still, it is not unusual for both parts to be used together in a dish.

SHALLOTS | 紅蔥頭

Although not universally used in Chinese cooking, shallots are found in the south, in the cuisines of Fujian, Taiwan, and Yunnan. Mostly cooked in stir-fries or braised dishes, it is also often thinly sliced and then deep-fried. This crunchy, nutty fried shallot is usually used to garnish a dish.

AROMATICS

GARLIC

SCALLIONS

GINGER

SHALLOTS

THAI BASIL

GARLIC CHIVE

CILANTRO

CHINESE LEEK

CHINESE CELERY

GARLIC CHIVE

MINT

HERBS

DILL

FRESH HERBS

The use of fresh herbs varies greatly among Chinese regional cuisines. Whereas southern cuisines use them generously, northern regions use them more sparingly. But in all cases they play a vital role in boosting flavors. When used as a garnish, fresh herbs create a nice sharp accent to whatever they accompany. When a large quantity is cooked in a dish, the herbs almost become another vegetable and contribute amazingly to the flavor of the dish.

CILANTRO | 香菜

Often compared to the smell of soap, cilantro's highly perfumed taste is not universally admired. Also known as fresh coriander, it has flat segmented leaves resembling those of Italian parsley, which belongs to the same family. The Chinese use cilantro leaves extensively as a garnish and sometimes as a flavoring herb. When used in cooking, cilantro is often used in a large quantity. Coriander seeds are used only in rare instances in the flavor-potting broth for meat.

CHINESE CELERY | 芹菜

With its firm, hollow stalks and leafy tops, this light green vegetable definitely looks like celery. Because its taste is stronger and its stalks narrower than the thick-stalked celery common in the West, Chinese celery is probably closer to the original wild variety. When it is younger and smaller, Chinese celery is easily confused with its cousin Italian parsley because the leaves look very similar. Chinese celery is consumed both raw and cooked. Both stems and leaves are used in soups and stews, or lightly cooked and served as a separate course.

GARLIC CHIVES | 韭菜

The Chinese eat both the leaves and the unopened flower buds of garlic chives. Heartier and more robust than Western chives, garlic chives have a slight hint of garlic and are used more as a vegetable than as a garnish in Chinese cooking. Garlic chives have flat blue-green blades, whereas regular chives have cylindrical grass-green leaves. Yellow garlic chives (韭黃), which are grown in the dark, have a more delicate taste and are highly sought after.

CHINESE LEEKS | 蒜苗

Also called green garlic or spring garlic, Chinese leeks are a northern Chinese staple. They look like a larger version of scallions, but like garlic chives, they have flat leaves. Sometimes the bulbs have a purple hue. Chinese leeks have a flavor that is considered mild for an allium but is somewhat more pungent than Western leeks. They also have a slight taste of garlic. Chinese leeks are eaten raw or cooked. Stir-fried beef with leeks is a common example.

DILL | 茴香

In the same family as celery, dill is an aromatic herb that has a mild grassy fennel flavor. It is used mostly in the northern and southwestern regions of China. When used as an herb, dill adds flavor to egg dishes and pancakes. More frequently, though, it is used in large quantities as a vegetable in a fish soup or as the dominant ingredient in fillings for dumplings and steamed buns.

THAI BASIL | 九層塔

Thai basil, sometimes called Asian basil, is a type of sweet basil. Used mostly in Taiwanese regional cooking in China, it is occasionally referred to as Taiwan basil. Different from its cousin, the Mediterranean sweet basil used in Italian cooking, Thai basil has narrower, darker leaves, rectangular purple stems, and mauve flowers. Although often used interchangeably in recipes with Italian basil, Thai basil has a slightly more assertive flavor and stands up better when cooked. Because of its warm, peppery anise flavor, it is sometimes called licorice basil or anise basil.

MINT | 薄荷

Mint is used most commonly in the southern provinces, where a tropical spearmint with fuzzy dark green leaves is popular. The cool, grassy, spicy flavor adds a distinctly Southeast Asian flair to Chinese dishes. It is almost always used as a garnish and is usually eaten raw, although in Yunnan fresh mint is combined with Thai basil and lemongrass to make an herbal marinade for grilled fish.

SPICES

Spices were originally used in Chinese cooking to preserve food and to maintain good health. Although their medicinal or health benefits remain an important consideration into the modern age, spices are currently used mainly as flavor enhancers.

STAR ANISE | 八角

Undoubtedly the most widely used spice in Chinese cooking, star anise is the brown star-shaped seed pod of a broadleaf evergreen plant native to Vietnam and southwest China. It is about ½ inch in diameter, with eight spiky seed compartments. The eight-pointed star gives rise to its Chinese name, "eight corners." The flavor is slightly sweeter than that of regular aniseed. Their shared licorice taste comes from the chemical anethole, but the two plants are not related. Star anise is used extensively in braising, boiling, pickling, and curing.

SICHUAN PEPPERCORNS | 花椒

Mistakenly called peppercorns, these seeds of a variety of prickly ash tree are in no way related to the pepper family. They do, however, physically resemble peppercorns. Also known as flower peppercorns or Chinese peppercorns, they originate from Sichuan province. They don't have the spicy heat characteristic of regular peppercorns, but rather they create a numbing sensation on the tongue. When combined with red chiles, Sichuan peppercorns create the distinctly hot and numbing *mala* (麻辣) taste characteristic of Sichuan food.

CASSIA BARK | 桂皮

Harvested from the *Cinnamomum cassia* tree, this fragrant bark is often referred to as Chinese cassia or Chinese cinnamon. Belonging to the same family as common cinnamon, the bark has a similar but subtler smell and flavor. Regular cinnamon stick can be substituted if cassia bark is unavailable. Unlike the Western use of ground cinnamon in sweet dishes, cassia bark is mostly used whole in braised dishes.

CLOVES | 丁香

Cloves are the aromatic flower buds of a tropical evergreen tree and are used mostly in marinades or braising liquids. Cloves complement the flavors of star anise and Sichuan peppercorns, with which they are regularly paired.

FENNEL | 小茴香

The seed of a flowering herb related to the celery family, fennel has an aniseed flavor that works well with other spices. It is used almost exclusively in marinades and braising liquids.

FIVE-SPICE POWDER | 五香

Five-spice powder is a mixture of ground spices, most commonly star anise, Sichuan peppercorns, cassia bark, cloves, and fennel. The formulas vary from one producer to the next, but the standard is to combine equal amounts of the five components. Some spice companies add additional spices to the mix to create their own special blend. The powder is used in barbecue rubs, marinades, and spiced salts. To incorporate the five-spice flavor during braising

SPICES

BAY LEAF

GOJI BERRIES

JUJUBE

CUMIN
SEEDS

LICORICE

GREEN CARDAMOM

BLACK CARDAMOM

TANGERINE PEEL

DRIED CHILE

STAR ANISE

CLOVES

SICHUAN
PEPPERCORNS

FIVE-SPICE
POWDER

CASSIA
BARK

FENNEL SEEDS

or boiling, whole spices are used because they can be removed easily; using five-spice powder in a braised dish will produce a sauce with a gritty texture.

LICORICE | 乾草

The dried stem of the licorice plant, this is often used in making herbal soups, especially in southern China. Licorice has a sweet anise flavor with a slightly bitter aftertaste and should be used sparingly.

BLACK CARDAMOM | 草果

Used mostly in southwestern China, black cardamom is almost always combined with other spices. Sichuan and Hunan cuisines regularly use this spice in braised dishes. It is also one of the staple spices in the Sichuan *mala* soup base used in hot pots.

GREEN CARDAMOM | 豆蔻

Also known as white cardamom, this is not as commonly used as black cardamom. It has a distinct strong aroma and can supply a fragrant depth to any spice mix. Mostly used in southern China, it often appears as one of the spices in the complex flavor-potting broth for duck or goose. In Sichuan it is sometimes added to a *mala* broth along with black cardamom.

CUMIN | 孜然

Cumin reached China from Persia by way of the Silk Road and influenced the cuisine of the Muslim population in Xinjiang province as well as other western regions. Originally used exclusively with lamb, this nutty, fragrant spice is now often found paired with other ingredients such as beef, chicken, and fish.

BAY LEAF | 香葉

The Chinese use bay leaves from Southeast Asia for pickling and braising. The leaf has a floral fragrance that imparts depth to any other spices with which it is combined. Mostly used in the southern provinces, it is often an ingredient in the Sichuan *mala* soup base and in Yunnan braised meat.

GOJI BERRIES | 枸杞

Goji berries, or wolfberries, have become popular among Western consumers recently because of their high antioxidant content and other as yet unproven health claims. The Chinese use them extensively in preparing soups and steamed dishes, where the berries are considered an herbal supplement to the daily diet. Goji berries do not have a distinct flavor and simply blend into the flavor of the dishes they are added to.

JUJUBE | 紅棗

Often incorrectly called Chinese dates, jujubes are not from the date palm family. Rather, they are the dried fruits of a deciduous plant native to northern China. Jujubes are commonly used in making soups, braised dishes, and sweet dishes. They have a sweet date-like taste and are often boiled until soft, mashed into a paste, and used as a pastry filling.

DRIED CHILES | 乾辣椒

Dried chiles are used extensively in southwestern China, especially in Sichuan. They are used in just about every cooking technique—whole, as flakes, or powdered. Thought to have been introduced to China from South America by Portuguese traders, chiles have become a staple in Chinese cooking.

TANGERINE PEEL | 陳皮

Produced in the southern provinces of China, tangerine peel is dried and used to infuse a fruit flavor into many different savory and sweet dishes. The dried peel has a much more intense citrus flavor than the fresh fruit and works well with other spices.

STARCHES

Starch is used extensively in Chinese cooking for thickening sauces and for coating fried foods. Although a huge variety of starches is available in Chinese markets, most of them have very similar characteristics, and they can generally be used interchangeably with good results. My personal favorite is tapioca starch; I believe it produces the smoothest sauce and crispiest fried crust. For convenience, though, cornstarch, which is readily available in any American market, can be used as a general-purpose starch. Here is a list of starches that can be used successfully in Chinese cooking.

Arrowroot starch
Cornstarch
Potato starch
Tapioca starch
Wheat starch

SAUCES

Chinese sauces have a very long history that most likely predates written records. The ancient sauces, known as *jiang* (醬), were originally made from meat or fish that was salted and fermented, producing a rich savory sauce similar to modern fish sauce. The process was later adapted for use with soybeans and grains that later became the soy sauce we know today.

SOY SAUCE | 生抽

A product of soybean fermentation, soy sauce is the most commonly used sauce in Asia. The sauce is thin and light in color, so it is often referred to as light soy sauce. In this case, the word "light" refers to the color and consistency and not to the fact that the sodium content has been reduced. This type of soy sauce is used as an ingredient in stir-fries, steamed dishes, and cold dishes, and as a condiment at the table.

DARK SOY SAUCE | 老抽

After the initial fermentation, soy sauce is aged in large clay jars for another 6 to 9 months to produce dark soy sauce. Darker and richer in flavor, this is used almost exclusively for braising meat and is never used as a condiment.

SWEET SOY SAUCE | 甜醬油, 醬油膏

In Fujian and Taiwan, soy sauce is sweetened, then reduced to a consistency similar to maple syrup. This sauce is commonly used as a condiment or for making dipping sauces. In the southwest provinces of Sichuan and Yunnan, a similar sweet soy sauce is spiced with star anise and Sichuan peppercorns.

OYSTER SAUCE | 蠔油

Oyster sauce was accidentally invented by Lee Kum Sheung, who founded the Lee Kum Kee Company in 1888 to market his invention. Lee, who was a chef, apparently left a batch of oysters boiling unattended and returned to find the liquid had reduced to a flavorful savory sauce. It has become popular not just in China but worldwide, and is a standard condiment for flavoring beef and meat dishes. It is a relative newcomer for a Chinese condiment, but its success has made it synonymous with Cantonese cooking.

PASTES AND CONDIMENTS

Flavorful pastes and condiments play a very important role in Chinese cooking, and every region in China has its own collection. But some pastes have become so popular that they are regularly used nationwide. I introduce a few of them here to help you understand their different flavors and uses.

FERMENTED BEAN PASTE | 豆瓣醬

Among the many varieties of fermented bean pastes, this basic brown paste made from soybeans is the most common. The paste is thick and contains broken pieces of soybeans. The strong, salty, and soy sauce–like flavor is excellent in braised dishes or when used to make a meat sauce.

SICHUAN CHILE BEAN PASTE | 四川辣豆瓣醬

This Sichuan version of fermented bean paste is spiced with pickled red chiles. The best pastes are supposedly made in Sichuan's Pixian County (郫縣). Chile bean paste is used extensively in Sichuan cooking for making sauces, stir-fries, and braised dishes. It is often combined with Sichuan peppercorns to enhance the numbing sensation that is typical of Sichuan flavors.

DRY FERMENTED BEANS | 豆豉

Because they turn a black color during fermentation, these fermented soybeans are also known as fermented black beans—but they are not made from black beans. Dry fermented beans are soybeans that have been fermented without liquid; they are most commonly used in southern China. The soybeans are usually packed in a clear plastic bag for easy identification and are excellent for stir-frying, steaming, and braising.

FERMENTED TOFU | 腐乳

Very common in the southern coastal province of Fujian, this tofu product, known as *furu* (腐乳), is fermented cubed tofu placed in brine. It can be either white or red depending on the type of yeast used in the processing. The specific name for the red version is *nanru* (南乳). There is a third version that is spiced with pickled red chiles. Fermented tofu can be used in stir-fries and braised dishes, and as a condiment to accompany rice porridge.

HOISIN SAUCE | 海鮮醬

Widely known in the West, hoisin sauce is a sweetened fermented soybean paste. The paste is finely ground so there are no visible pieces of soybean. Hoisin sauce is used mainly in the south, especially as the base for Cantonese barbecue sauce. It can be used in cooking or as a condiment. It is similar in flavor to the sweet bean paste popular in the north; many cooks use them interchangeably.

SWEET BEAN PASTE | 甜麵醬

This paste is very similar to hoisin sauce but is mostly used in northern China. Sweet bean paste is the defining sauce used for serving Peking duck and is often used in many northern-style stir-fries.

SESAME PASTE | 芝麻醬

Made from ground toasted white sesame seeds, sesame paste has a consistency and nutty fragrant taste reminiscent of peanut butter. Commonly used in making dressings for cold dishes and cold noodles, it can also be used as a dipping sauce for hot pot.

WHITE WINE LEES | 酒釀

Commonly known as *jiuniang*, white wine lees is glutinous rice fermented with wine yeast. It contains a small trace of alcohol and has a slightly tart flavor. This wine-flavored paste is very popular in the Yangtze River Delta region and is a common ingredient in *Huaiyang* cuisine. Traditionally *jiuniang*

WINE YEAST BALL

RED YEAST RICE

was the actual residue, or lees, from the winemaking process. Today it is manufactured separately. It is a very simple process and is often made at home.

WHITE WINE LEES | 酒釀

MAKES 3 CUPS

1½ cups glutinous rice
1 ball (about ½ ounce) wine yeast

Soak the glutinous rice in 2 cups water for at least 12 hours or overnight.

Drain the rice and spread it over a cheesecloth-lined bamboo steamer. Put the steamer over simmering water in a wok, cover, and steam until tender, 1 hour. Cool the steamed rice to room temperature.

In the meantime, boil 1 cup water and then let it cool. Crush the wine yeast ball into a powder and add it to the cooled boiled water. (The yeast ball can be crushed by using a rolling pin or a small mortar and pestle.) Combine the cooked glutinous rice and the yeast water in a wide-mouth 1-quart glass or plastic container. Stir the mixture until the rice and yeast are well combined.

Cover the container with plastic wrap and poke a few tiny air holes in it with a metal skewer or the sharp point of a knife. Let stand at room temperature to ferment. It will be ready to use after 36 to 48 hours, when the rice is soft and a layer of wine appears on the top. Cover and refrigerate for up to 3 months.

RED WINE LEES | 紅糟

The residue, or lees, from making red rice wine, this paste is common in southern coastal China. Closely identified with Hakka cuisine, red wine lees has a very strong alcohol flavor that is great for making braised dishes and stir-fries. The red color comes from the use of red yeast, now readily available in Chinatown markets. Commercially produced red wine lees is available, but the homemade variety can provide a much fresher taste without the use of additives and preservatives.

RED WINE LEES | 紅糟

MAKES 2 CUPS WINE LEES AND 2 CUPS WINE

1½ cups glutinous rice
½ ball (about ¼ ounce) wine yeast
¼ cup red yeast rice

Soak the glutinous rice in 2 cups water for at least 12 hours or overnight.

Drain the rice and spread it over a cheesecloth-lined bamboo steamer. Put the steamer over simmering water in a wok, cover, and steam until

DUCK SAUCE | 蘇梅醬

Also known as plum sauce and made from preserved plum and citrus, this sauce has a fragrant sweet-and-sour flavor beloved by many Americans. It is most commonly used as a dipping sauce with roast duck. It is also excellent for making a sweet-and-sour dressing for salads and cold dishes. Squeeze some lime juice into this sauce and add some pickled chiles and you have a great dressing to use with tropical Chinese ingredients such as green papaya.

SHRIMP PASTE | 蝦膏

To make this paste, tiny shrimp are salted and fermented before being ground into a purple-gray paste with a very strong anchovy smell. When used sparingly, shrimp paste can impart a rich savory flavor to any dish. It is very similar to other shrimp and fish pastes widely used in Southeast Asian cooking, and they can be used interchangeably. Mostly used by the Cantonese, it is excellent in stir-fries.

OSMANTHUS BLOSSOM SYRUP | 糖桂花

The tiny yellow blossom of the *Osmanthus fragrans* plant is used in Chinese cooking the way vanilla is used in Western cooking. It has a subtle but fragrant vanilla-like smell and is usually used with sugar. The dried blossoms can be steeped in hot water to make tea, or added to sugar syrup for use in cooking; use about 2 tablespoons dried osmanthus blossoms with each cup of simple syrup.

SWEET-AND-SOUR SAUCE | 甜酸醬

Although it is possible to purchase commercially produced sweet-and-sour sauce as a condiment, it is so simple to make that there is no reason not to prepare it in your kitchen. Garlic, ketchup, sugar, and vinegar are the major components of this sauce, which is excellent with fried wontons, egg rolls, or fried rolled meat.

tender, 1 hour. Cool the steamed rice to room temperature.

In the meantime, boil 2 cups water and let it cool. Crush the wine yeast ball into a powder and add it to the cooled boiled water. (The yeast ball can be crushed by using a rolling pin or a small mortar and pestle.) Combine the cooked glutinous rice, red yeast rice, and the yeast water in a wide-mouth 1-quart glass or plastic container. Stir the mixture until the rice and yeast are well combined.

Cover the container with plastic wrap and poke a few tiny air holes in it with a metal skewer or the sharp point of a knife. Let stand at room temperature to ferment for 30 to 45 days. By the end of the fermentation period, a layer of wine will have developed on top. The lees can be strained from the wine and stored in a separate container if desired. Both the wine and the lees can be used for cooking. Refrigerate for up to 1 year.

SWEET-AND-SOUR DIPPING SAUCE | 甜酸醬汁

<small>MAKES ½ CUP</small>

1 tablespoon vegetable oil

1 tablespoon minced garlic

2 tablespoons ketchup

1 teaspoon white rice vinegar

1 tablespoon sugar

¼ teaspoon salt

1 tablespoon tapioca starch

1 tablespoon toasted sesame oil

Heat the vegetable oil in a saucepan over medium heat until hot, about 30 seconds. Add the garlic and stir-fry until fragrant, about 30 seconds. Add the ketchup, rice vinegar, sugar, salt, and ⅓ cup water and mix well. Bring the mixture to a boil.

In a small bowl, whisk the tapioca starch with 3 tablespoons water to make a slurry. Add this to the pan and cook, stirring, until thickened, about 1 minute. Add the sesame oil just before removing from the heat. Serve the sauce immediately, while still hot.

XO SAUCE

Created during the 1980s in Hong Kong, this fancy spicy sauce was originally used as a condiment for dipping. Made with expensive ingredients such as dried scallops, ham, and dried shrimp, the sauce was initially served only at high-end restaurants—its name was meant to conjure up the chic image of the XO-grade cognac beloved by the Hong Kongers. XO sauce has become so popular that it is no longer used just as a table condiment; many dishes have been created using the sauce as a flavoring ingredient.

XO SAUCE

MAKES 2 CUPS

4 dried medium scallops, rehydrated (see page 80)

1 cup vegetable oil

1 tablespoon minced shallots

2 tablespoons minced garlic

1 ounce dry-aged Virginia ham, minced

¼ cup dried shrimp, rehydrated (see page 80) and minced

1 ounce dried salted fish, minced

¼ cup minced fresh red chiles

2 tablespoons minced fresh Thai bird's-eye chiles

1 teaspoon sugar

Steam the scallops in a small bowl set over boiling water in a steamer for about 20 minutes. Remove from the steamer and shred the scallops.

Heat the oil in a saucepan over medium heat until it is just beginning to shimmer or registers about 350°F. Add the shallots and garlic and fry for about 45 seconds or until slightly browned. Reduce the heat to low and add the ham, shredded scallops, dried shrimp, and dried fish. Gently cook the ingredients in the oil for about 5 minutes or until they turn golden brown. Add both types of chiles and continue to cook for about 5 minutes, until the chiles are soft. Add the sugar and mix well. Remove from the heat and let cool before transferring to a glass jar. Cover and refrigerate for up to 9 months.

COOKING WINES

The term "Chinese rice wine" is very much a misnomer. It is not wine in the Western sense of fruit alcohol, but rather it is grain liquor. There are two main classifications for Chinese rice wine: yellow rice wine and white rice wine. Both wines are made from combinations of regular and glutinous rice. The yellow color comes from the toasting of the grain before fermentation.

Yellow rice wine, with an alcohol content of between 14 and 20%, is a nondistilled grain liquor made by simple fermentation. White rice wine, on the other hand, is distilled and the alcohol content can be more than 40%, making it more closely related to the distilled liquors of the West. Rice wine is as important for enhancing flavors in Chinese cooking as grape wine is in Western cooking.

SHAOXING COOKING WINE | 紹興料酒
The best-known yellow rice wine used for cooking comes from the town of Shaoxing. It has become the most common cooking wine used throughout China. The nutty grain taste of Shaoxing wine is reminiscence of dry sherry, which can be used as a substitute. It is used in all types of cooking.

LAOJIU WINE | 老酒
Laojiu literally means "aged wine." Made by aging yellow rice wine, it has the signature nutty wine taste, but the aging process makes its flavor more pronounced. Used in all manners of cooking, *laojiu* is popular in Fujian and Taiwan, where it is produced.

WHITE RICE WINE | 白米酒
White rice wine, commonly known as *baijiu*, is a high-alcohol-content liquor. Although it does not have the nutty flavor of yellow rice wine, *baijiu* does have the characteristically sharp grain alcohol aroma. It is used extensively in the north for all kinds of cooking.

SAN CHENG CHEW | 三蒸酒
San cheng wine is white rice wine that has been distilled three times; it is produced specifically for cooking and not for drinking. Many chefs claim the extra distillation steps add depth to the flavor. Manufactured in Guangdong province, it is used by the locals in all their cooking.

VINEGAR

Chinese vinegar is made from rice wine and is generally milder and less acidic than the vinegar sold in American markets. Three different types of vinegar are produced: white, red, and black. White and red vinegar are mild and slightly sweet. Black vinegar is aged and supplemented by other grains and fruits, giving it a richer sweet taste reminiscence of balsamic vinegar.

WHITE RICE VINEGAR | 白米醋
White rice vinegar is made from glutinous rice wine and is the basic vinegar used for cooking in China. It is used throughout the country as an ingredient in sweet-and-sour sauces and in hot and sour soup. It is also used for pickling.

RED RICE VINEGAR | 紅醋
Red rice vinegar is made from rice wine that has been fermented with red wine yeast, giving it a pinkish color. Red rice vinegar has a more floral fragrance than white rice vinegar, with the same slightly sweet mellow taste. Not as widely used as white and black vinegar, red rice vinegar can be used as a cooking ingredient or as a condiment in a dipping sauce.

CHINKIANG BLACK VINEGAR │ 鎮江香醋

Black vinegar is made from rice wine with additional grains, fruits, and herbs. It is aged from 3 to 6 months. Although it is made in many parts of China, the black vinegars from the city of Chinkiang, or Zhenjiang (鎮江) in Mandarin, in Jiangsu province are considered to be the best. Black vinegar is mostly used as condiment for dipping or made into sauces for cold dishes, although there are braised dishes that also call for it.

COOKING FATS

It is important to discuss the choice of cooking fat because of the unique requirement of high temperatures in Chinese cooking. For stir-frying in particular, it is necessary to use a fat that can withstand temperatures as high as 400°F without breaking down and beginning to turn rancid.

Traditionally, the most common and beloved cooking fat in China was lard. Its relatively high smoke point makes it perfect for use in stir-frying, and it adds flavor when used as a supplemental fat in pastry filling or with steamed glutinous rice. Unfortunately, ever since the health-care community demonized lard, it has fallen out of favor worldwide. The reality is that lard is no more unhealthy than butter or any other animal fat. In moderation, lard is not necessarily such an unhealthy choice.

LARD │ 熟豬油

Naturally rendered lard is one of the most delicious and potentially healthful fats available. It is great for Chinese cooking because its smoke point is relatively high. Always use freshly rendered lard and not the commercial hydrogenated variety. The best way to render lard for Chinese cooking is to dry-render leaf lard, cut it into ¼-inch cubes, and then cook it directly over low heat until melted. The alternative wet rendering of lard with water is not suitable for use with Chinese cooking because that process introduces too much moisture.

VEGETABLE OILS │ 素菜油

Vegetable oils have long been recommended as an alternative to animal fat, but there are health implications that are not fully understood by the general consumer. Cold-pressing is a method of extracting oil without high heat and without solvents. Because of this the oil remains in its natural condition and is usually healthier. The other method of extracting oil uses high heat and chemical solvents and changes the structure of the oil, sometimes leaving trace amounts of toxins in the process.

Smoking Point Temperature of Common Vegetable Oils		
Oil	°C	°F
Almond	216	421
Avocado	271	520
Canola (rapeseed)	230	446
Coconut (virgin)	177	351
Corn	238	460
Cottonseed	232	450
Grapeseed	216	421
Olive (virgin)	160	320
Peanut	229	444
Rice Bran	213	415
Safflower	266	511
Sesame (toasted)	177	351
Soybean	245	473
Sunflower	209	408
Walnut	204	399

Certain oils, such as olive, avocado, walnut, almond, coconut, and grapeseed, are extracted using the cold-press method. These oils have a much more pronounced flavor than refined vegetable oil. Except for a few oils such as those extracted from avocado and grapeseed, very few natural oils have a smoke point that is high enough to make them suitable for stir-frying.

Oils extracted with the high heat method are more common; these include canola, corn, peanut, soybean, rice bran, and cottonseed. These oils are often further refined to give them a higher smoke point.

Choosing which oil to use for Chinese cooking is a bit of a dilemma. Avocado oil, which has a high smoke point, is rare and expensive. On the other hand, the more readily available oils such as canola, corn, soybean, and rice bran are all highly refined and may have as yet unidentified negative health effects. The oil you choose to buy will depend on its availability, the cost, and your health concerns.

FLAVORED OILS

To infuse aromatic hints into a dish, many recipes call for adding a flavored oil. Although many different flavored oils are used in Chinese cooking, sesame and chile oil are the most common. Not only do they add flavor, but they often improve the overall texture and mouthfeel as only fats can.

TOASTED SESAME OIL | 芝麻油

Toasted sesame oil is generally made from toasted black sesame seeds. (This oil is different from the untoasted white sesame oil available in Middle Eastern markets.) It is fragrant and has a nutty taste, and is used both as an ingredient in cooking and as a condiment. It is always used in cold dishes and salad dressings.

Sesame oil has a low smoke point, so it breaks down easily when cooked. To avoid overcooking it, it should be added at the last minute just before a dish is removed from the heat.

CHILE OILS | 辣椒油

Chile oil, a versatile flavoring ingredient that can be used in both hot and cold dishes, is made by infusing dried red chiles in vegetable oil. It is a great way to kick up the spicy heat level in a dish. Although available commercially, a homemade version will be hotter and will have a far superior flavor.

SIMPLE CHILE OIL | 辣油

MAKES 2 CUPS

1 cup Chinese red chile powder
2 cups vegetable oil

Put the chile powder in a heat-proof 3-quart bowl.

Heat the vegetable oil to about 250°F. Pour the hot oil over the chile powder and stir around to make sure the powder is spread evenly throughout the oil. Let infuse for 24 hours.

Strain the oil through a fine-mesh sieve and store it in a covered glass jar for up to a year.

SICHUAN SPICED CHILE OIL
四川辣油

MAKES 4½ CUPS

½ cup Sichuan peppercorns

4 cups vegetable oil

1 (1-inch-long) piece of fresh ginger

2 scallions

2 tablespoons whole cloves

1 (1-inch) square of cassia bark

4 whole star anise

2 black cardamom pods

2 cups dried whole red chiles

¼ cup crushed Chinese red chile flakes

2 tablespoons Chinese red chile powder

Soak the Sichuan peppercorns in the oil for at least 8 hours or overnight.

In a large saucepan, heat the oil and peppercorns over low heat to about 250°F. Add the ginger, scallions, cloves, cassia bark, star anise, black cardamom, and dried whole red chiles. Simmer in the oil for about 20 minutes.

Put the red chile flakes and powder in a heat-proof 3-quart bowl. Strain the oil through a wire-mesh strainer into the bowl. Discard the strained spices. Let the oil steep overnight before using.

Both the oil and the chile flakes can be used in recipes. Store in a covered glass jar for up to a year.

PICKLED INGREDIENTS

Brine-pickling helps preserve the harvest's bounty and provides flavorful ingredients to use during the rest of the year. The method is similar to the Western pickling process, but the Chinese pickle a wider variety of ingredients, including cabbage, mustard greens, radishes, and sour plums. Some of the pickles are stored for the long term while others are served soon after pickling.

PICKLED MUSTARD GREENS | 酸菜

Made from *gai choy*, mustard greens that resemble cabbage, this pickle is widely produced in southern China. The entire head of greens is brined and then allowed to ferment. The process creates salty and sour crunchy greens with a faint mustard taste—but without the bitterness usually present in the fresh ingredient. These pickled mustard greens, known as *suan cai* in Chinese, are served in a variety of ways; they can be stir-fried, made into soups, or even eaten as is.

PICKLED SOUR PLUM | 酸梅

The Chinese sour plum is a small round fruit with sour flesh and a large pit. The pickling process mellows the taste slightly but leaves the plum with a nice fruity aroma. Normally sold whole, pickled plums are usually pitted and mashed before use. They are excellent as a sauce for steamed dishes, as an ingredient in braising, or made into the familiar plum sauce to accompany roast duck.

Feast or Famine Food?

Whenever exotic Chinese cooking ingredients are discussed, poverty and famine are invariably cited to explain why the Chinese eat such items as dog meat and insects. Although China has known deprivation during turbulent times, especially during the last two hundred years, it is perhaps more instructive to look at what was eaten during periods of peace and prosperity. In the calm and booming era of the Song Dynasty, Chinese culinary art developed into a sophisticated enterprise using exotic ingredients and complex techniques. Attesting to the wealth of the society, ingredients such as sea cucumbers from the southern ocean and snake wine from the southwest hills were transported thousands of miles to the kitchens of the imperial capital in the Central Plain.

At the archeological site of Mawangdui (馬王堆), in Hunan province, the tomb of a Han aristocrat contains bamboo tiles used to record the items in the tomb's kitchen. The inventory of meat includes venison, rabbit, and dog, indicating that these ingredients were considered luxury foods.

So is poverty the impetus that drove the Chinese to eat these foods, considered disgusting by Westerners? I believe it is the adventurous nature of the Chinese culinary culture that drives the Chinese diners to seek out so many exotic foods.

SALTED AND CURED INGREDIENTS

For millennia people in China have been using salt to preserve both meats and vegetables. It is a process that also transforms the ingredients through chemical reaction into highly flavorful products. Different regions in China have developed their own curing techniques, and salted and cured items have had a big influence on the development of local cuisines.

HAM | 火腿

Chinese ham is cured using a dry-aging process and is never smoked. The process is more akin to making prosciutto than to smoking ham. There are three regions in China that have become well known for their ham: Jinhua (金華) in Zhejiang, Xuanwei (宣威) in Yunnan, and Rugao (如皋) in Jiangsu. Among these three, Jinhua ham is the most sought after. Chinese ham generally is used as a flavor-enhancing ingredient in soups, steamed dishes, and stir-fries. However, one exception to this rule is Steamed Ham in Osmanthus Blossom Sauce (page 351), where the ham is the star ingredient; this is admittedly one of the most luxurious dishes in Chinese cuisine.

CHINESE BACON | 臘肉

Known as Chinese bacon, pork belly is routinely cured using salt, soy sauce, spices, and herbs before being air-dried. This curing process, known as *la* (臘) in Mandarin, is also used with many different types of meat. Cured pork belly is commonly used as a flavor-enhancing ingredient in stir-fries, braised dishes, steamed dishes, and flavored rice. Cured pork belly is sometimes smoked, in which case it is known as smoked pork belly (燻肉) or Chinese smoked bacon.

CURED DUCK | 臘鴨

Similar to cured pork belly, cured duck is salted in an aromatic brine first, then air-dried. After the curing process the duck meat develops a subtle waxy texture and a mild aroma that's not as gamy as the fresh meat. The cured duck is often served by itself after being simply steamed, or combined with other ingredients to make braised dishes or flavored rice.

SALTED PORK | 鹹肉

Salted pork is slightly different from the previously described cured meats in that the pork is not air-dried. The pork is usually prepared with lean meat and is kept moist in brine. The flavor and texture are similar to regular ham, but salted pork has a fresher taste. This is a common ingredient in the Yangtze River Delta region and is used in stir-fries and soups.

SALTED EGGS | 鹹蛋

Salted eggs are ubiquitous in Chinese cooking. They are duck eggs that have been soaked in a simple brine and left for 30 and 40 days. Salted eggs have numerous uses as ingredients in stir-frying and steaming, or as part of the sweet paste filling of certain pastries.

CENTURY EGGS | 皮蛋

Known by many different names, such as preserved eggs, thousand-year-old eggs, and millennium eggs, these are duck eggs that have been preserved in a clay coating of alkali and salt. After curing, the yolk becomes dark grayish green and the white turns into a clear brown gel. It has a strong phosphorous smell that can be offensive to some. This egg is often eaten as is with a dipping sauce, cooked with rice porridge, or stir-fried with other ingredients.

FERMENTED DRIED MUSTARD GREENS | 梅乾菜

A specialty of Hakka cuisine, these dried greens are made from select varieties of leafy mustard greens such as shepherd's purse and mizuna. The entire mustard plant is first salted, then allowed to ferment for 15 to 20 days before being dried in the sun. The mustard greens become dark brown and have a strong nutty mustard aroma. Called *meigan cai,* they are used mostly in braised dishes (see photograph on page 38).

CURED RADISH | 蘿蔔乾

Dried daikon radish is a southern specialty, especially in Fujian and Taiwan. Daikon radishes are cut into long thick strips, pickled in brine with sugar, and then dried in the sun before being stored. The dried radish has a spicy sweet and salty taste that is especially appetizing. It is most frequently used as an ingredient in a special Fujian omelet.

TIANJIN PRESERVED VEGETABLE | 冬菜

Although best known as a preserved vegetable called *dongcai* in Mandarin, which literally means "winter vegetable," it originates from Tianjin in northern China and is used in the cooking of other regions as well. The preservation process starts by adding salt, garlic, and spices to season a variety of napa cabbage known as Tianjin cabbage before the vegetable is sun-dried and packed in a clay jar.

Dongcai is never eaten directly but rather used as a seasoning and flavoring ingredient in stir-fries, soups, noodles, and scramble-fried eggs. It is full of umami.

DRIED SPECIALTIES

Drying is the best way to efficiently prepare specialty ingredients, especially seafood, for transport over long distances. Not only does drying preserve the ingredients, it also reduces their weight. Since ancient times the Chinese have shipped dried seafood from the coast to satisfy the demand of dynastic palaces in inland capitals. Many of the dried seafood ingredients are considered treasured delicacies and are often sold at very high prices.

DRIED SHIITAKE MUSHROOMS | 香菇

The most common Chinese dried ingredient has to be shiitake mushrooms. The ones that are most highly prized are called flower mushrooms (花菇); the cap of this shiitake mushroom has a cracked pattern and has a potent earthy flavor. Rehydrated, they are used in all sorts of dishes including stir-fries, braised dishes, steamed dishes, and soups.

DRIED WOOD EAR | 木耳

Wood ear is a large fungus that grows on tree trunks. There is a black and a white variety, both of which are used extensively in Chinese cooking. Often used in stir-fries and soups, they contribute very mild flavor and a nice crunchy texture to any dish.

DRIED DAYLILY BUDS | 金針花

The dried unopened blossoms of daylilies have a subtle floral fragrance that is pleasant in braised dishes. They are most commonly used in the cooking of southern China, where the lilies are abundantly grown. The Chinese name for this flower means "golden needles flower," in reference to its long brownish yellow buds.

DRIED WOOD EAR
(BLACK AND WHITE)

DRIED SHIITAKE

DRIED SEAFOOD

DRIED SCALLOPS

DRIED ABALONES

DRIED FISH MAW

DRIED SEA
CUCUMBER

DRIED SCALLOPS | 乾貝

Scallops are considered a delicacy, and the dried type is highly prized because of its concentrated flavor. Often used to enhance flavor in a broth or stock, dried scallops, which are full of umami, can also be used in braised or steamed dishes.

DRIED FISH MAW | 花膠, 魚肚

Fish maw, the air bladder of a fish, is a delicacy from the southern coastal region of China, where it is used quite extensively. Rehydrated, it has a spongy texture and a rather appealing seafood taste that goes well in braised dishes and soups.

DRIED SEA CUCUMBER | 海參

Together with dried abalone and dried shark fin, dried sea cucumber is considered one of the three most precious ingredients in Chinese cuisine. The sea slugs, which come in various sizes and varieties, are harvested or farmed along the coastal regions and then dried. The most sought-after variety is the medium-size spiky slug. They are great in stir-fries, braised dishes, and soups.

DRIED ABALONE | 鮑魚

Dried abalone is known to cost thousands of dollars per pound, and it is not surprising. The subtle nutty seafood flavor, along with the slightly chewy, tender texture, make it one of the most luxurious food sensations one can experience. The mollusks are harvested and farmed along the coastal region and come in many different sizes. At their most elegant they are served whole in a rich aromatic sauce.

DRIED SHARK FIN | 魚翅

It is impossible to ignore shark fin in the context of Chinese cooking, even though I wish I could. Shark fin has been consumed by the Chinese since the Song Dynasty around the 10th century, and became popular during the Ming Dynasty. In fact American traders first entering the China market brought shark fin from the warm waters of the Indian Ocean and Southeast Asia to trade for tea, porcelain, silk, cotton, and other Chinese merchandise. The Americans, though, were not the only traders in shark fin. European as well as Arab and Southeast Asian traders also imported it into China. The trade grew steadily over the centuries until the economic reform in the 1980s, when it began to expand exponentially.

To satisfy this burgeoning demand from China's nouveau riche, large numbers of shark fins are harvested. The relentless pursuit of profit by the people involved in this industry is destroying the shark population worldwide in a sinister and inhumane way. Instead of marketing the entire fish, only the fins are cut off and the shark is thrown back, still alive, into the water. Unable to swim, the shark eventually dies from suffocation or is eaten by predators. Although "shark finning" has been outlawed in many countries, the practice continues in international waters. The only way to reduce this trade is to abstain from consuming shark fin.

The shark fin business in its current state is unsustainable and criminal. As such it is important that all consumers understand the implications of supporting such an industry. For me this is an enterprise that my conscience cannot support. Instead of shark fin soup made with real shark fin, an alternative recipe for mock shark fin soup made with Japanese yam cake is provided on page 278.

CHAPTER FOUR

Basic Ingredient Preparation

WHEN DESCRIBING A PERFECTLY EXECUTED DISH, THE CHINESE USE THE EXPRESSION *SE XIANG WEI CHUAN* (色香味全), MEANING "EXCELLENCE IN PRESENTATION, FRAGRANCE, AND FLAVOR." This idiom recognizes that we appreciate our food first by its appearance, then by its smell, and finally by its taste. The first step toward a successful presentation is proper preparation of the ingredients.

Basic ingredient preparation is similar across culinary cultures; the differences are in the details. In Chinese cooking, knife techniques rank high in importance, and there are cuts that can be considered uniquely Chinese. Another important skill is knowing how to prepare the multitude of Chinese dried ingredients, such as mushrooms and seafood. Finally, preparation of special ingredients such as offal, pig's ear, and jellyfish is not very well understood by most casual cooks. For the intrepid, I have included instructions on how to handle the most common of these exotic ingredients.

KNIFE TECHNIQUES

Have you ever wondered what some of those funny-sounding names in Chinese dishes mean? Such as "Chicken Almond Ding" or "Moo Goo Gai Pan"? The answer has something to do with Chinese knife cut definitions. The "ding" in Chicken Almond Ding is a term that means to cut the chicken into about ½-inch cubes. And the "pan" in Moo Goo Gai Pan simply means to cut the chicken into slices.

BIAS CUT | *PIAN* 片

To slice a vegetable, hold the knife over the vegetable with the blade even with the long edge of the ingredient. Rotate the knife 30 degrees so that it now rests diagonally over the vegetable. Holding the blade vertically, cut straight down into the vegetable. Continue slicing at the same angle, making parallel cuts at the width specified in the recipe you are following.

To cut meat, hold the knife over the meat, against the grain, with the blade even with the short edge of the ingredient. Move the knife in about 2 inches from the short edge, still keeping it parallel with the short edge. Tilt the knife about 30 degrees away from that short edge. Holding the blade at this angle, cut diagonally down into the meat. Continue slicing by making parallel cuts at the width specified in the recipe.

JULIENNE | *SI, TIAO,* AND *DUAN* 絲 條 段

After being sliced using the bias cut, an ingredient can then be julienned. Essentially this is the same as the Western julienne technique, in which slices about 2 inches long are further cut parallel to the long side to produce strips of different thicknesses. In Chinese, thinly cut strips are called *si* and slightly thicker ones, batons in English or French, are called *tiao*. If the ingredient being cut is naturally long and thin, such as scallions, chives, or string beans, then the shape is called *duan*.

DICE | *DING* OR *MI* 丁 米

A julienned strip can be cut crosswise into cubes of different sizes; this is normally known as dicing in the West. Larger cubes, up to ¾ inch thick, are known as *ding*, and *mi*, which means "rice," is used for smaller cubes that can be as tiny as ⅛ inch across.

ROLL CUT | *KUAI* 塊

This is a uniquely Chinese cutting technique that has found acceptance all over the world. It is used exclusively for solid vegetables and calls for a bias cut at a 45-degree angle. After the first cut the ingredient is rolled about one-third of the way away from the cook before another cut is made. This process is repeated until the entire ingredient is cut. The result is a series of irregularly shaped pieces. Ingredients cut this way are usually used for braising or boiling.

MINCE | *MO* OR *SUI* 末 碎

For aromatics and vegetables, the ingredients are roughly chopped into very fine pieces, known as *mo*. Sometimes the flat side of the knife is then used to further crush the pieces to create the consistency of a paste. When mincing meat, the Chinese use two chopping cleavers, one in each hand, and alternately chop until it becomes a paste, or *mo*. *Sui* refers specifically to minced flat leafy ingredients, such as cilantro.

BASIC KNIFE TECHNIQUES

BIAS CUT
FINE DICE
ROLL CUT
THICK JULIENNE
THIN JULIENNE
DICE
MINCE

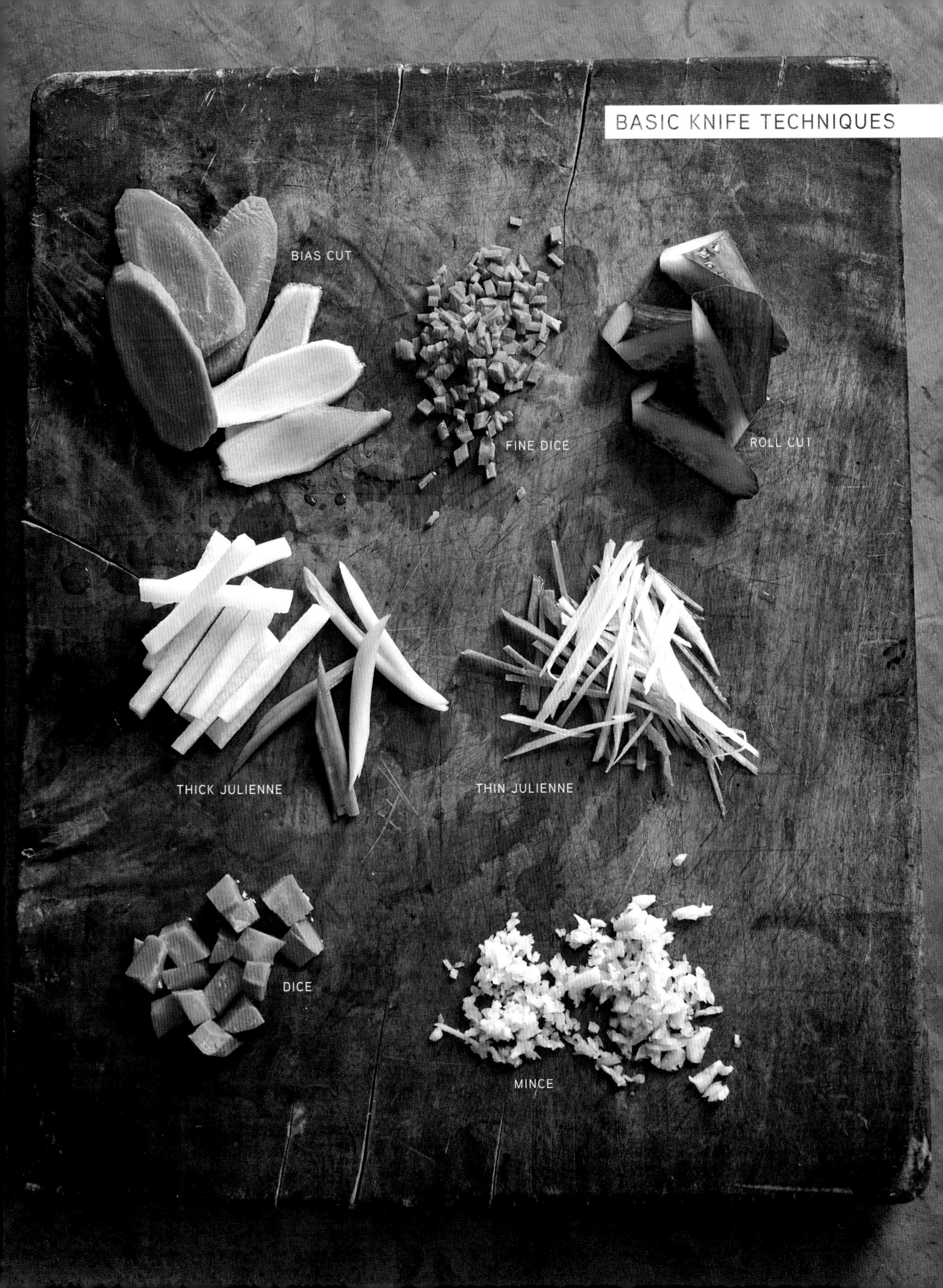

USING KNIFE TECHNIQUES

What you are cooking and how you are cooking it determines how the ingredient should be cut. Here are basic guidelines that you can use as a reference.

VEGETABLES

Stir-frying is the predominant technique used to cook solid and root vegetables. It is best to cut them on the bias into thin slices, between $\frac{1}{16}$ and $\frac{1}{8}$ inch thick. But some tender vegetables, like zucchini, may be cut into large blocks and stir-fried efficiently. When added to soups or braised with meat, the vegetables should be cut into large chunks using the bias or roll cut.

Leafy vegetables are either picked off the stem, or with larger leaves, cut with a knife into bite-size pieces about 2 inches wide.

CHICKEN AND POULTRY

The Chinese consume a wide variety of poultry, but only a handful of birds are eaten regularly at home. They include chicken, duck, goose, squab, quail, and silky chicken. Except for chicken, these fowl are generally butchered in the standard way and are almost always cooked whole. A special technique is reserved for preparing a whole duck for roasting: the abdomen is kept intact and openings to remove the internal organs are made in the neck, under one wing, and in the anus (see page 297).

Chicken is undeniably the most popular type of poultry. Deboned breast meat and thigh meat are regularly used for stir-frying. The breast is best sliced using the bias cut, and the thigh is best diced into about ½-inch cubes.

PORK

Pork is the staple meat in China. It is so ubiquitous that when the name of a dish simply says "meat," as in "stir-fried julienned meat with yellow chives," the meat is understood to be pork.

For braising the popular cuts are pork belly, pork shoulder, and country-style ribs. They are always cut into about 1-inch cubes for easy cooking. For stir-frying the most common cuts of pork are loin and tenderloin. Tenderloin is prepared using the bias cut or julienned.

BEEF AND LAMB

Both beef and lamb are eaten in many parts of China, but they are especially popular among the large Muslim communities in the western and southwestern regions. Properly butchered, both these meats can be halal.

Diced into 1-inch cubes, beef chuck shoulder and lamb shoulder are the best cuts for braising. For stir-frying, beef flank steak and tenderloin or boneless lamb leg are best, sliced using the bias cut.

Cutting Whole Cooked Fowl for Serving

In Chinese cooking, it is customary to cook a whole fowl and then cut it up into pieces for serving. A cleaver or a heavy chef's knife will do a good job.

For small birds, such as squab and quail, cut along the breast all the way to the back to separate the bird into halves, and then cut across the halves to make quarters.

For larger birds such as chicken and duck, first remove the legs and wings at the joint. Then cut each wing into two pieces by separating the drumette from the wingette at the joint. Cut the leg into three pieces by first separating the drumstick from the thigh and then cutting the thigh crosswise into two pieces. Remove the breast meat from the breastbones, and then cut each breast crosswise into four or six pieces. Arrange all the pieces in the shape of the bird on a serving platter. The carcass can be reserved for making stock.

SEAFOOD

Whole Fish | Many Chinese fish recipes call for cooking the fish whole. Not only does a whole fish stay fresh longer than fillets, but by cooking the fish whole, you get the added advantage of extracting delicious flavor from the bones. Ask your fishmonger to clean and scale the fish and remove the gills but leave the tail and fins on. At home, use the back of a knife to scrape off any stray scales, especially on the head and belly area, which can be missed by the fishmonger. Before cooking, cut a few slits on the bias in the body of the fish, spacing them about ¾ inch apart. It will now be ready for steaming, deep-frying, or pan-frying.

Butterflied Fish | To cook fish quickly so the meat doesn't fall apart, you can butterfly it. There are three common ways to butterfly a whole fish Chinese-style.

The first way is to separate the meat from the ribs on both sides of the fish (see photographs, above): Lay the fish on its side. Insert a boning knife between the ribs and the top layer of flesh just behind the gill

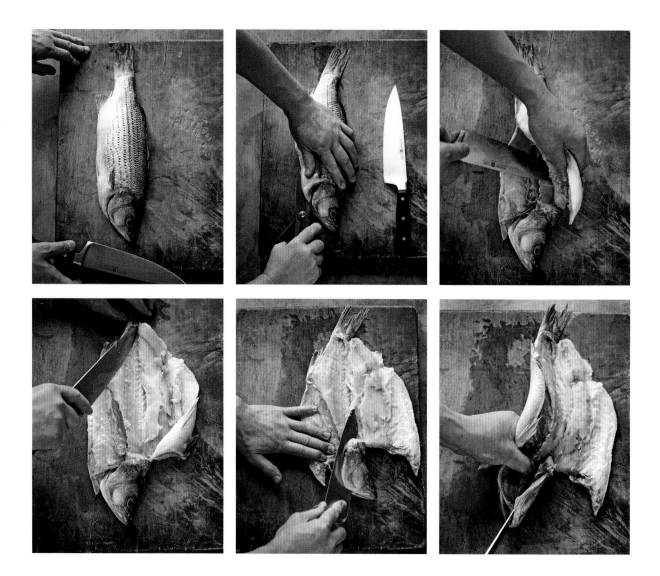

slit. Then slowly slide the knife along the backbone toward the tail, leaving as little flesh as possible still attached to the bones. Be careful not to slice through the skin near the top fin. Flip the fish over and repeat the process on the other side. Arrange the fish with the flesh spread apart on the sides with the backbone propped up vertically as support. The fish is now ready to be cooked.

The second way is similar to the first except that the backbone is removed. After separating the flesh from the ribs on both sides, use kitchen shears to cut the backbone twice, once near the head and again

near the tail. Remove the backbone and all the top fins in one piece. When this butterflied fish is dipped in hot oil and fried, the meat will curl up and the fish will assume a beautiful posture.

The last way to butterfly a fish involves splitting the whole fish in half while keeping the sides joined along the top fin (see photographs, above and right). Separate the meat from the ribs on one side, slicing all the way along the backbone so the tail is cut away from this side of the fish. Be careful not to slice through the skin near the top fin. Do not flip the fish over. Now use a large knife and split the head in half

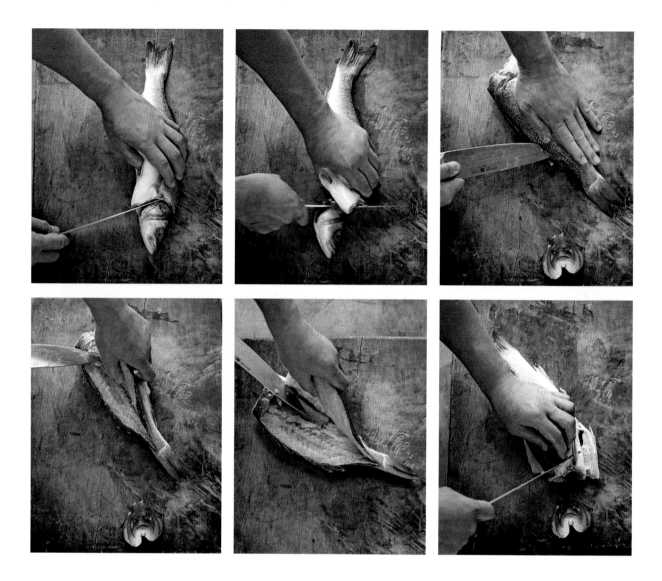

by cutting it from the bottom of the head all the way through the top. When the two sides are flipped open, they will look like two conjoined fish attached by the top fin. This technique is generally used to quickly boil fish.

Squirreled Fish | This unique way to butterfly a whole fish, called squirreling, originated in the Yangtze River Delta area. When the squirreled fish is deep-fried, the tail and the edges flip up, the cross-hatched flesh resembles fur, and many people think the fish comes to resemble a flying squirrel.

The first step in squirreling is to cut the head off the body just behind the gill covers. Then split the jaw and spread the two sides of the head apart far enough so that it can sit upright. Set aside for later use. Lay the fish on its side. Insert a boning knife between the ribs and the top layer of flesh, starting at the front of the fish. Slide the knife slowly along the backbone toward the tail, leaving as little flesh as possible still attached to the bones. Leave the fillet attached to the tail. Turn the fish over and repeat the process on the other side. Now use kitchen shears to cut the backbone away from the tail. You should now

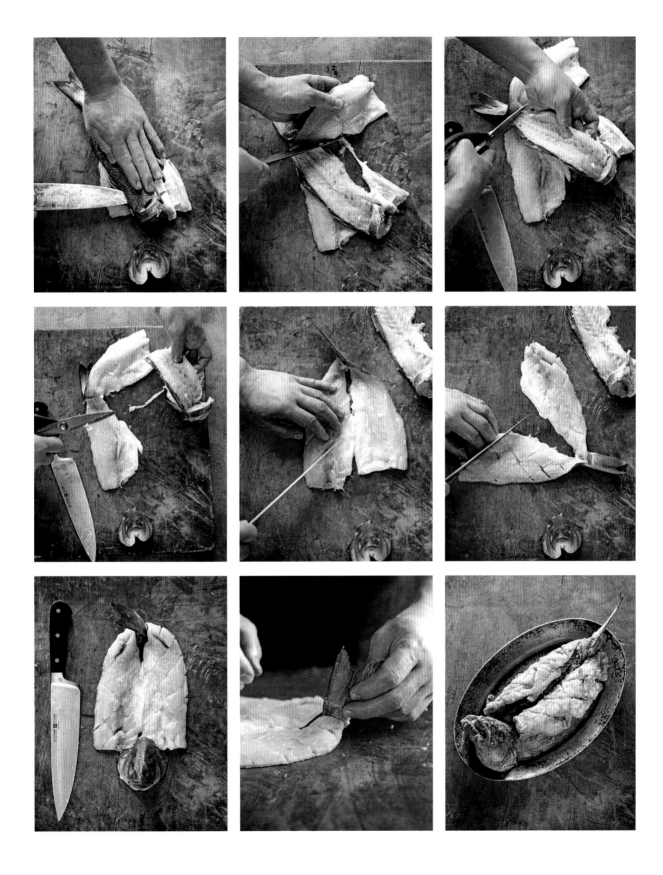

have two fillets attached to one tail. Put the fish on a cutting board and turn the fillets so they are skin-side down. Cut crisscross slits about ½ inch apart all over the exposed flesh. Cover both the fish head and the fillets, including the tail, generously with tapioca starch. You are now ready to deep-fry them.

Swamp Eel | Freshwater swamp eel is popular along the southeast region of China and is now readily available in the United States. When you purchase this fish, the fishmonger should remove the internal organs and clean the cavity, otherwise leaving the fish intact. There are no scales on a swamp eel.

   The first step in preparing the eel is to blanch it in boiling salted water for about 1 minute. The meat will be partially cooked and the slime on the skin will be boiled off.

   After draining the eel, cut off the head and tail. The body of the eel has a central backbone with three rows of ribs radiating from it. The ribs separate the body into three sections: one that holds the internal organs and two others that hold the meat. Use a boning knife to separate the two long coils of meat from the ribs, keeping the skin attached. The coils can either be cut into 2-inch-long sections and braised, or julienned and crisp-fried in oil or stir-fried with yellow chives.

Shellfish | Common shellfish such as clams, mussels, and oysters require very minimal preparation beyond scrubbing the shell and soaking them in water with cornmeal overnight so they expel any sand trapped inside.

   For sea snails such as conch and whelk, the shell is either cracked open to harvest the meat or it is blanched for a short time, allowing the cook to pull the meat out and preserving the shell for presentation. When preparing sea snails, the digestive sac and other organs should be removed; only the main body and foot muscle are consumed. The meat is always sliced very thin, to a thickness of about 1/32 inch, and cooked very quickly to prevent it from getting tough.

RECONSTITUTING DRIED INGREDIENTS

Drying concentrates flavors and makes dried ingredients excellent for enhancing dishes. For use in cooking, they all have to be rehydrated.

DRIED BEANS AND SEEDS

Dried beans and seeds such as soybeans, mung beans, red beans, and lotus seeds are common ingredients in Chinese cooking as well. They should all be soaked in cold water for at least 4 to 6 hours before using. Put them in a container that is double the volume of the dried beans, as they will expand as they rehydrate.

DRIED LOTUS AND BAMBOO LEAVES

Dried lotus and bamboo leaves are used for wrapping loose ingredients before cooking. They both have distinct fragrances that will infuse into the main ingredient. Soak them in cold water for about 2 hours before using.

DRIED MUSHROOMS, FLOWERS, AND KOMBU

Many different types of dried mushrooms—such as shiitake, king oyster, bamboo pith, and tea plant—can be gradually rehydrated by soaking in cold water. It will likely take 1 to 2 hours to completely rehydrate these mushrooms. But boiling water can expedite the process without greatly affecting the quality. The liquor from the soaking has an intense mushroom flavor and can be strained and then used in place of water in dishes that include these mushrooms as ingredients.

   Wood ear mushrooms come in black and white varieties and are shipped dried globally. Cut off the tough woody root end after rehydrating in cold water, which should take only 15 to 20 minutes.

   Daylily buds are one of the most delicious dried ingredients in Chinese cooking. They are sold as dried flowers and can be rehydrated with cold water.

RECONSTITUTED WOOD EAR
(WHITE AND BLACK)

RECONSTITUTED SHIITAKE

Just like wood ear, they reconstitute quickly and also produce a scented soaking liquor. The stem end of the flower bud can be tough, so trim it off before cooking.

To rehydrate dried kombu, or kelp, soak the seaweed with enough cold water to cover it completely. It should only take about 30 minutes to rehydrate before it can be drained and cut to whatever size is called for in a recipe.

DRIED ABALONE

Preparing dried abalone requires patience. Start by submerging the abalone in clean cold water in a nonreactive container such as a stainless steel, ceramic, or glass bowl. Add 2 tablespoons baking soda to every 1 quart water to help tenderize it, and mix well. Soak for 12 hours in the refrigerator. Then drain the liquid and replace it with fresh water every 12 hours for 2 full days (four times total, not

including the initial baking soda soak). Do not add baking soda after the first soaking. Small abalones are often cooked whole, but larger ones are cut into slices about 1/16 inch thick. Cut straight down vertically, starting from the elongated end.

DRIED SEAFOOD (SCALLOPS, SHRIMP, OYSTERS, FISH MAWS)

If you're a Chinatown regular, you are probably aware that countless types of dried seafood are sold there, including clams, oysters, scallops, shrimp, fish maws, anchovies, and all kinds of fish, commonly displayed in barrels arranged in front of the store. Even though it may take a long time, rehydrating seafood is best done with cold water, so do plan ahead. Dried fish maws and oysters can take more time, needing as much as 6 to 8 hours to properly rehydrate, but most seafood will take about 2 hours. Dried shrimp usually take much less time; it is possible to soak them successfully for less than 30 minutes.

DRIED SEA CUCUMBER

Dried sea cucumbers must be rehydrated and parboiled before using. Use enough water to completely submerge the sea cucumbers in a nonreactive container. The sea cucumbers will generally expand to three or four times their original volume, so be sure to use a large enough container. Refrigerate for 12 hours. Repeat four more times for a total soaking time of 48 hours.

Drain the sea cucumbers and cut a slit from end to end on the underside of each one. Remove the intestines and rinse the inside completely. Small sea cucumbers are often cooked whole and make for an elegant presentation. Sometimes larger sea cucumbers need to be cut into bite-size pieces. Now they are ready for parboiling.

PARBOILING LIQUID

MAKES ENOUGH FOR ABOUT 8 OUNCES
DRIED SEA CUCUMBERS

4 cups water

½ cup Shaoxing cooking wine

1 (1-inch-long) piece of fresh ginger, peeled and
crushed with the flat side of a knife

2 scallions, cut into 2-inch-long sections

Combine all the ingredients in a large saucepan and
bring to a boil. Add the sea cucumbers and cook
for about 30 minutes or until a fork can easily prick
through them.

Drain the sea cucumbers and halve them
lengthwise; then, using the bias cut, cut the halves
into ½-inch-thick slices. Sliced sea cucumber can be
used in stir-fries, braised dishes, or soups.

DRIED SQUID

When rehydrating dried squid, a tenderizing agent
is needed to restore the chewy texture. Make a
solution of 2 tablespoons baking soda to every
1 quart water. Use a nonreactive container, such
as one made of stainless steel, ceramic, or glass, to
soak the squid. Add enough baking soda solution to
completely cover, then cover and soak the squid in
the refrigerator for about 6 hours. Drain completely,
cover the squid with plain water, cover the container,
and continue to soak in the refrigerator for another
12 hours. In some cases the cartilage in the center
needs to be removed before using, but otherwise the
squid is now ready for use.

PREPARING OTHER SPECIALTY INGREDIENTS

Eating an entire animal from head to tail is a growing
trend in the United States. Artisanal butchers have
begun selling previously discarded organ meats
to avant-garde chefs, who are creating new and
exciting dishes. The movement has gained further
momentum as more people learn about the negative
environmental impact of wasting edible cuts of meat.
As it takes a good amount of energy to raise animals
for food, consuming a larger part of each animal
makes sense.

American home cooks are often intimidated by
specialty meats because they are not only unfamiliar
with the cuts but also unskilled in the techniques for
cleaning and preparing them. However, most of these
specialty meats, such as kidney, liver, and tripe, are
now available in markets and butcher shops, already
completely cleaned and ready to cook.

For the handful of ingredients that may require
further preparation at home, here are some notes.

PIG'S EAR

Pig's ear is enjoyed the world over. In Spain and
Portugal it is boiled, then roasted until crisp; in parts
of Eastern Europe it is boiled, smoked, or braised;
and in the southern United States it is cooked in many
different ways. The Chinese mostly braise the ears
and then serve them either cold or stir-fried with
other vegetables.

Inspect the ear to make sure there are no stray
hairs, which should be shaved with a clean razor or
plucked with a tweezer, or singed by placing the ear
directly near the flame of a gas burner. Once cleared
of hair, the pig's ear should be parboiled in water for
about 10 minutes. Skim off any scum that forms on
the surface of the liquid. Drain the water and rinse
the pig's ear. It is now ready to be used in a recipe.

HEART

Pig's heart and beef heart are common in Chinese cooking. Although it may be an ingredient that a local butcher will need to special-order for you, some Chinatown or Asian butchers will carry it. The heart can be stir-fried, braised, or made into a soup.

For stir-frying, the heart muscle meat is the only part that is used. Cut the heart into halves and remove the arteries and tough membranes. Then cut the red muscle crosswise into 1/16-inch-thick slices. Stir-fry for a very short time to keep the heart tender.

The whole organ can be braised in an aromatic broth. It needs to be cooked for an extended period of time so that the muscle will be tender when done. After it cools, halve the heart lengthwise and then cut crosswise into thin slices.

Chicken and duck hearts are also regularly used in Chinese cooking. Make sure you cut off the top of the heart, where the arteries can be tough, and use only the muscle itself.

KIDNEY

Done well, there are few things more delicious than kidney; cleaned improperly, however, there is nothing more unpleasant. Chinatown markets usually sell only pork kidney. Beef, veal, and lamb kidneys are available from many butchers and are equally appetizing in Chinese recipes. Most butchers sell kidney whole and already soaked, but it still needs to be split open and rinsed. Here is how to properly complete this task:

Lay the kidney flat on a cutting board and halve it horizontally. This will expose the white tissue in the middle. Use a sharp knife to cut off all the white tissue. Slice off a little extra of the kidney surrounding the white tissue. As this organ filters urine, it is important to remove all the white tissue.

Put the kidney halves in a bowl of water set under a dripping tap. Let the water run for about 20 minutes to completely rinse them. Drain the kidneys completely.

SALTED JELLYFISH

Jellyfish is usually packed in salt to be transported, so it needs to be soaked to wash the salt away. Put the jellyfish in a plastic container and add enough cold water to completely submerge it. Refrigerate it, replacing the water every 2 hours, for about 8 hours. Drain well.

There are two different parts of the jellyfish that are edible: the bell-shaped dome (known as jellyfish skin in Chinese) and the paddles that look like coral (jellyfish head). Regardless of which part of the jellyfish you're working with, it has to be quickly blanched first. Put the jellyfish in a colander in the sink. Pour about ½ cup boiling water over every 1 pound jellyfish. The jellyfish will shrink a little from the blanching; too much hot water will shrink it excessively.

For the jellyfish dome, roll it up into a tight cylinder, then cut down vertically to make slices about ¼ inch wide. The result will be strands of jellyfish that look like thick cellophane noodles.

For the jellyfish paddles, put them flat on the cutting board, and then use a knife to bias cut them horizontally into 1-inch squares.

FRESH BAMBOO SHOOTS

Fresh bamboo shoots have the most delicate flavor and a remarkably crunchy texture. If available in the market they should be favored over canned ones. However, they do need to be prepared before being used in a recipe. Cut each shoot in half lengthwise. Then twist each half to loosen and separate the heart from the outer sheath; discard the sheath. Cut off the dried bottom of the shoot and discard it as well.

Put the bamboo shoots in a medium saucepan. Add enough water to cover. Gently boil for 10 minutes until the shoots are cooked through. Drain the bamboo shoots thoroughly and cool completely before using.

FRESH BAMBOO SHOOTS

CHAPTER FIVE

Chinese Stocks

GLUTAMATE COMPOUNDS OCCUR NATURALLY IN FOOD AND PRODUCE A SAVORY FLAVOR KNOWN AS *UMAMI* IN JAPANESE OR *XIAN* (鮮) IN CHINESE, WHICH HAS BEEN RECOGNIZED AS THE FIFTH TASTE AFTER SWEET, SOUR, SALTY, AND BITTER. For centuries cooks everywhere have enhanced their food by using stock made from bones and aromatic vegetables without understanding the science behind what they were doing: extracting the naturally occurring glutamates from the bones. In 1908 Professor Kikunae Ikeda at Tokyo Imperial University isolated MSG from kelp and identified it as the chemical compound associated with umami. Since then the artificial form of MSG has been commercially produced and marketed all over the world.

In the April 4, 1968, issue of the *New England Journal of Medicine*, a letter to the editor by Dr. Robert Ho Man Kwok was published. Dr. Kwok described a few uncomfortable and disturbing symptoms that he experienced after eating at Chinese restaurants. Among the possible causes he suggested was monosodium glutamate, or MSG. He titled his letter "Chinese Restaurant Syndrome." That was the beginning of the controversy over adding MSG to Chinese food.

Although processed food products we consume every day contain MSG as a flavor enhancer, it is most closely identified with Chinese food because of Dr. Kwok's letter. Despite the fact that extensive studies, including one done by the Federation of American Societies for Experimental Biology in 1992, have concluded that there is no evidence of adverse side effects from MSG consumption, it continues to be viewed as a villain—and especially in Chinese cuisine.

In theory I don't condemn the use of extracted MSG, but still I prefer to use natural glutamates to enrich my food. The best way to do this is by making and using rich, savory stocks. In Chinese cooking there are four recognized categories of stock: simple stock, compound stock, supreme stock, and milky stock.

Simple stocks (清湯), similar to those found in Western cooking, are made from a single type of meat such as chicken, pork, duck, or fish. Generally a simple meat stock is used to enhance the flavor of a dish made with the same meat. However, chicken stock has much broader usage because of its mild complementary flavor and so it is routinely added to seafood dishes as well as pork and vegetable dishes. The key to a simple stock is that it should improve but not overpower the final dish; it should have a simple, delicate flavor but be rich in umami.

On the other hand, compound stocks (高湯), which are made from combinations of different fresh and sometimes cured meats, are regularly used as a main liquid ingredient in soups and braised dishes; these stocks should be complex enough to stand on their own. For this reason, compound stock is used in dishes such as winter melon soup or braised pig's feet with black-eyed peas, where the broth lifts up the savory taste of the main ingredients. Additionally, I like to use compound stock for herbal recipes; the richness of these stocks blends with the herbal flavors seamlessly to create a complex aroma in the final dish. For vegetarian dishes, a fragrant stock is made from a combination of aromatic and root vegetables to infuse lots of umami into the liquid.

The ultimate stock in Chinese cooking is known as supreme stock (上湯) and is frequently used for such luxurious delicacies as abalone soup and braised lion's head meatballs. Supreme stock is simple stock that is further clarified until it is similar to consommé. It is so full of flavor that using it is almost like adding pure MSG to a dish.

One unusual type of stock not found in Western cooking is milky stock (奶湯), which is made by cooking the ingredients at a rolling boil over a long period of time. The boiling action creates a cloudy stock that in addition to being rich and savory has a silky mouthfeel. This stock is standard in stew and braise recipes with fish, pig's feet, or other odd bits of meat.

Stock vs. Broth

In Western cuisine, stock is made from bones and intended as a foundation liquid, whereas broth is made from bones with meat and can be a finished dish. In Chinese cooking there is no such distinction. The Chinese believe that bones and meat together produce a much more flavorful stock than just bones alone. So it is not unusual to find a recipe that calls for stock made with an entire chicken or a ham hock.

SIMPLE STOCK | 清湯

Clear stock can be made from many different kinds of bones, including fresh uncooked chicken, pork, beef, or lamb bones. In order to keep the stock clear, the bones should be parboiled. Be sure to diligently skim off any scum from the surface of the parboiling liquid and to wash off any particles clinging to the bones before making the stock, which should be simmered over very low heat for a long period of time to ensure a clear result.

CHICKEN STOCK | 雞清湯

Often simply known as clear stock (清湯), chicken stock is the most versatile of all stocks. The mild chicken flavor works well with seafood and vegetable dishes. It is also excellent as a soup base. I regularly throw chicken feet into the pot in addition to fresh chicken carcasses to enhance the flavor and give depth to the stock. And when I occasionally find a rooster for sale in Chinatown, I use this whole bird in place of the bones to make the best chicken stock ever. | MAKES 3 QUARTS

2 pounds chicken bones

4 scallions, cut into 2-inch-long pieces

1 (2-inch-long) piece of fresh ginger, smashed with the flat side of a knife

1 cup Shaoxing cooking wine

Put the chicken bones in an 8-quart stockpot and add enough cold water to cover them completely. Bring the water to a gentle boil and cook for about 5 minutes. Drain and discard the liquid. Rinse the bones under cold running water to remove any scum from the parboiling.

Return the bones to the pot, add the scallions, ginger, wine, and 4 quarts water, and slowly bring to a simmer over low heat. Skim off any scum that forms on the surface of the liquid. Simmer uncovered for 4 hours.

Use tongs to remove the solid ingredients and then strain the liquid through a very-fine-mesh sieve. Let cool, then cover and refrigerate for up to 5 days or freeze for up to 6 months.

PORK STOCK | 豬清湯

Clear pork stock is most commonly used as a soup base. It can also be used to enhance the flavor of any braised pork dish. Pork stock is almost never used in cooking with other types of meat. While pork shoulder bones yield the best result, fresh ham bones and neck bones are excellent options as well. | MAKES 3 QUARTS

Follow the directions for chicken stock, substituting pork bones for the chicken bones.

BEEF STOCK | 牛清湯

Unlike its common Western counterpart, Chinese beef stock is not a brown stock. It is in fact a clear beef broth that can be used either as a soup base or as a flavor enhancer for any beef dish. I add dried shiitake mushrooms and Sichuan peppercorns to further develop umami in the stock. For best results, use knuckle, shoulder, or shank bones. | MAKES 3 QUARTS

Follow the directions for chicken stock, substituting beef bones for the chicken bones. Add 1 ounce dried shiitake mushrooms and 1 teaspoon Sichuan peppercorns when you add the scallions and ginger.

LAMB STOCK | 羊清湯

Just as beef stock is reserved for beef dishes, clear lamb stock is used only in making lamb soup or enhancing lamb dishes. To neutralize the gaminess of lamb, Sichuan peppercorns and bay leaf are added to the pot. | MAKES 3 QUARTS

Follow the directions for chicken stock, substituting lamb bones for the chicken bones. Add 1 ounce dried shiitake mushrooms, 1 teaspoon Sichuan peppercorns, and 1 bay leaf when you add the scallions and ginger.

VEGETARIAN STOCK | 素清湯

Chinese vegetarian cooking uses soy and gluten products to simulate the texture of meat ingredients. These imitative ingredients are largely flavorless, so it is often up to the accompanying sauces to saturate them with sufficiently intense flavor. Many vegetable ingredients—among them mushrooms, soybeans, corn, and radishes—contain high amounts of glutamates and can be cooked in a stock. This vegetarian stock can be used as a general-purpose stock. If soybean sprouts are not available, use 4 ounces dried soybeans, but rehydrate them first (see page 78). | MAKES 3 QUARTS

12 ounces soybean sprouts

2 ears fresh corn

1 ounce dried shiitake mushrooms

1 pound daikon radish

4 scallions, cut into 2-inch-long pieces

1 (2-inch-long) piece of fresh ginger, smashed with the flat side of a knife

1 ounce dried kombu (about two 6 by 4-inch pieces)

1 cup Shaoxing cooking wine

Put all the ingredients in an 8-quart stockpot, add 4 quarts water, and slowly bring to a simmer over low heat. Simmer uncovered for 1½ hours.

Use tongs to remove the solid ingredients and then strain the liquid through a very-fine-mesh sieve. Let cool, then cover and refrigerate for up to 5 days or freeze for up to 6 months.

COMPOUND STOCK	複合湯

SUPREME STOCK	上湯

When making soup with a mild-flavored ingredient such as winter melon or daikon radish, a strong stock with full-bodied flavor will help bring out the ingredient's character. A compound chicken and pork stock can be used when making seafood soup, eight treasures winter melon soup, or hot and sour soup, for example. The combination of chicken, pork, and ham, on the other hand, produces a much more complex stock, often used in expensive, luxurious dishes such as abalone soup or braised sea cucumber.

CHICKEN AND PORK STOCK
高湯

The key to making a good compound stock is to use types of bones whose flavors are compatible. Chicken and pork make a classic combination. | MAKES 3 QUARTS

Follow the directions for chicken stock (page 88), using 1 pound chicken bones and 1 pound pork bones.

CHICKEN, PORK, AND HAM STOCK | 火腿高湯

For many of the luxurious dishes made with expensive seafood such as abalone and sea cucumber, a complex and full-bodied stock is essential. The combination of chicken, pork, and ham produces plenty of umami without creating flavors that will overwhelm the main seafood ingredients. | MAKES 3 QUARTS

Follow the directions for chicken stock (page 88), using 1 pound chicken bones, 1 pound pork bones, and 1 pound smoked ham on the bone.

Many lavish banquet menus include sumptuous soups made with abalone, sea cucumber, and other exotic ingredients and use a base of supreme stock, the most luxurious of all stocks. Unlike the Western technique of making consommé using egg white and ground meat, the Chinese clarification process uses only ground meat.

SUPREME CHICKEN STOCK
雞上湯

This stock is not only used for special soups and stews, but it is also regularly used to cook vegetable dishes. The rich flavor of the stock is excellent for enhancing the flavor of leafy vegetables such as spinach, pea shoots, and watercress. | MAKES 2 QUARTS

2½ quarts chicken stock (page 88), cold
1 pound ground chicken breast

Combine the chicken stock and chicken meat in a 4-quart saucepan and mix well. Bring the stock slowly to a simmer and cook uncovered over very low heat for 30 minutes.

Line a strainer with several layers of cheesecloth and set it over a bowl. Using a ladle and avoiding the meat particles, carefully scoop the clear stock into the strainer. Discard the ground meat. Let cool, then cover and refrigerate for up to 5 days or freeze for up to 6 months.

SUPREME CHICKEN AND PORK STOCK | 上湯

In addition to making an excellent soup base for exotic seafood, this stock is often used in pork and ham dishes. | MAKES 2 QUARTS

Follow the directions for Supreme Chicken Stock, using Chicken and Pork Stock (opposite), 8 ounces ground chicken, and 8 ounces ground pork.

MILKY STOCK 奶湯

Meatballs, pork, and seafood are often braised in a milky white broth in a clay pot. Cooked at a steady boil to churn protein and fat particles into the liquid, milky stock is most commonly made from pork, ham, or fish.

MILKY PORK AND HAM STOCK 火腿奶湯

The combination of fresh pork bones and smoked ham produces the most concentrated and aromatic flavors to enhance a pork dish. This rich stock blends very well with the flavors of pig's feet and pork belly and hence is commonly used for braising them. It is also a great complementary broth for napa cabbage and tofu dishes. | MAKES 3 QUARTS

Follow the directions for pork stock (page 89), adding 1 pound smoked ham when you add the scallions and ginger. Instead of simmering the stock, boil it over medium heat, adding more water as needed to keep the ingredients covered.

MILKY FISH STOCK | 魚骨奶湯

Milky fish soup and fish stews are classic dishes in many parts of China. They always require a base stock of rich fish broth. The bones of cod, haddock, flounder, and pollack are recommended rather than those of oily fish such as salmon or mackerel. Fish heads are excellent for making fish stock but only after the gills have been removed. | MAKES 2 QUARTS

6 cups vegetable oil

3 pounds white fish bones

4 scallions, cut into 2-inch-long pieces

1 (2-inch-long) piece of fresh ginger, smashed with the flat side of a knife

1 ounce dried kombu, reconstituted in 1 cup water (see page 78)

1 cup white rice wine

Heat the vegetable oil in a wok to about 350°F. Fry the fish bones in the oil for about 15 minutes or until they turn brown. Drain, then put the bones on a paper towel to absorb any excess oil.

Put the bones, scallions, ginger, drained kombu, wine, and 3 quarts water in an 8-quart stockpot and slowly bring the liquid to a boil over medium heat. Skim off any scum that forms on the surface of the liquid. Boil uncovered for 30 minutes.

Use tongs to remove the solid ingredients and then strain the liquid through a very-fine-mesh sieve. Let cool, then cover and refrigerate for up to 3 days or freeze for up to 6 months.

CHAPTER SIX

Harnessing the Breath of a Wok

THERE IS NO COOKING TECHNIQUE THAT IS RECOGNIZED AS MORE CHARACTERISTICALLY CHINESE THAN STIR-FRYING. It wields the greatest influence on the culinary landscape throughout East Asia, including the cuisines of Southeast Asia, Korea, and Japan, and has also become part of the standard vocabulary in Western cooking. Yet it is one of the most misunderstood techniques outside of Asia.

Known as *chao* (炒) in Mandarin Chinese, there was no equivalent word in the English language until "stir-fry" was introduced to Western audiences in a cookbook in 1945. Buwei Yang Chao described the technique in *How to Cook and Eat in Chinese*, which is one of the first English-language Chinese cookbooks in America. Her Harvard linguist husband, Yuen Ren Chao, coined the term. She explained it as "big-fire-shallow-fat-continual-stirring-quick-frying of cut-up material with wet seasoning." That is a mouthful, but it accurately represents the overall concept.

Two distinctive characteristics define stir-frying: high cooking temperature and constant stirring. Ingredients are rapidly tossed and turned in a small quantity of oil over very high heat. This sears and seals the ingredients, reducing the absorption of oil during cooking. Cooked in a well-seasoned wok, stir-frying produces a dish that exudes an intense aroma the Cantonese calls *wok-hay*, aptly described by Grace Young in her book as "the breath of a wok."

Volumes have been written on the subject of stir-frying since the publication of Buwei Yang Chao's seminal book. Most, though, concentrate on presenting recipes without discussing the technique in depth. Stir-frying actually has very rigid definitions in professional restaurant kitchens. In fact, I've uncovered up to eight formalized stir-frying techniques described in various professional Chinese cooking textbooks. However, as several of them are similar, I believe there are basically five techniques that are distinct enough to be discussed in detail for the home cook. They are simple stir-fry, dry stir-fry, moist stir-fry, dry-fry, and scramble stir-fry.

Simple stir-fry is the most basic of the five techniques: cooking a single ingredient with aromatics and sauces. The next two techniques, dry stir-frying and moist stir-frying—both commonly known to American cooks—involve cooking a combination of protein and vegetable ingredients. The only difference between the two procedures is in the sauce: dry stir-frying uses a small amount of liquid, resulting in a light sauce coating, while moist stir-frying is laden with a gravy-like sauce. Dry-frying, a typically Sichuan style of cooking, fries the main ingredient in a pool of oil before it is stir-fried normally. Finally, scramble stir-fry is reserved for making egg custard.

With the exception of scramble stir-fry, the stir-frying techniques follow a standard procedure: Protein is first parcooked, then removed from the wok. (This step is moot when cooking with a precooked protein ingredient.) Aromatics are quickly fried in hot oil until fragrant before the vegetable is added. The protein is returned to the wok to finish cooking before a sauce is finally added.

Almost any ingredient that cooks quickly is appropriate for stir-frying. For meat, tender cuts are most suitable. The quick high-heat cooking is not long enough to tenderize tough meat such as shank or brisket. But with precooking, some tougher cuts of meat such as pork belly or animal innards can be successfully stir-fried. Seafood such as fish, shrimp, and scallops are all excellent choices; they cook quickly and are full of flavor. Vegetable proteins, made of soy and gluten, are also common in stir-fries.

These proteins are always cooked with aromatics and often with vegetables. It is this balance of protein and vegetable that makes stir-frying one of the healthier ways of cooking. In terms of pairing ingredients, the general rule is to match mild ingredients together and strong ingredients together.

Pork, poultry, and seafood are generally considered mild-flavored, whereas beef, lamb, and game meats are considered strong-flavored. Sample dishes of mild flavor combinations are Stir-Fried Shrimp with Sweet Peas (青豆蝦仁) and Stir-Fried Chicken with Mushrooms (or Moo Goo Gai Pan, 蘑菇雞片, page 121). For strong flavor combinations we have dishes such as Stir-Fried Pepper Steak (青椒牛肉絲) and Stir-Fried Lamb with Leeks (乾煸羊肉). These and other popular combinations have been immortalized in traditional recipes.

For vegetarian proteins, whose flavors are often neutral and delicate, the accompanying vegetables will contribute the dominant flavor. Shiitake mushrooms, Chinese celery, garlic chives, and other fragrant vegetables are excellent choices. It is also customary to add strong-flavored sauces or spices to enhance the vegetarian protein. A good example of a vegetarian protein dish is Stir-Fried Chive Blossoms with Tofu (豆干炒韭菜花).

For a simple stir-fry, only one main ingredient is used. It can be a vegetable or a meat. Leafy vegetables should always be prepared as a simple stir-fry. They have a high moisture content and produce a puddle of liquid after stir-frying, which is unappealing when combined with other ingredients. Some common examples of leafy vegetables are pea shoots (豆苗), spinach, water spinach (空心菜), bok choy (白菜), and Chinese broccoli (芥蘭菜). Legumes and gourds, such as string beans, long beans (豇豆), loofah (絲瓜), and bitter melon (苦瓜), are all classic choices. A simple stir-fry of meat or seafood is also very common. Good selections include shrimp, scallops, sliced beef, and sliced lamb.

In the end, what really matters is some common sense and a little bit of creativity. Use fresh local ingredients and innovate with flavors. This is how families in China cook. Vegetables and meat are bought daily at the neighborhood markets and dinner is made from the purchases. Stir-fries, which are almost always part of the meal, are created from whatever seasonal ingredients are available.

PREPARING INGREDIENTS

The rapid-fire nature of this cooking technique makes it necessary to cook without interruption once it begins. It is not unusual for an entire recipe to require only 3 to 5 minutes of cooking time. Therefore, all ingredients must be ready and organized before starting the stir-frying process. Any interruption increases the risk of overcooking or burning.

Cooking with high heat requires a few precautions. Hot oil and moisture can be a dangerous combination, so make sure that whatever ingredients you're preparing for stir-frying are kept dry. Dry all vegetables after washing and before cutting. Leafy vegetables in particular should be well drained after washing. Drying in a salad spinner may not be necessary, but it can't hurt. Be sure to pat seafood and meat dry, too. These precautions will prevent the violent splattering associated with cooking in hot oil and reduce the chance of burn injuries.

Three common cutting techniques are regularly employed to prep the protein ingredients: slicing, julienning, and dicing. (These techniques are discussed in detail in Chapter 4.) Proteins with a chewy and tougher texture should be sliced or julienned, whereas tender cuts of meat do well when diced. For example, pork belly and flank steak are excellent when sliced thin or julienned, and beef tenderloin or chicken thighs can be stir-fried successfully when diced. Fish works best when sliced so it will cook evenly and hold its shape. Large chunks of fish risk flaking off on the outside while the interior remains uncooked.

For vegetable ingredients, the two common cutting techniques are slicing and julienning. When combining protein with vegetable ingredients in a stir-fry, it is customary to cut them in similar shapes and sizes. There are two reasons for this: First, it is easier to control the doneness of the ingredients when they are of similar proportions. Second, uniformly shaped ingredients are easier to manipulate with chopsticks at the dining table. Stir-Fried Shredded Beef and Green Bell Pepper is a good example where all the ingredients are julienned. The finished dish turns into a beautiful pile of evenly cut morsels of tender beef and crunchy peppers.

Regardless of which stir-frying technique is used, a sauce is often added to flavor the dish. It, too, should be premeasured and mixed before starting the cooking process. Sauces for stir-frying come in a wide variety. They range from simple soy sauce and cooking wine combinations to more elaborate ones using fermented soybeans or minced pickled vegetables. These sauces often contain thickening agents such as starches, so it's important to stir them thoroughly just before pouring them into the wok; otherwise they may separate.

MANAGING THE TEMPERATURE

In her book *The Key to Chinese Cooking*, Irene Kuo writes that her family cook in Shanghai said, "Once you toss in the ingredients for a sizzling stir, even if the stove catches on fire and the fire is spreading with leaping flames, pick up the pan and let it ride the crest of the heat to completion before you put out the fire." Such is the importance of heat in stir-frying! No other cooking technique in the world requires such intense heat. This technique, created more than three thousand years ago, is a very efficient way of utilizing scarce fuel. The round-bottomed pot, now known as a wok, maximizes the contact surface between food and heat, and the quick cooking process consumes very little fuel.

This cooking method makes it necessary to use oil with a high smoke point (see page 57). There are many options for you to choose from, and your decision will depend on your health concerns and how much you're willing to spend.

Meat Marinating Time

Marinating meat before stir-frying enhances the flavor, but caution must be used to determine how long to marinate. Chinese marinating mixtures often include sauces or pastes that are full of salt or vinegar, which can draw moisture out from the meat. Therefore, it is important to keep the marinating time at a minimum. It is customary to marinate the meat for only about 20 minutes or so. Any longer and you run the risk of the meat becoming too dry.

Once the ingredients are ready for stir-frying, the oil must be heated to the appropriate temperature. Although the oil temperature needs to be as high as possible, it is not always a good idea to heat the oil to the point of smoking. When cooking oil reaches the smoke point, it begins to break down and can result in an unpleasant flavor. The best way to heat the cooking oil quickly without burning it is to preheat the wok: Heat an empty wok over high heat for 3 minutes or just until a droplet of water evaporates immediately when flicked onto its surface. At this point the oil can be added and swirled around the wok, about halfway up to the rim. Tip and rotate the wok until the oil has completely coated the bottom; then it is ready for cooking.

As home cooks in American kitchens, we often face the reality that most of our stoves are designed with moderate heat output of 10,000 to 12,000 BTU per hour, which is adequate for general stir-frying purposes. (Professional gas ranges in restaurants can have ratings of up to 150,000 BTU per hour.) However, if you find yourself with a stove that is not as powerful, it can be challenging to create stir-fry dishes that produce the depth and complexity of *wok-hay*, a Cantonese term used to describe the flavor and aroma a hot wok can impart. On these appliances the temperature of the wok often drops dramatically when ingredients are crowded into it. In this situation I recommend cooking a dish in two batches: Divide all the ingredients in half and follow the instructions for cooking the dish twice. At the end combine the two batches for a few extra seconds in the wok before garnishing and plating.

THE VELVETING TECHNIQUE 上漿

Go to any classic Shanghainese restaurant in Asia and you'll find a dish called Simple Stir-Fried Shrimp (清炒蝦仁). The shrimp is cooked with only sliced ginger, rice wine, and chopped scallions. Each individual shrimp is surrounded with a velvety-smooth coating. It is a dish that showcases the freshness of the shrimp perfumed by the ginger with no distraction from any other flavors. The only embellishment is the silky starch texture enclosing the crunchy shrimp within. This technique of coating the shrimp is uniquely Chinese and is called "velveting," or *shang jiang* (上漿) in Mandarin.

This technique is most commonly used in stir-frying, although occasionally it is also used for cooking meat in soup. Velveting creates a silky texture that feels luxurious on your tongue while sealing in the moisture and flavor of the meat.

The velveting mixture is simply moistened starch with or without the addition of egg white. Tapioca starch is the most commonly used ingredient, although cornstarch works well also. The egg white is usually added for white meat such as chicken and seafood, whereas the moistened starch alone is usually used for red meat.

It is also common practice in Asia to add tenderizer to the velveting marinade. Red meat such as beef or lamb usually has a tougher texture in Asia. Baking soda is regularly used for tenderizing

these red meats, resulting in a rather spongy texture. Many Chinese cooks continue to use this practice in America, but I don't advocate it. If the proper cuts of beef and lamb for stir-frying have been selected, they should already be sufficiently tender and not require additives to make them palatable.

THE PASS-THROUGH TECHNIQUE 過油

Diners at Chinese restaurants in America often complain about greasy stir-fry dishes that swim in pools of oil. This is the result of not properly executing the "pass-through" technique. In this technique protein ingredients, coated with a velveting mixture, or uncoated vegetables are gently fried in hot oil for just a few seconds before being thoroughly drained and then stir-fried. If done properly, this technique should not produce oily meat but instead juicy, flavorful meat surrounded by a velvet coating.

The optimum oil temperature for this "pass-through" process is around 350°F, which is at a level where the food will not brown quickly. In the absence of an oil thermometer it is possible to judge when this temperature has been reached by observing the oil heating in the wok: A slight swirling and gentle rolling of the oil indicates that the oil is ready for pass-through.

Of equal importance is the time the food spends being passed through. For most meat proteins it should take no more than 30 seconds. For vegetables it should take from only a few seconds to about a minute. When passing-through meat, observe the changes in the color: When the outside of the meat has completely changed color but the inside is still slightly uncooked, it is ready to be removed from the oil. Remember that the meat will continue to cook once removed from the oil (residual heat) and also will be returned for further stir-fry, so it should not be cooked completely.

This process can sometimes be problematic for home cooks because it calls for quite a large amount of oil before stir-frying. But passing-through the ingredients in two batches with a smaller amount of oil is a practical compromise.

Is Stir-Frying Really Healthy?

Whenever there is a discussion about stir-frying, someone will invariably ask if it is really a healthy way of cooking. There are many claims about the superiority of the stir-frying technique in preserving natural nutrients, but I didn't know if they are real or fiction. So I went in search of a definitive answer. My quest brought me to Professor Chi Fai Chau at the Department of Food Science and Biotechnology of the National Chung Hsing University in Taichung, Taiwan. He helped me to understand the science behind stir-frying and to clarify the validity of some of these claims.

It is true that high-temperature quick cooking does not break down most nutrients in food ingredients. So stir-frying does indeed retain all the ingredients' nutrients better than long, slow cooking. For heat-sensitive compounds such as vitamin C, this benefit is especially significant. Since vegetables usually contain large quantities of vitamin C, stir-frying them to al dente can help preserve this nutrient.

But Professor Chau cautioned that the type and quantity of fat used in stir-frying can be of concern. Using vegetable oil, such as canola, rice bran, or avocado, is much healthier than animal fat, such as lard. Although many recent research studies suggest that fat does not contribute to obesity as much as originally thought, one should always drain as much of the fat as possible after "passing-through" the oil during the first step of stir-frying.

SIMPLE STIR-FRY | 清炒

At just about every meal in a Chinese household, there's a stir-fry of a single leafy vegetable, more often than not seasoned only with salt and white pepper—no thickener, no soy sauce. Sliced ginger or garlic is just about all one would add to give it a little extra kick. This is what is known as simple stir-fry (清炒) because it uses only a single main ingredient.

This emphasis on simplicity doesn't mean that you cannot add other, stronger-flavored ingredients to enhance a simple stir-fry. Fermented black beans (豆豉), shrimp paste (蝦醬), and fermented tofu (腐乳) are often added at the end of the cooking process as part of the seasoning step.

Perhaps the reason that Americans are not familiar with this technique is because Chinese restaurants rarely list simple stir-fries on their menus. A Chinese patron would normally ask the waiter or waitress what kind of green vegetables are in season and available in the kitchen, then order one for simple stir-fry.

A few tips are in order to help you with simple stir-fry. When cooking leafy vegetables it is almost always sufficient to just let them cook in their own moisture, without covering the wok. However, when cooking vegetables that contain less moisture, such as legumes or gourds, you can add a few splashes of water or stock during cooking and cover the wok with a lid; repeat this a few times, stirring the vegetable each time, until cooked.

Stir-Frying Leafy Vegetables Evenly

Special steps should be taken when stir-frying leafy vegetables. In order to cook them evenly, cut the leaves from the stems and place them in separate containers. First cook the stems until they begin to sweat; then add the leaves and cook until completely done. Remember not to overcook vegetables—this process may take just a few seconds.

GARLIC STIR-FRIED GREENS
蒜炒青菜
HOME-STYLE

This recipe can be used for cooking any leafy greens, such as spinach, bok choy, or chrysanthemum greens. I chose to use pea shoots here because they are my favorite. Pea shoots are the young leaves and tendrils of sweet peas. You can buy them very young as sprout-like greens, or most commonly as more mature but still tender leaves and tendrils. When buying pea shoots, be sure to select those with young tender leaves. Pea shoots are full of vitamins A and C and are an excellent source of fiber. | SERVES 2 OR MORE, AS A SIDE DISH

2 tablespoons vegetable oil

2 garlic cloves, thinly sliced

12 ounces pea shoots, cut into 2-inch pieces

½ teaspoon salt

¼ teaspoon ground white pepper

Heat a wok over high heat until a droplet of water sizzles and evaporates immediately upon contact. Swirl the vegetable oil around the bottom and sides of the wok to coat it evenly. Add the garlic slices to the wok and stir-fry until fragrant, about 30 seconds. Add the pea shoots and mix them in with the garlic. Cover the wok and let the vegetable steam for about 1 minute.

Uncover the wok and add the salt and pepper. Stir-fry for about 1 minute more. The vegetable is ready when the leaves are just wilted.

STIR-FRIED SHRIMP

STIR-FRIED SHRIMP | 清炒蝦仁

SHANGHAI

A classic dish from the Yangtze River Delta region, this simple yet delicious stir-fry should be made with very fresh shrimp, full of natural sweetness and flavor. The ideal size for the shrimp is 25 to 30 count per pound. | SERVES 2 OR MORE, PAIRED WITH A VEGETABLE DISH SUCH AS GARLIC STIR-FRIED GREENS (PAGE 100)

VELVETING MIXTURE

1 large egg white

1 tablespoon Shaoxing cooking wine

1 tablespoon tapioca starch

1 teaspoon salt

¼ teaspoon ground white pepper

12 ounces small shrimp, shelled and deveined

½ cup vegetable oil

6 very thin slices fresh ginger

2 garlic cloves, thinly sliced

In a bowl, combine all the ingredients for the velveting mixture and mix well. Add the shrimp and mix well.

Heat the vegetable oil in a wok over high heat until it begins to shimmer, about 350°F. Add the shrimp to the oil and cook, stirring continuously, until the shrimp is about three-quarters done or until it just turns pink, about 45 seconds. Scoop the shrimp out and put them in a skimmer set over a bowl to collect the excess oil. Pour the oil out of the wok, reserving 2 tablespoons, and quickly rinse the bottom of the wok with water, scraping off any residue.

Dry the wok and return it to the heat. Return the reserved 2 tablespoons vegetable oil to the wok. Add the ginger and the garlic and stir-fry until fragrant, about 30 seconds. Return the shrimp to the wok and stir-fry for another minute or so, until they are cooked through.

STIR-FRIED CHINESE WATER SPINACH WITH SHRIMP PASTE
空心菜炒蝦醬

HOME-STYLE

A staple in typical Chinese home meals, water spinach is often stir-fried simply with garlic or cooked with shrimp paste. Water spinach grows in moist soil near wetlands and is commonly found in southern China and Southeast Asia. It is now grown in the United States and Europe as well. The leaf is arrow-shaped and the stem is hollow. Water spinach stays crunchy even after cooking, which makes it very popular with both kids and adults. | SERVES 2 OR MORE, AS A SIDE DISH

1 pound water spinach

2 tablespoons vegetable oil

2 garlic cloves, thinly sliced

2 tablespoons white rice wine

2 tablespoons shrimp paste

¼ teaspoon salt

¼ teaspoon ground white pepper

A few slices of fresh red chile (optional)

Snap the spinach leaves off the stems, keeping the leaves and stems separate. Cut the stems into 2-inch lengths.

Heat a wok over high heat until a droplet of water sizzles and evaporates immediately upon contact. Swirl the vegetable oil around the bottom and sides of the wok to coat it evenly. Add the garlic slices to the wok and stir-fry until fragrant, about 30 seconds. Add the spinach stems and wine and stir-fry for about 1 minute. Add the spinach leaves and mix them in with the stems. Cover the wok and let the vegetable steam for about 1 minute.

Uncover the wok and add the shrimp paste, salt, and pepper. Stir-fry for about 1 minute more. The vegetable is ready when the leaves are just wilted. Turn the heat off and mix in the chile slices if desired.

STIR-FRIED PORK LIVER
WITH GINGER | 清炒豬肝
HOME-STYLE

Simple fried pork liver is an everyday home-cooked meal in many Chinese households. Liver is considered excellent for healing anemia and improving vision. Do not overcook it. | SERVES 2 OR MORE, PAIRED WITH A VEGETABLE DISH

10 ounces pork liver, cut into ⅛-inch-thick slices

VELVETING MIXTURE
1 teaspoon tapioca starch
½ teaspoon salt

1 cup vegetable oil
2 tablespoons thinly julienned fresh ginger
2 tablespoons Shaoxing cooking wine
2 teaspoons soy sauce
¼ teaspoon ground white pepper

Combine the liver slices with the velveting mixture in a small bowl and mix well.

Heat the vegetable oil in a wok over high heat until the surface begins to shimmer, about 350°F. Add the liver to the wok and quickly stir the slices around for about 15 seconds. Remove the liver and place it in a skimmer set over a bowl to drain off the excess oil. Pour the oil out of the wok, reserving 2 tablespoons, and quickly rinse the wok with water, scraping off any residue.

Dry the wok and return it to the heat. Return the reserved 2 tablespoons vegetable oil to the wok. Add the ginger and stir-fry until fragrant, about 30 seconds. Add the wine, soy sauce, and pepper and cook for about 30 seconds to reduce the sauce slightly. Return the liver slices to the wok and stir-fry for another 30 seconds, until just cooked through. The sauce should be reduced enough to lightly coat each slice of liver.

SESAME OIL–FRIED PORK
KIDNEY | 麻油腰花
TAIWAN

Pork kidney can be a challenge to cook simply because of the nature of the organ. If not cleaned properly, the strong taste can ruin the dish. This Taiwanese kidney dish is a classic and a wonderful way of using toasted sesame oil to bring out the flavor of the organ. The quick, simple stir-fry technique also guarantees that the texture will be perfect. | SERVES 2 OR MORE, PAIRED WITH A VEGETABLE DISH

12 ounces pork kidney, cleaned (see page 82)
¼ cup toasted sesame oil
4 thin slices fresh ginger
3 tablespoons white rice wine
1 tablespoon soy sauce
¼ teaspoon ground white pepper

Cut the kidney into pieces about 1 inch by 2 inches. Score the inside surface of the pieces with a crisscross pattern to promote easy cooking.

Heat a wok over high heat until a droplet of water sizzles and evaporates immediately upon contact. Add the sesame oil to the wok and heat it for about 30 seconds. Add the ginger slices and stir-fry for 30 seconds or until they are just about to turn brown. Add the kidney pieces and stir-fry for about 30 seconds. Add the wine, soy sauce, and pepper and continue to stir-fry for about 3 minutes, until the kidney is cooked through but still tender and slightly crunchy.

SESAME OIL-FRIED PORK KIDNEY

DRY STIR-FRY | 煸炒

Dry stir-fry is easily the least understood of all the stir-fry techniques. We are so used to the gooey, sticky sauce of Chinese takeout food that we often assume all stir-fries are finished with a sauce. But that is hardly the case. In dry stir-fry the finished dish does not have a wet gravy; instead, the sauce only lightly coats the ingredients.

The dry stir-fry technique follows the general stir-frying procedure very closely in that protein ingredients are first parcooked in the wok, then removed. Vegetables are then cooked before the protein is returned to the wok to finish the dish. A small amount of sauce is added at the very end to season and lightly coat the ingredients.

STIR-FRIED GARLIC SCAPES
WITH CHINESE BACON | 蒜薹炒臘肉
GUANGDONG

Garlic scapes are a delicious spring vegetable that is now widely available in farmer's markets and gourmet markets. Unlike Western cooking, where the garlic scape is often used as an herb, in Chinese cooking it is treated as a vegetable. This recipe pairs it with rich Chinese bacon. | SERVES 2 OR MORE, AS A SIDE DISH

SAUCE

¼ cup chicken stock (see page 88) or water

1 tablespoon soy sauce

1 teaspoon tapioca starch

1 teaspoon sugar

¼ teaspoon ground white pepper

2 tablespoons vegetable oil

1 garlic clove, thinly sliced

3 thin slices fresh ginger

4 ounces Chinese bacon, thinly sliced

1 small carrot, julienned

8 ounces garlic scapes, cut into 2-inch pieces

¼ cup Shaoxing cooking wine

3 ounces canned baby corn, drained

1 ounce dried shiitake mushrooms, reconstituted (see page 78) and cut into ⅛-inch-thick julienne

¼ cup chicken stock (see page 88) or water, or less, if needed

Combine the sauce ingredients in a small bowl and mix well.

Heat a wok over high heat until a droplet of water sizzles and evaporates immediately upon contact. Swirl the vegetable oil around the bottom and sides of the wok to coat it evenly. Add the garlic and ginger and stir-fry until fragrant, about 30 seconds. Add the Chinese bacon and stir-fry for about 30 seconds. Add the carrot and garlic scapes. Pour the wine into the wok and stir-fry for about 30 seconds. Cover and let the vegetables steam in the wok for about 1 minute.

Uncover the wok, add the baby corn and mushrooms, and stir-fry for another 30 seconds. (If the vegetables are dry when stir-frying, add up to ¼ cup chicken stock or water.) Pour the sauce mixture into the wok and cook for 30 seconds or until it thickens.

STIR-FRIED SHRIMP WITH BITTER MELON | 蝦仁炒苦瓜

HUNAN

Thought to have originated in Hunan province, in the southwest of China, fermented black beans are now used throughout southern China and are commonly available in Chinatown markets. They are probably best known to Westerners as an ingredient in the black bean sauces of Cantonese cooking. | SERVES 2 OR MORE, PAIRED WITH A VEGETABLE DISH

¼ cup vegetable oil

4 ounces medium shrimp, shelled and deveined

1 teaspoon minced garlic

1 teaspoon minced fresh ginger

1 large bitter melon (about 10 ounces), seeded and cut into 1-inch squares

2 tablespoons Shaoxing cooking wine

½ teaspoon salt

¼ teaspoon ground white pepper

1 tablespoon fermented black beans, coarsely chopped

1 tablespoon chopped fresh red chile (optional)

Heat the vegetable oil in a wok over high heat until it begins to shimmer, about 350°F. Add the shrimp to the wok and stir-fry until they just begin to turn pink, about 2 minutes. Remove the shrimp from the wok and place them in a skimmer set over a bowl to drain off the excess oil. Pour the oil out of the wok, reserving 2 tablespoons, and quickly rinse the bottom of the wok with water, scraping off any residue that's stuck there.

Dry the wok and return it to the heat. Return the reserved 2 tablespoons vegetable oil to the wok. Add the garlic and ginger and stir-fry until fragrant, about 30 seconds. Add the bitter melon, wine, and ¼ cup water. Cover the wok and let cook for about 2 minutes. Uncover, stir the bitter melon, then cover again and continue to cook for another 3 minutes. If the mixture is too dry, add another splash of water to prevent it from burning. The bitter melon is cooked when it turns brownish green. Take a piece of bitter melon out and taste it for doneness. The texture should be soft and crunchy, but not mushy.

Return the shrimp to the wok and add the salt, pepper, black beans, and chile if desired. Stir-fry for another minute to combine.

Cooking Wine (噴酒)

Adding cooking wine at different points during the cooking process can produce different results. Occasionally, cooking wine is poured in just after the aromatics have been fried but before the main ingredient is added. This will slightly caramelize the wine, creating a distinct nutty taste in the final dish. Another approach is to add the cooking wine after the main ingredient has been added to the wok. In this situation the cooking wine steams the ingredient, infusing it with a mild wine flavor.

KUNG PAO CHICKEN | 公保雞丁

SICHUAN

Kung Pao Chicken is one of those takeout dishes that is usually covered by a landslide of sickeningly sweet brown sauce. It would not be recognized by anyone arriving in the United States from China. Kung Pao Chicken is in fact a dry stir-fry dish. The spicy sauce should only lightly coat the chicken pieces, giving them enough flavor to delight the palate and provide subtle contrast to the crunchy peanuts. | SERVES 2 OR MORE, PAIRED WITH A VEGETABLE DISH SUCH AS GARLIC STIR-FRIED GREENS (PAGE 100)

CHICKEN MARINADE

1 tablespoon vegetable oil

½ teaspoon tapioca starch

¼ teaspoon salt

¼ teaspoon ground white pepper

1 pound boneless, skinless chicken thighs, cut into ¾-inch cubes

SAUCE

3 tablespoons Shaoxing cooking wine

1 tablespoon soy sauce

1 teaspoon toasted sesame oil

1 teaspoon tapioca starch

1 teaspoon sugar

½ teaspoon Sichuan peppercorn powder

1 cup dried whole red chiles

½ cup vegetable oil

4 very thin slices fresh ginger

2 garlic cloves, thinly sliced

½ cup unsalted dry-roasted peanuts

3 scallions, cut into ¼-inch pieces

Combine all the marinade ingredients in a bowl and mix well. Add the chicken and toss thoroughly. Set aside for about 20 minutes.

Combine all the ingredients for the sauce in another bowl.

Cut the chiles with kitchen shears into 1-inch-long pieces and remove the seeds.

Heat the vegetable oil in a wok over high heat until the surface begins to shimmer, about 350°F. Add the chicken to the wok and quickly stir-fry for about 1 minute or until the chicken is about three-quarters done. Remove the chicken from the wok and place it in a skimmer set over a bowl to drain off the excess oil. Pour the oil out of the wok, reserving 2 tablespoons, and quickly rinse the bottom of the wok with water, scraping off any residue that's stuck there.

Dry the wok and return it to the heat. Return the reserved 2 tablespoons vegetable oil to the wok. Add the ginger and garlic and stir-fry until fragrant, about 30 seconds. Add the dried chiles and stir-fry for another minute. (The chiles will create a stinging steam as they fry, so make sure your kitchen is well ventilated.)

Add the chicken to the wok and stir-fry for about 3 minutes, until cooked through. Be sure to keep stirring so the chicken will be cooked evenly. Pour the sauce into the wok. Continue cooking until the sauce coats the chicken, about 30 seconds. Add the peanuts and scallions and stir-fry for another 30 seconds.

STIR-FRIED FLY HEAD | 炒蒼蠅頭
SICHUAN

No one knows for certain how this dish got the name "fly head," but most sources refer to the fact that the fermented black beans look like little fly heads among the ground pork and chopped chive blossoms. Although considered Sichuanese, this dish is very popular in Taiwan and has been closely identified with cooking from the island. | SERVES 2 OR MORE, PAIRED WITH A SEAFOOD OR VEGETABLE DISH

12 ounces lean ground pork

2 teaspoons soy sauce

¼ teaspoon ground white pepper

3 tablespoons vegetable oil

1 tablespoon minced garlic

6 ounces garlic chive blossoms,
cut into ¼-inch pieces

2 tablespoons fermented black beans

1 large fresh red chile, cut crosswise into
¼-inch-thick rings

3 tablespoons white rice wine

½ teaspoon salt

In a bowl, mix the pork with the soy sauce and pepper. Let marinate for 10 minutes.

Heat a wok over high heat until a droplet of water sizzles and evaporates immediately upon contact. Swirl 2 tablespoons of the vegetable oil around the bottom and sides of the wok to coat it evenly. Add the pork to the wok and stir-fry for about 30 seconds. Add ¼ cup water and simmer for 1 minute or until it has evaporated. Remove the pork from the wok.

Return the wok to the heat and swirl the remaining 1 tablespoon vegetable oil around the sides of the wok. Add the garlic and stir-fry until fragrant, about 30 seconds. Add the garlic chive blossoms and stir-fry for about 30 seconds. Return the pork to the wok and add the black beans, chile, wine, and salt. Continue to stir-fry for 1 minute to blend.

STIR-FRIED PRESSED TOFU
WITH GARLIC CHIVE BLOSSOMS
香乾炒韭菜花
HOME-STYLE

Garlic chive blossoms have a slightly grassy and garlicky taste that is perfect for a stir-fry dish. It makes a great complementary vegetable to pressed tofu, which can be found in Chinatown markets in either smoked or five-spice flavor. Regardless which tofu you choose, this recipe will produce a most delicious combination of flavors. | SERVES 2 OR MORE, AS A SIDE DISH

1 tablespoon vegetable oil

1 teaspoon minced garlic

8 ounces pressed tofu, cut into ⅛-inch-thick strips

1 small carrot, julienned into strips about ⅛ inch thick

2 tablespoons Shaoxing cooking wine

4 ounces Chinese chive blossoms,
cut into 2-inch pieces

¼ cup vegetarian stock (page 89) or water

½ teaspoon salt

½ teaspoon ground white pepper

Heat a wok over high heat until a droplet of water sizzles and evaporates immediately upon contact. Swirl the vegetable oil around the bottom and sides of the wok to coat it evenly. Add the garlic to the wok and stir-fry until fragrant, about 30 seconds. Add the tofu, carrot, and wine and continue to stir-fry for about 1 minute. Add the chive blossoms, stock, salt, and pepper and stir-fry for another 2 minutes, until the liquid is reduced to a sauce that just coats all the ingredients.

STIR-FRIED PRESSED TOFU
WITH GARLIC CHIVE BLOSSOMS

SHRIMP AND ASPARAGUS FRIED RICE | 蘆筍蝦球炒飯

GUANGDONG

Shrimp and asparagus make a winning combination, especially with fried rice. What puts this recipe over the top is the addition of a little bit of dried shrimp, which has an intense umami taste. | SERVES 2 AS A MAIN COURSE, 4 AS A SIDE DISH

3 tablespoons vegetable oil

8 ounces medium shrimp, shelled and deveined

1 tablespoon minced garlic

3 ounces dried shrimp, rehydrated (see page 80) and chopped

4 ounces asparagus, cut into ½-inch pieces

3 cups leftover cooked rice

1 teaspoon salt

¼ teaspoon ground white pepper

1 large egg, lightly beaten

2 scallions, cut into ¼-inch pieces

Heat a wok over high heat until a droplet of water sizzles and evaporates immediately upon contact. Swirl 2 tablespoons of the vegetable oil around the bottom and sides of the wok to coat it evenly. Put the fresh shrimp in the wok and stir-fry until they turn slightly pink and are partially cooked, about 1 minute. Remove the shrimp from the wok.

Swirl the remaining 1 tablespoon vegetable oil evenly around the sides of the wok. Add the garlic and dried shrimp to the wok and stir-fry until browned and crisp, about 2 minutes. Add the asparagus and the leftover rice. Break up any lumps of rice and stir-fry for another 3 minutes. Return the shrimp to the wok and add the salt and pepper. Continue to stir-fry for another minute.

Push the rice toward one side of the wok to expose about a quarter of the bottom surface. Pour the egg into the open space in the wok and scramble it slightly. Then push the rice over the egg and let the egg continue to cook. At this stage you want to let the rice sit without stirring so that the bottom of the rice browns slightly, providing the dish's characteristic caramelized flavor. This should take about 1 minute. Then stir the rice around and once again let the rice on the bottom brown. Stir the rice once again and repeat this browning for a third time.

Turn the heat off, add the chopped scallions to the rice, and mix well.

FRIED RICE

Although China shares traditions of boiling raw rice and cooking flavored rice with many of the world's other cuisines, stir-frying cooked rice is uniquely Chinese. This technique has proven to be so popular that it has spread all over Asia. Countless variations of fried rice have been developed, based on local ingredients and taste preferences. But the frying process, a slight modification of the dry stir-frying technique, is the same everywhere.

The process usually involves parcooking the protein, browning the aromatics, and finally adding the rice and vegetables. The protein is returned to the wok and egg is added to finish the frying. However, many Chinese cooks have adapted this process and often simply start by first cooking the aromatics, then adding the vegetables and rice before finishing with the egg.

There are also various ways to incorporate the egg. Some people scramble the eggs first while others pour the whole raw egg into the wok. Yet others serve a whole fried egg on top of the rice.

But the real secret to making perfect fried rice is to use leftover rice. Newly cooked rice that has not had enough time to absorb all the moisture from the cooking process will stick together and become mushy when you try to fry it. Too much moisture in the rice will also inhibit the browning process. Leftover rice, on the other hand, will become fluffy and brown nicely. It is this caramelization that imparts the smoky taste to the rice.

STIR-FRIED NOODLES

Cooked noodles can also be stir-fried. Using the dry stir-frying method, the noodles are added along with the vegetable, after the protein has been parcooked. Eggs are occasionally added at the end, just as in fried rice. Some caramelization of the noodles is also desirable.

Be sure to drain the noodles thoroughly after boiling. Toss them with a little vegetable oil to keep them from sticking together before stir-frying. Finally, do not overcook.

STIR-FRIED LO MEIN WITH BARBECUED PORK | 叉燒撈麵
GUANGDONG

Found in just about every Chinese takeout restaurant, this noodle dish is a popular example of Cantonese comfort food. Lo mein noodles are egg- and flour-based noodles similar to fettuccine; fresh noodles can be found already cooked in Chinatown markets. Alternatively, you can buy 8 ounces dried and cook them yourself for this recipe. | SERVES 2 AS A MAIN COURSE, 4 AS A SIDE DISH

2 tablespoons vegetable oil

2 garlic cloves, thinly sliced

3 thin slices fresh ginger

1 small carrot, julienned into strips about 1/16 inch thick

6 ounces Barbecued Pork (page 302), julienned into strips about 1/8 inch thick

12 ounces cooked fresh lo mein noodles

6 ounces mung bean sprouts

2 tablespoons white rice wine

1 teaspoon salt

1/4 teaspoon ground white pepper

2 scallions, cut into 1½-inch pieces

Heat a wok over high heat until a droplet of water sizzles and evaporates immediately upon contact. Swirl the vegetable oil around the bottom and sides of the wok to coat it evenly. Add the garlic and ginger to the wok and stir-fry until fragrant, about 30 seconds. Then add the carrot and stir-fry for about 30 seconds. Continue by adding the barbecued pork, noodles, and bean sprouts and stir-fry for another 30 seconds. Add the wine, salt, and pepper and stir-fry for another 30 seconds or until all the ingredients are mixed together. Turn the heat off, add the scallions, and mix together.

STIR-FRIED HO FAN WITH BEEF AND YELLOW CHIVES | 牛肉炒河粉

GUANGDONG

A favorite at dim sum restaurants and Hong Kong diners, known as cha chaan teng, *this rice noodle dish can be served as a one-dish meal or as a starch dish in a multi-course meal. The light garlicky taste of yellow chives and the crunchy texture of bean sprouts enhance the tender beef, making this a great dish for all occasions. Fresh rice noodles are available in sheets or pre-cut in Chinatown. If you're using the sheets, cut them into ½-inch-wide strips before cooking.* | SERVES 2 AS A MAIN DISH, 4 AS A SIDE DISH

BEEF VELVETING MIXTURE

2 tablespoons white rice wine

1 tablespoon dark soy sauce

1 tablespoon vegetable oil

1 tablespoon tapioca starch

6 ounces flank steak, cut into ⅛-inch-thick slices

½ cup vegetable oil

2 garlic cloves, thinly sliced

3 thin slices fresh ginger

12 ounces fresh rice noodles

4 ounces mung bean sprouts

4 ounces yellow Chinese chives, cut into 1½-inch pieces

1 teaspoon soy sauce

1 tablespoon dark soy sauce

¼ teaspoon ground white pepper

2 scallions, cut into 1½-inch pieces

Combine all the ingredients for the velveting mixture in a medium bowl and mix well. Add the beef, stir, and marinate for about 20 minutes.

Heat the vegetable oil in a wok over high heat until it begins to shimmer, about 350°F. Drop the beef into the oil and quickly stir the slices around, making sure they do not stick together. Cook the beef to about three-quarters done or just until no longer red on the outside, about 1 minute. Remove the beef from the wok and place it in a skimmer set over a bowl to drain off the excess oil. Pour the oil out of the wok, reserving 2 tablespoons, and quickly rinse the bottom of the wok with water, scraping off any residue that's stuck there.

Dry the wok and return it to the heat. Return the reserved 2 tablespoons vegetable oil to the wok. Add the garlic and ginger slices and stir-fry until fragrant, about 30 seconds. Then add the rice noodles, bean sprouts, and yellow Chinese chives and stir-fry for about 30 seconds. Return the beef to the wok and continue to stir-fry for another 30 seconds. Add both soy sauces as well as the pepper and stir-fry for another 30 seconds or until the noodles are evenly coated with the soy sauce. Turn the heat off, add the scallions, and mix them into the noodles.

MOIST STIR-FRY | 滑炒

If dry stir-fry is the least known stir-fry variation in America, moist stir-fry is the best known. The gooey sauces in chop suey and Moo Goo Gai Pan found in so many Chinese-American restaurants rely on this technique. It is unfortunate that some takeout restaurants have given this technique a bad name. An expertly prepared moist stir-fry can be a very satisfying, smooth, and flavorful dish.

The cooking procedure for moist stir-fry follows the general dry stir-fry procedure very closely. The main difference is that a sauce mixture is added at the end to create a thickened gravy.

The sauce is the key to the success of a moist stir-fry dish because it is what defines the flavor, so it is important to choose a sauce that complements the main ingredient. Look through Chinese stir-fry recipes on the Internet and you'll find plenty that call for hoisin sauce. It is the base for all the universal and uniformly uninteresting "brown sauces" that seem to have flooded so many Chinese restaurant menus.

Don't simply cook with the one-dimensional flavor of hoisin sauce, but create more pronounced and nuanced flavors by using other sauces from the many regions of China. In Cantonese cooking, oyster sauce, abalone sauce, and garlic sauce are common. Sichuan cooking uses a variety of hot and spicy sauces, many based on hot bean paste and pickled red chiles.

STIR-FRIED BEEF WITH BLACK PEPPER | 黑椒炒牛肉
GUANGDONG

In Chinese cooking, black pepper is commonly used as spice, not a seasoning. In this recipe the black pepper is the star, not a bit player. It should be coarsely cracked, not ground. This dish has a European accent as the onions, black pepper, and oyster sauce create a savory steak sauce. | SERVES 2 OR MORE, PAIRED WITH A VEGETABLE DISH SUCH AS GARLIC STIR-FRIED GREENS (PAGE 100)

VELVETING MIXTURE

1 tablespoon Shaoxing cooking wine

1 teaspoon soy sauce

1 teaspoon tapioca starch

12 ounces beef tenderloin, cut against the grain into 1/8-inch-thick slices

SAUCE

2 tablespoons oyster sauce

1 tablespoon dark soy sauce

2 tablespoons Shaoxing cooking wine

1 teaspoon sugar

1/3 cup beef stock (see page 89) or water

2 teaspoons tapioca starch

1/2 cup vegetable oil

6 thin slices fresh ginger

2 garlic cloves, thinly sliced

1 medium onion, cut into 1/8-inch-thick slices

1 tablespoon black peppercorns, coarsely cracked

Cilantro sprigs

In a bowl, combine all the ingredients for the velveting mixture and mix well. Add the beef and mix well. Let marinate for 20 minutes.

Mix the sauce ingredients together in another bowl.

Heat the vegetable oil in a wok over high heat until it begins to shimmer, about 350°F. Add the beef to the wok and quickly fry it for about 1 minute, until the meat is about three-quarters done or the exterior has turned brown. Remove the beef from the wok and place it in a skimmer set over a bowl to drain off the excess oil. Pour the oil out of the wok, reserving 2 tablespoons, and quickly rinse the bottom of the wok with water, scraping off any residue that's stuck there.

Dry the wok and return it to the heat. Return the reserved 2 tablespoons vegetable oil to the wok. Add the ginger, garlic, and onion to the wok. Stir-fry until fragrant, about 30 seconds. Return the beef to the wok and add the black peppercorns. Stir-fry for about 15 seconds, then add the sauce mixture. Cook until the sauce thickens, about 2 minutes. Serve garnished with cilantro sprigs.

MOO GOO GAI PAN | 蘑菇雞片

GUANGDONG

In many American Chinese restaurants Moo Goo Gai Pan is made with a psychedelic array of colorful vegetables. Yet the name simply means "stir-fried chicken slices with mushrooms." This recipe stays true to the name by using only the namesake ingredients, with bamboo shoots added for extra crunch. However, if you wish to add color to the dish, choose your favorite non-leafy vegetables. | SERVES 2 OR MORE, PAIRED WITH A VEGETABLE DISH

12 ounces boneless, skinless chicken breast, cut against the grain into ⅛-inch-thick slices

VELVETING MIXTURE

1 egg white, lightly beaten

2 teaspoons tapioca starch

½ teaspoon salt

½ teaspoon ground white pepper

SAUCE

½ cup chicken stock (see page 88) or water

¼ cup white rice wine

2 tablespoons oyster sauce

1 tablespoon soy sauce

1 tablespoon tapioca starch

½ cup vegetable oil

2 garlic cloves, thinly sliced

4 thin slices fresh ginger

4 ounces cremini or button mushrooms, stemmed and halved

4 ounces shiitake mushrooms, stemmed and halved

¼ cup chicken stock (see page 88) or water

½ fresh or 4 ounces canned bamboo shoots, cut into ⅛-inch pieces

1 teaspoon toasted sesame oil

Sliced scallion greens

Cilantro sprigs

Put the chicken slices in a bowl, add all the velveting ingredients, and mix well.

In another bowl, mix all the sauce ingredients together.

Heat the vegetable oil in a wok over high heat until it begins to shimmer, about 350°F. Drop the chicken slices into the hot oil and stir to keep them separate. Cook until three-quarters of the way done, or until the outside of the chicken turns white but the center is still slightly pink. Remove the chicken from the wok and place it in a skimmer set over a bowl to drain off the excess oil. Pour the oil out of the wok, reserving 1 tablespoon, and quickly rinse the bottom of the wok with water, scraping off any residue that's stuck there.

Dry the wok and return it to the heat. Return the reserved 1 tablespoon vegetable oil to the wok. Add the garlic and ginger slices and stir-fry until fragrant, about 1 minute. Add the mushrooms and the chicken stock and stir-fry for about 30 seconds. Cover the wok and cook for 1 minute.

Uncover and return the chicken to the wok. Add the bamboo shoots and stir-fry for 30 seconds. Add the sauce to the wok. Be sure to stir the mixture to ensure that the starch is completely combined. Stir-fry until the sauce thickens, about 1 minute. Turn the heat off, swirl in the sesame oil, and quickly mix together before removing from the wok. Serve garnished with scallion slices and cilantro sprigs.

YU XIANG STIR-FRIED PORK | 魚香肉絲

SICHUAN

Yu Xiang *literally means "fish fragrance." It is fragrant, but there is no fish in this dish. Legend has it that one night, when her husband arrived home early, a devoted but harried housewife quickly put together a pork stir-fry and tossed in some leftover fragrant sauce that was originally made for a fish dish. The pork was such a hit with her husband that she started using the sauce in more and more dishes. Although a misnomer, the name has stuck. This is a very spicy dish that relies on heat from pickled chile, which can be purchased at Chinatown markets. In Sichuan many cooks would likely double the amount of chile I specify. You can adjust the amount to suit your own taste.* | SERVES 2 OR MORE, PAIRED WITH A VEGETABLE DISH SUCH AS GARLIC STIR-FRIED GREENS (PAGE 100)

VELVETING MARINADE

1 tablespoon vegetable oil

1 tablespoon tapioca starch

½ teaspoon salt

12 ounces pork loin, cut into strips 2 inches long and ⅛ inch thick

SAUCE

2 teaspoons soy sauce

2 tablespoons Chinkiang black vinegar

1 tablespoon Shaoxing cooking wine

2 tablespoons chopped pickled red chile

1 tablespoon sugar

1 tablespoon tapioca starch

2 tablespoons vegetable oil

1 tablespoon minced garlic

1 tablespoon minced fresh ginger

1 tablespoon finely chopped scallions

½ fresh or 4 ounces canned bamboo shoots, cut into ⅛-inch pieces

½ ounce dried black wood ear mushroom, rehydrated (see page 78) and cut into ⅛-inch-thick slices

In a bowl, combine all the ingredients for the velveting marinade and mix well. Add the pork and mix well. Let marinate for 20 minutes.

Combine all the sauce ingredients in another bowl and mix well.

Heat a wok over high heat until a droplet of water sizzles and evaporates immediately upon contact. Swirl the vegetable oil around the bottom and sides of the wok to coat it evenly. Add the pork to the wok and quickly stir-fry to separate the strips. Cook until the meat just starts to color, about 30 seconds. Remove the pork from the wok and place it in a skimmer set over a bowl to drain off the excess oil. Pour the oil out of the wok, reserving 1 tablespoon, and quickly rinse the bottom of the wok with water, scraping off any residue that's stuck there.

Dry the wok and return it to the heat. Return the reserved 1 tablespoon vegetable oil to the wok. Add the garlic, ginger, and scallions to the wok and stir-fry until fragrant, about 30 seconds. Add the bamboo shoots and wood ear and stir-fry for about 1 minute.

Return the pork to the wok and add the sauce mixture. Continue to stir-fry until the sauce has thickened, about 1 minute.

DOUBLE WINTER DELIGHT | 蠔油炒雙冬

GUANGDONG

Winter bamboo is one of the most eagerly anticipated seasonal ingredients in China. Arriving in markets in early winter, it is tender and crunchy and full of flavor. Shiitake mushrooms, known as "winter mushrooms" in Chinese, are paired with the bamboo shoots to become the "double winter." This Cantonese dish is flavored with oyster sauce, but you can use a vegetarian stir-fry sauce if you wish to make a vegetarian version. Dried shiitake mushrooms, rehydrated, can be substituted for fresh ones. | SERVES 2 OR MORE, PAIRED WITH A MEAT, SEAFOOD, OR ANOTHER VEGETARIAN DISH

1 head fresh winter bamboo shoots
(1 pound with the husk)

SAUCE

¾ cup chicken stock (see page 88), vegetarian stock (see page 89), or water

2 tablespoons oyster sauce or vegetarian stir-fry sauce

2 tablespoons Shaoxing cooking wine

1 teaspoon soy sauce

¼ teaspoon ground white pepper

8 baby bok choy, halved lengthwise

2 tablespoons vegetable oil

1 teaspoon minced garlic

8 fresh shiitake mushrooms, stems removed

1 teaspoon tapioca starch

Follow the instructions on how to prep fresh bamboo shoots on page 82. Then cut them crosswise into slices about ⅛ inch thick.

Combine all the sauce ingredients in a bowl and mix well.

In a saucepan, bring 4 cups water to a boil. Add the bok choy and blanch for 1 minute. Drain well, and arrange them in a circle on a round plate. Keep warm.

Heat a wok over high heat until a droplet of water sizzles and evaporates immediately upon contact. Swirl the vegetable oil around the bottom and sides of the wok to coat it evenly. Add the garlic and stir-fry until fragrant, about 30 seconds. Add the bamboo shoots and mushrooms and continue to stir-fry for another minute. Be sure to stir continuously to prevent burning. Add the sauce mixture to the wok and turn the heat down to medium. Simmer the vegetables, covered, for about 5 minutes.

Mix the tapioca starch with 2 tablespoons water to make a slurry. Uncover the wok and add the slurry. Simmer for 1 minute to thicken. Scoop the bamboo shoots and mushrooms over the bok choy and arrange decoratively.

One of the most distinctive Sichuan preparations is a stir-fried string beans dish that looks as though the vegetable has been mistakenly overcooked to the point of scorching and shriveling. It is commonly known as Dry-Fried String Beans (乾煸四季豆). Once you try the smoky string beans accompanied by their spicy sauce, you will not be able to resist having second and third helpings. The texture of the string beans is transformed into something crunchy yet tender.

This dish showcases a technique that's generally known as dry-fry—but don't confuse this with the dry stir-fry technique. It is used frequently in Sichuan, less so elsewhere. The key to this technique is to fry the main ingredient, which is cut into thin strips, in shallow but very hot oil until scorched on the outside and slightly dehydrated inside. At this point, not only is the ingredient's flavor concentrated, but any flavoring that's introduced will be immediately absorbed. Other common dry-fried dishes include Dry-Fried Beef (page 127), Dry-Fried Lamb, and Dry-Fried Lotus Root (this page).

Although the expression "dry-frying" can be easily confused with "dry stir-fry," I've decided to stick with it because of the popularity of the term. The confusion arises from translating the Chinese characters literally. In Mandarin Chinese dry-frying is called *gan bian* (乾煸). The first character, *gan*, means "dry" and the second character, *bian*, means "dry stir-fry." With double "dry" built into the name, there is no mistaking that the dish is a very dry stir-fry.

DRY-FRIED LOTUS ROOT
乾煸藕絲
SICHUAN

Lotus root is usually cut crosswise to expose the wheel-like pattern, but for this recipe it is cut lengthwise into matchsticks to better coat the pieces with starch for crisping when fried. The crisp texture and the mala *taste transform this mild root vegetable into a thoroughly different and unexpected vegetable sensation: abundantly spicy and crunchy.* | SERVES 2 OR MORE AS A SIDE DISH

12 ounces lotus root, cut lengthwise into matchsticks
¼ cup tapioca starch

SAUCE
2 tablespoons white rice wine
1 teaspoon soy sauce
1 teaspoon sugar
½ teaspoon Chinkiang black vinegar
½ teaspoon salt

4 cups vegetable oil
1 teaspoon minced fresh ginger
1 teaspoon minced garlic
½ ounce dried red chiles, cut into ½-inch pieces and seeded
1 teaspoon Sichuan peppercorn powder
1 teaspoon white sesame seeds, toasted
2 tablespoons chopped scallions

In a bowl, soak the lotus root in cold water to cover for 5 minutes. Drain, and dry thoroughly on paper towels. Put the lotus root in a large bowl, sprinkle with the tapioca starch, and mix well.

Combine all the sauce ingredients in another bowl and mix well.

Heat the vegetable oil in a wok over high heat until it is just beginning to smoke, about 395°F. Fry

the lotus root in two batches for about 3 minutes each or until the edges begin to turn brown. Drain the lotus root on paper towels to absorb any excess oil. Pour the oil out of the wok, reserving 2 tablespoons.

Dry the wok and return it to the heat. Return the reserved 2 tablespoons vegetable oil to the wok. Add the ginger and garlic and stir-fry until fragrant, about 30 seconds. Add the chiles and Sichuan peppercorn powder and continue to stir-fry for another 20 seconds. Add the sauce mixture and stir for about 10 seconds. Return the lotus root to the wok and stir-fry for another 10 seconds or until the pieces are completely coated with the sauce. Turn the heat off, add the sesame seeds and scallions, and stir to combine.

DRY-FRIED STRING BEANS | 乾煸四季豆

SICHUAN

Widely served in Sichuan restaurants in the United States, this string bean dish appears in many variations. The classic version calls for pork, ya cai, *and Sichuan chile bean paste. Ya cai is a Sichuan pickled green that's only recently became available, so it is forgivable that restaurants would omit it or substitute other Chinese pickles. Similarly, fermented black beans often take the place of the Sichuan chile bean paste. This version preserves the original recipe.* | SERVES 2 OR MORE, AS A SIDE DISH

SAUCE

2 tablespoons white rice wine

1 tablespoon soy sauce

1 tablespoon chile bean paste

1 teaspoon sugar

3 cups vegetable oil

12 ounces string beans, ends trimmed, cut into 1½-inch pieces

1 tablespoon minced garlic

1 tablespoon minced fresh ginger

¼ ounce dried red chiles, cut into ½-inch pieces and seeded

½ teaspoon Sichuan peppercorn powder

2 ounces ground pork

2 tablespoon minced *ya cai* (Sichuan pickled greens; optional)

Combine all the sauce ingredients in a bowl and mix well.

Heat the vegetable oil in a wok over high heat until it is just beginning to smoke, about 395°F. Put the string beans into the oil and fry them for about 2 minutes or until they have shriveled a little bit. Remove the string beans from the wok and place them in a skimmer set over a bowl to drain off the excess oil. Pour the oil out of the wok, reserving 2 tablespoons.

Return the wok to the heat. Return the reserved 2 tablespoons vegetable oil to the wok. Add the garlic, ginger, chiles, and Sichuan peppercorn powder and stir-fry over high heat until fragrant, about 1 minute. Add the pork and *ya cai* and continue to stir-fry for about 30 seconds. Return the string beans to the wok and then add the sauce mixture. Stir-fry the string beans for another minute, until the sauce has evaporated.

DRY-FRIED BEEF | 乾煸牛肉絲

SICHUAN

Leaner beef loin is better than more marbled flank steak or hanger steak for this crisp fried dish. The beef will cook quickly during the initial frying and will absorb the sauce just before it finishes cooking. The result is incredibly flavorful beef mingled with crisp celery for a contrasting texture. | SERVES 2 OR MORE, PAIRED WITH A VEGETABLE DISH

SAUCE

¼ cup white rice wine

1 tablespoon chile bean paste

1 tablespoon soy sauce

1 teaspoon sugar

3 cups vegetable oil

12 ounces beef loin, cut into strips 2 inches long and ⅛ inch thick

2 garlic cloves, thinly sliced

6 very thin slices fresh ginger

1 teaspoon Sichuan peppercorn powder

½ ounce dried red chiles, cut into ½-inch pieces and seeded

3 ounces Chinese celery stalks, cut into 2-inch pieces

2 tablespoons chopped scallions

Combine the sauce ingredients in a small bowl and mix well.

Heat the vegetable oil in a wok over high heat until it is just beginning to smoke, about 395°F. Add the beef to the oil and quickly stir the pieces to separate them. Cook the beef for about 2 minutes or until it is thoroughly cooked but not browned. Remove the beef from the wok and place it in a skimmer set over a bowl to drain off the excess oil. Pour the oil out of the wok, reserving 2 tablespoons.

Return the wok to the heat. Return the reserved 2 tablespoons vegetable oil to the wok. Add the garlic and ginger and stir-fry until fragrant, about 30 seconds. Add the peppercorn powder and chiles and stir-fry for about 30 seconds. Add the celery and stir-fry for about 1 minute.

Return the beef to the wok and add the sauce mixture. Continue to stir-fry for another 30 seconds or until all the sauce has been absorbed by the beef.

Serve garnished with the chopped scallions.

SCRAMBLE STIR-FRY | 軟炒

Scrambling eggs with aromatic ingredients was very common for our family meal. Our cook used to make scrambled egg with scallion and tomato, which resembles the common scrambled eggs served in the West. It was delicious and satisfying, but never awe-inspiring. For years I dismissed Chinese scrambled eggs as a common home-style cooking that's great as a last-minute dish when you're in a hurry—but not something to serve to guests. That was until I was invited to James Zhang's home in Shanghai for a dinner with friends. James is a software developer and a very talented cook. Among the dishes he served that night was a mound of pillowy egg studded with a confetti of garlic chives, red sweet peppers, and tender tiny shrimp. The egg was filled with little pockets of flavorful liquid that burst open in my mouth. I had never had scrambled egg like this before. What James introduced me to was egg cooked using a technique known as "scramble stir-fry."

As you may have guessed, the scramble stir-fry technique involves "stir-frying" custard with a little oil over low temperature. The egg is beaten, seasoned, and mixed with all the other accompanying ingredients, including an aromatic broth. James's recipe uses four parts egg to one part liquid by weight. The egg is stirred with a circular motion while it is cooked in the wok. This stirring motion allows the egg to trap moisture and incorporate it into the cooked custard. Temperature control is the key to successfully heating the custard to a silky texture and not overcooking it. A little oil is drizzled in a few times during the scrambling process to give a smooth sheen to the finished dish.

Many scramble stir-fry dishes are made with just the egg whites, but there are variations using the whole egg as well. The technique is the same; just make sure enough starch is added to the custard to create a smooth and silky feel.

SCRAMBLED EGG WHITE WITH MINCED CHICKEN | 軟炒雞蓉菜花

GUANGDONG

The chicken used in this dish should be minced to the point of becoming a paste. After mixing it with the starch and egg, it will have an incredibly smooth texture when cooked. The cauliflower adds a bit of crunch and the ham gives more depth to the flavor, making this one of the great egg custard dishes. | SERVES 2 OR MORE, PAIRED WITH A VEGETABLE DISH

6 ounces cauliflower florets

1 (1½-inch-long) piece of fresh ginger, thinly sliced

5 tablespoons vegetable oil

1 ounce ham, minced

4 ounces ground chicken breast

¾ cup chicken stock (see page 88)

6 large egg whites, lightly beaten

1 tablespoon tapioca starch

1 teaspoon salt

¼ teaspoon ground white pepper

2 tablespoons chopped scallion greens

Pour 3 cups water into a medium saucepan and bring it to a boil. Blanch the cauliflower in the boiling water for 2 minutes, until slightly translucent. Drain and cut into pieces about ½ inch thick.

Using a mortar and pestle, mash the ginger with ¼ cup water until completely pulverized. Strain the ginger juice through a fine-mesh sieve into a small bowl, discarding the pulp.

Heat 2 tablespoons of the vegetable oil in a wok over medium heat until it is just beginning to smoke, about 395°F. Add the ham and fry, stirring, until lightly browned, 2 minutes. Remove the ham from the wok and let it cool on paper towels to absorb any excess oil.

In a medium bowl, combine the ground chicken, chicken stock, and ginger juice until they are completely blended into a paste. Slowly add the egg whites and tapioca starch, mixing well. Add the cauliflower and ham and mix well. Stir in the salt and pepper.

Heat a wok over medium heat for about 30 seconds. Add 1 tablespoon of the vegetable oil to the wok and swirl the oil around the bottom and sides to coat the wok evenly. Turn the heat down slightly and pour the egg mixture into the wok. Immediately use a spatula to stir the egg mixture in a circular motion, scraping the mixture off the bottom as you stir. At the same time, slowly drizzle the remaining 2 tablespoons vegetable oil, 1 teaspoon at a time, around the edge of the hardening egg mixture. Continue to do this until all the vegetable oil has been used, about 4 minutes. The egg mixture should already have become a soft custard at this point.

Serve in a shallow bowl, garnished with the chopped scallion greens.

SCRAMBLED MILK CUSTARD WITH SEAFOOD | 海鮮炒牛奶

GUANGDONG

Crab and shrimp with egg is a natural combination because the egg adds a nice smooth texture to the rich seafood flavor. This dish is an elegant way of presenting the luxurious Chinese fried custard. | SERVES 2 OR MORE, PAIRED WITH A VEGETABLE DISH SUCH AS DOUBLE WINTER DELIGHT (PAGE 123)

6 large egg whites

1 cup whole milk

1 tablespoon tapioca starch

4 ounces cooked crabmeat

2 ounces cooked shrimp, finely chopped

1 ounce ham, minced

2 tablespoons minced scallion whites

½ teaspoon salt

¼ teaspoon ground white pepper

3 tablespoons vegetable oil

2 tablespoons chopped scallion greens

In a medium bowl, whisk together the egg whites, milk, and tapioca starch until completely blended. Then stir in the crabmeat, shrimp, ham, scallion whites, salt, and pepper.

Heat a wok over medium heat for about 30 seconds, until a droplet of water sizzles and evaporates immediately upon contact. Add 1 tablespoon of the vegetable oil to the wok and swirl the oil around the bottom and sides of the wok to coat it evenly. Turn the heat down slightly and pour the egg mixture into the wok. Immediately use a spatula to stir the egg mixture in a circular motion, scraping the mixture off the bottom as you stir. At the same time, slowly drizzle the remaining 2 tablespoons vegetable oil, 1 teaspoon at a time, around the edge of the hardening egg mixture. Continue to do this until all the vegetable oil has been used, about 4 minutes. The egg mixture should already have become a soft custard at this point.

Serve in a shallow bowl, garnished with the chopped scallion greens.

CHAPTER SEVEN

Explosion in the Wok

I VISITED CHENGDU, THE CAPITAL OF SICHUAN PROVINCE, IN THE SPRING OF 2013 AND MET WITH CHEF HE SHUNBIN, WHO WAS THE ASSOCIATE PROFESSOR AT THE SICHUAN HIGHER INSTITUTE OF CUISINE. Chef He, who had cooked in many leading restaurants all over China before accepting a faculty position at the school, became quite animated when describing how to make a certain spicy beef dish. To underline how hot the oil in the wok must be, he leapt up from his chair and gestured flames shooting up that according to him reached one *zhang* (the equivalent of about ten feet). This explosive technique is called *bao* (爆). It is similar to Western flash-frying but even more dramatic.

    Bao is the Chinese term for "explosion," and this name truly befits the cooking method. As is the case with the pass-through technique in stir-frying (page 99), the main ingredient of the dish is parcooked before being stir-fried. The difference is that the temperature of the cooking medium is raised to an extremely high level, which commonly results in an enormous splattering when the ingredient is dropped into the hot oil. It is the most rapid cooking method in the entire Chinese cooking repertoire. The standard steps consist of precooking or blanching the ingredient in water, then flash-frying it in oil before finally stir-frying it in some flavoring sauce. A variation of this technique that is popular in western China and Beijing uses water instead of oil to flash-cook, and I call that method "flash-poaching."

FLASH-FRY | 油爆

What makes this method so compelling is the short cooking time, which keeps tough cuts of meat from overcooking. After flash-frying, the ingredient retains a chewy, crunchy texture that is still tender to the bite. Commonly used ingredients for this technique include beef, lamb, tripe, stomach, gizzard, and heart. Seafood ingredients such as squid, conch, and abalone are also suitable, as are certain vegetables. Eggplant, for example, is perfect since the high temperature of flash-frying cooks it slightly without soaking it with oil.

To make sure that the ingredients will be fully cooked in such a short period of time, they are either sliced very thin or scored in a crisscross pattern before being cut into bite-size pieces about 1 inch wide. Kidney and gizzard are prime candidates for the crisscross scoring. When cooked, the pieces bloom into a beautiful flower shape. Other much tougher cuts of meat, such as stomach and intestine, will need to be precooked until tender.

To ensure that the ingredients are cooked thoroughly, there are usually three steps in this Chinese flash-fry technique, requiring three cooking vessels: a pot with boiling water, a pot with hot oil, and a wok for stir-frying. For certain ingredients, such as beef, lamb, whelk, and conch, blanching is not needed, so the cooking can be accomplished in two steps. I do not recommend flash-frying and stir-frying in the same wok. A large quantity of very hot oil would have to be drained from the wok, and it can be very dangerous to do so before the oil cools.

When flash-frying, the oil temperature should be raised almost to the smoke point, which calls for caution when using this technique at home. High-smoke-point vegetable oil is ideal since the temperature can be raised to near 395°F. If the

ingredient has been parboiled, make sure it has been well drained before transferring it to the extremely hot oil. Adding water to hot oil will cause bubbling. To prevent any boil-over of the hot oil, do not fill the pot more than one-third full; this will allow the oil to expand as it sizzles. When cooking on a home stovetop, you may want to work in batches to prevent a large-scale splattering and to ensure that the ingredients cook quickly and evenly.

FLASH-FRIED FRESH SQUID | 油爆鮮魷

HOME-STYLE

Stir-frying seafood with ginger and scallions is typical of simple home-style cooking. This recipe is straightforward enough to use for a last-minute meal. I use squid as the single seafood ingredient for this recipe, but shrimp, scallops, and clams are all excellent options. | SERVES 2 OR MORE, PAIRED WITH A VEGETABLE DISH

1½ pounds fresh squid

MARINADE

2 tablespoons Shaoxing cooking wine

½ teaspoon salt

¼ teaspoon ground white pepper

2 cups vegetable oil

1 teaspoon tapioca starch

6 very thin slices fresh ginger

6 dried red chiles, cut into ½-inch pieces and seeded

2 scallions, cut on the bias into ¼-inch pieces

4 cilantro sprigs

Clean the squid bodies and cut them into tubes about ½ inch wide or into 1-inch squares. Clean the tentacles and cut them into 1½-inch lengths. Dry the squid well on a paper towel and put it in a small bowl. Add the marinade ingredients, mix well, and let marinate for 10 minutes.

Heat the vegetable oil in a stockpot over high heat until it is just beginning to smoke, about 395°F. Carefully add the squid to the hot oil and cook for about 5 seconds or until the pieces start to curl. Be sure to use a spider skimmer to stir the squid pieces around so they don't stick to one another. Remove the squid from the pot and place it in a skimmer set over a bowl to drain off the excess oil.

Mix the tapioca starch with 2 tablespoons water to make a slurry.

Heat a wok over high heat until a droplet of water sizzles and evaporates immediately upon contact. Scoop out 2 tablespoons of the hot oil you used to cook the squid and transfer it to the wok. Swirl the oil around the bottom and sides of the wok to coat it evenly. Add the ginger and the chiles to the wok and stir-fry until fragrant, about 30 seconds. Return the squid to the wok and stir-fry for another 15 seconds. Add the tapioca slurry and cook until the sauce thickens and coats the ingredients, about 30 seconds. Turn the heat off, add the scallions, and mix well.

Serve garnished with the cilantro sprigs.

FLASH-FRIED LAMB WITH LEEKS | 蔥爆羊肉

SHANDONG

This is a classic lamb dish that's very popular in northern China. It is commonly made with a variety of Chinese leek that is not as big as its American cousin, but the flavor is very similar and regular leeks can be used here. The combination of leeks and cumin, which suggests an influence from the Muslim Xinjiang region, is simply divine. | SERVES 2 OR MORE, PAIRED WITH A VEGETABLE DISH

VELVETING MIXTURE

1 tablespoon vegetable oil

1 tablespoon dark soy sauce

1 tablespoon soy sauce

1 tablespoon tapioca starch

1 teaspoon sugar

½ teaspoon ground cumin

½ teaspoon ground white pepper

1 pound boneless lamb loin or leg, cut against the grain into ⅛-inch-thick slices

2 medium leeks

2 cups vegetable oil

2 tablespoons minced garlic

6 very thin slices fresh ginger

8 dried red chiles, halved and seeded

1 teaspoon salt

4 cilantro sprigs

Combine all the velveting mixture ingredients in a bowl, add the lamb slices, and mix together. Let marinate for about 20 minutes.

Cut the leeks on the bias into ⅛-inch-thick slices. Thoroughly clean the leek slices by washing them in a large bowl of water to make sure there is no soil lodged between the leaves. Drain well.

Heat the vegetable oil in a stockpot over high heat until it is just beginning to smoke, about 395°F. Flash-fry the lamb slices in the oil for about 10 seconds, stirring to prevent the pieces from sticking to one another. Remove the meat from the pot and place it in a skimmer set over a bowl to drain off the excess oil.

Heat a wok over high heat until a droplet of water sizzles and evaporates immediately upon contact. Scoop out 2 tablespoons of the hot oil you used to cook the lamb and transfer it to the wok. Swirl the oil around the bottom and sides of the wok to coat it evenly. Add the garlic and ginger to the wok and stir-fry until fragrant, about 30 seconds. Add the lamb and leeks and stir-fry until the meat is cooked through, about 30 seconds. Add the chiles and salt and continue to stir-fry for another 30 seconds or so to combine.

Serve garnished with the cilantro sprigs.

FLASH-FRIED PIG STOMACH WITH CILANTRO | 芫爆肚絲

SHANDONG

Although there are many different ways of cooking pig stomach, pairing it with cilantro is classic. This Shandong recipe is a favorite of home cooks yet still elegant enough for entertaining. Don't be surprised by the amount of cilantro that goes into the dish; here the herb is treated like a vegetable. | SERVES 2 OR MORE, PAIRED WITH A VEGETABLE DISH

8 ounces pig stomach, cleaned by your butcher

2 cups vegetable oil

4 thin slices fresh ginger

2 garlic cloves, thinly sliced

1 small onion, cut lengthwise into ⅛-inch-thick slices

3 tablespoons Shaoxing cooking wine

1 teaspoon white rice vinegar

½ teaspoon salt

¼ teaspoon ground white pepper

1 scallion, julienned

1 medium bunch cilantro (4 ounces), including stems, cut into 2-inch pieces

Put the pig stomach in a medium saucepan and add enough water to completely cover it. Bring the water to a boil over medium heat and boil gently until tender, about 1½ hours. Drain the stomach and pat dry. Cut the stomach into strips 1½ inches long and ⅛ inch wide. Pat dry again.

Heat the vegetable oil in a stockpot over high heat until it is just beginning to smoke, about 395°F. Flash-fry the stomach slices in the oil for about 10 seconds, stirring to prevent them from sticking to one another. Remove the stomach from the pot and place it in a skimmer set over a bowl to drain off the excess oil.

Heat a wok over high heat until a droplet of water sizzles and evaporates immediately upon contact. Scoop out 2 tablespoons of the hot oil you used to cook the stomach and transfer it to the wok. Swirl the oil around the bottom and sides of the wok to coat it evenly. Add the ginger and garlic to the wok and stir-fry until fragrant, about 30 seconds. Return the stomach to the wok and add the onion, wine, vinegar, salt, and pepper. Stir-fry for another 30 seconds. Add the scallion and cilantro and turn off the heat. Toss everything around for another 10 seconds before serving.

FLASH-POACHING | 水爆

Most commonly used in northern China, flash-poaching is a version of the *bao* (爆) technique where water is used as the cooking medium instead of oil. It is used almost exclusively to cook beef or lamb stomach and intestines, and is popular among the Muslim community of western China in Beijing.

As is the case with flash-frying, the ingredients for flash-poaching should be sliced very thin in order to make sure they cook through. Sliced innards are dropped into boiling water to cook for a very short time, typically only 20 to 25 seconds. This short cooking time ensures that the meat does not overcook. It is common to cook these ingredients a small portion at a time so as not to reduce the temperature of the water too much. Unlike with the flash-frying technique, the cooked food is not seasoned but instead is served with a dipping sauce, making this method similar to that of hot pot cooking (see page 245). But here the water is used only for cooking and not intended to be eaten as a soup.

BEIJING POACHED BEEF TRIPE
老北京爆肚
BEIJING

Both beef and lamb tripe are used interchangeably to make this dish. Buy fresh leaf tripe and make sure to cut it very thin. Try this on a cold winter night and you'll understand why it is such a popular dish in Beijing. | SERVES 2 OR MORE

1 pound beef leaf tripe, cut into ⅛-inch-thick slices

SAUCE

½ cup Chinese toasted sesame paste

¼ cup white rice wine

2 tablespoons soy sauce

2 tablespoons chile oil

2 tablespoons minced garlic

2 tablespoons garlic chive paste (optional)

1 tablespoon fermented tofu

1 teaspoon sugar

4 cilantro sprigs

1 cup white rice wine

1 (1-inch-long) piece of fresh ginger, crushed with the flat side of a knife

2 scallions, cut into 2-inch pieces

1 teaspoon Sichuan peppercorns

6 ounces napa cabbage, cut into 1-inch-wide pieces

Put the tripe in a saucepan and add water to cover. Bring the water to a boil over medium heat and cook the tripe uncovered for 2 hours, replenishing the water if needed during this time. Drain well and cut it into ⅛-inch-thick slices.

Combine all the sauce ingredients in a serving bowl and mix well. Garnish with the cilantro sprigs and set aside.

Put the rice wine, ginger, scallions, and Sichuan peppercorns in a stockpot, add 2 quarts water, and bring the liquid to a boil. Boil gently over medium heat for about 15 minutes. Use a strainer to remove and discard all the solid ingredients. Turn the heat up to high and bring the water to a rolling boil.

Use a spider skimmer to scoop up a handful of the tripe. Lower the skimmer into the boiling water, submerging the tripe, and boil for about 3 seconds. Then lift the skimmer out of the water and let the water come to a rolling boil again. Repeat the blanching action two more times and then put the tripe in a serving bowl. Blanch the rest of the tripe following the same process.

Put all the napa cabbage into the boiling water and cook for about 10 seconds. Drain the cabbage and put it in a separate serving bowl.

Serve the tripe, cabbage, and sauce together. Each diner takes a small quantity of the sauce, then dips the tripe and cabbage in the sauce to eat.

CHAPTER EIGHT

Dipping in Oil

IN FEBRUARY 1951, THE CHIEF EDITOR OF THE EVENING EDITION OF *SING TAO DAILY* (星島日報) IN HONG KONG STARTED WRITING A FOOD COLUMN FOR THE MORNING PAPER.

His name was Chen MengYin (陳夢因) and he was an accomplished cook and gourmet. He called his column the "Dining Chronicle" (食經) and used as a nom de plume "Executive Proofreader" (特級校對), a playful reference to the fact that as the chief editor of the evening edition he did everything from reporting to editing and proofreading. He wrote about his cooking experiences at home, dining discoveries at restaurants, and other musings about the culinary culture in Hong Kong. The column was a sensation and appeared regularly until late 1960s, when he retired. Chen was the original Chinese food blogger!

In one of his early articles, Chen lamented that Western writers often confused the definition of stir-frying with that of deep-frying, failing to differentiate between *chao* (炒) and *zha* (炸). He likened *chao* to Western sautéing (although they are not really comparable), which uses a minimal amount of oil, and *zha* to deep-frying, which requires a large quantity of oil. Although the term "stir-frying" was beginning to gain acceptance in the West, Chen was probably not aware of it and continued to criticize the use of "frying," which implicitly referred to deep-frying, as the description for *chao*.

After writing about the nuances of both stir-frying and deep-frying, Chen went on to explain in detail the different ways of deep-frying in Chinese cooking. He divided deep-frying into sub-techniques of light frying (嫩油), deep-frying (老油), oil steeping (油浸), and yin-yang frying (陰陽油).

I was impressed by the clarity of these sub-techniques and decided to embrace his simple classification. Deep-frying is probably easily understood as it is the same technique used in many other cultures where food items are fried in a pool of hot oil until golden brown. The Chinese use this method to cook many different ingredients, some coated with batter and others simply fried as is until crisp.

The other frying methods, however, will probably need more explanation. Light frying, for example, is a method where the oil is kept well below the smoke point, thus frying the food item without browning it. This method is commonly used for delicate ingredients such as fish and vegetables. A light flour or batter coating is often applied to protect the main ingredient.

A uniquely Chinese technique, oil steeping calls for ingredients to be dropped into extremely hot oil, where they are immediately sealed. Then the heat source is turned off and as the oil cools down the food is gently cooked. A representative dish of this technique is oil-steeped whole fish.

A curious counterintuitive frying technique is the yin-yang method, in which cold oil is poured into sizzling hot oil right after the ingredient is dropped in. Unlike the oil steeping method, the heat is not turned off, so the oil temperature rises again and continues to crisp the ingredient. This is a Cantonese technique that's regularly used for making crisp fried foods.

Pan-frying is serious business in Chinese cooking. Not only are there different variations of pan-frying, but each one is represented by its own single Chinese character. The Chinese language is very compact, and each character expresses a very specific idea. You could cram one-third of Hamlet's "To be, or not to be . . ." soliloquy into one Twitter post of 140 Chinese characters. Some examples of pan-frying techniques include *jian* (煎), *tie* (貼), and *ta* (塌), but because the various techniques are very similar, I will explain only *jian* in detail.

The Chinese frying technique known as *jian* is a simple shallow-oil frying similar to other pan-frying techniques around the world. Food is fried on each side to thoroughly cook until crisp and browned, and then served with a simple seasoning of spiced salt or with a dipping sauce. (The other pan-frying techniques include a Sichuan method known as *tie* that layers different ingredients together and pan-fries them in shallow oil, and *ta*, a Dongbei cooking method, where ingredients are covered in an egg batter, pan-fried, and then flavored with a sauce.)

LIGHT FRYING | 嫩油

When frying delicate food such as fish fillets and vegetables, it is important to protect them from being overcooked. A tried-and-true method is to cover the ingredients with a light flour coating or an airy whipped egg white batter, then fry them in warm oil until cooked. This is precisely the method the Japanese use for making tempura.

For a very simple coating, a few different starches such as tapioca starch, potato starch, and cornstarch are all suitable. Sometimes flour by itself or in combination with one or more of these starches can be used. To apply, pat the ingredients dry, then lightly roll them in a bowl of the starch seasoned with salt, ground white pepper, and sometimes spices.

For a light batter, a mixture of whipped egg white, water, flour, and starch is ideal. For the best results, according to many tempura chefs, use cake flour and ice-cold water to make the batter. The coating will turn out light and crisp.

The coated food is then fried in medium-hot oil at a temperature of about 350°F. At this heat level the ingredient will be cooked gently while the outside will not brown, yet it will still crisp.

THE LEFTOVER OIL DILEMMA

What to do with the leftover oil from frying is a perennial problem for home cooks. In professional kitchens the oil can be used for a couple of days before it is discarded. However, it is not common to make fried food for consecutive meals at home. Differing opinions abound on whether to discard or to save the oil for future use.

In order to come up with an appropriate answer we must first understand the effect the elevated temperature has on the quality of the oil. Cooking oil begins to break down as it reaches the smoke point, which is around 450°F for vegetable oil or 375°F for animal fat. So after the oil is used for frying, it is beginning to turn rancid. This is why good restaurants keep frying oil for only one or two days. For household purposes, discarding the oil after frying only once seems rather extravagant, so it is common to save the oil for later use at home.

But how long can the recycled oil be stored? The reply to this question is that there is no one definitive answer. Much depends on the type of oil, what was fried in it, and how hot it was during the frying. Saturated fat does not break down as easily as unsaturated fat, so animal fat such as tallow or lard will usually stay fresher longer. But it does have a lower smoke point. If you're frying food that does not have a strong odor, such as chicken or vegetables, then reusing the oil can be acceptable. But you may want to consider discarding the oil after frying fish, or at least storing that oil separately and using it only for frying other fish. The oil will also turn rancid much faster if you repeatedly raise the temperature to near the smoke point. So if you're doing a lot of high-temperature browning, you may not want to keep the oil for too long.

There are also a few tests to help in the decision. The most important is to smell the oil. If you detect a rancid odor or a very strong residual smell from the food cooked in it, then discard the oil. Another indicator is the color of the oil. As the oil is used repeatedly, it will darken. A good rule of thumb is that no recycled oil should be kept for more than a month.

Many people advocate using only fresh oil for stir-frying, and there is a good reason for that. Vegetable oil deteriorates with repeated use, lowering the smoke point temperature. So oil that's been used for repeated deep-frying may not be suitable for stir-frying.

SALT AND PEPPER FRIED FISH FILLET | 椒鹽魚片

GUANGDONG

Salt and black pepper is a combination typical of Cantonese cooking. Sprinkled over crisp battered fried fish, it creates a wonderful sensation that is very appetizing. The green chile slices provide added heat for those who like their food even spicier. | SERVES 2 OR MORE, PAIRED WITH A VEGETABLE DISH

4 cups vegetable oil

1 tablespoon minced fresh ginger

1 tablespoon minced garlic

BATTER

½ cup cake flour

½ cup tapioca starch

1 teaspoon baking soda

¼ teaspoon salt

1 large egg white

1 pound skinless tilapia fillet, cut into ⅛-inch-thick slices

2 tablespoons coarse sea salt

1 teaspoon ground black pepper

1 green longhorn chile, cut on the diagonal into ¹⁄₁₆-inch-thick slices

6 cilantro sprigs

Heat ¼ cup of the vegetable oil in a wok over high heat until it is shimmering or about 375°F. Add the minced ginger and garlic to the wok and stir-fry until only lightly browned, about 2 minutes. Use a fine-mesh skimmer to remove the ginger and garlic from the oil and transfer them to a paper towel to drain. The aromatics will continue to brown as they cool.

To make the batter, combine the flour, tapioca starch, baking soda, and salt in a medium bowl and mix well. In a separate bowl, whip the egg white until it holds soft peaks. Whisk ½ cup ice-cold water into the flour mixture. Fold in the egg white.

Pour all the remaining vegetable oil into the wok and heat until it starts to shimmer, about 350°F. Working with 4 to 6 slices of fish at a time, coat them in the batter and deep-fry them for about 2 minutes. Remove the fish from the oil when the batter coating turns pale brown. Do not overcook. Put the fried fish on paper towels to absorb the extra oil.

Stir together the coarse salt and pepper, and sprinkle this over the fish, tossing the slices gently to distribute. Serve garnished with the green chile and cilantro.

SICHUAN CRISP FRIED WILD MUSHROOMS | 川味椒鹽菇

SICHUAN

The batter used in this recipe is based on Japanese tempura batter. It is light and crisp while having the effect of bringing out the mushroom flavor. But the spicy and numbing flavor of the Sichuan spiced salt, made with dried red chile and Sichuan peppercorns, is all Chinese. This is a great vegetarian finger food for a party. | SERVES 4 OR MORE AS AN APPETIZER, 2 OR MORE WHEN PAIRED WITH ANOTHER VEGETABLE DISH

7 ounces enoki mushrooms
3½ ounces white beech mushrooms
3½ ounces brown beech mushrooms

SICHUAN SPICED SALT
6 to 7 dried red chiles, to taste
2 tablespoons Sichuan peppercorns
2 tablespoons coarse sea salt

BATTER
½ cup cake flour
⅔ cup tapioca starch
¼ teaspoon salt
1 large egg white

4 cups vegetable oil
½ cup toasted sesame oil
Chopped scallions
Chopped cilantro

Trim off and discard the root end of the mushrooms and pull them all apart as much as you can. Combine the three types of mushrooms in a bowl. Do not wash them.

To make the spiced salt, put the chiles and Sichuan peppercorns in a dry wok. Toast the spices over low heat, tossing them around to make sure not to burn them. When you start to smell the fragrance from the spices, after about 3 minutes, turn off the heat. Transfer the spices to a plate to cool. Pulse the cooled spices a few times in a blender or mini food processor until they are pulverized. They don't have to be ground into a fine powder. Combine with the coarse sea salt in a bowl and mix well.

To make the batter, combine the cake flour, tapioca starch, and salt in a bowl and mix well. In a separate bowl, whip the egg white until it holds soft peaks. Whisk 1½ cups ice-cold water into the flour mixture. Don't worry if the resulting batter is a little lumpy. Fold in the egg white.

Heat the vegetable and sesame oils together in a wok to about 350°F, or to the point when a drop of the batter sizzles and rolls in the oil. Separate the mushrooms into four equal batches. Put one portion in a small bowl and ladle about one-quarter of the batter over it. Coat the mushrooms evenly in the batter and then drop them into the hot oil. Fry the mushrooms for about 3 minutes and then turn them over. Continue to fry for another minute, until crisp and creamy in color but not browned. Using a skimmer, transfer the mushrooms to a paper towel to drain. Immediately start to fry the next batch. Work as quickly as possible so you can serve the mushrooms hot.

Sprinkle chopped scallions and cilantro over the mushrooms and serve with the spiced salt alongside.

DEEP-FRYING | 老油

Similar to the common deep-frying technique in Western cooking, the Chinese deep-frying method calls for cooking food in oil that is heated to just below its smoke point. This browns the ingredient evenly without burning it, and creates a crisp texture on the outside while keeping the interior succulent and tender.

Deep-frying is the method most commonly used for frying meat or firm solid ingredients. They can be fried directly, covered with a heavy batter, or crusted with a dry coating. The key is to quickly brown and crisp the outer layer without overcooking the inside. The optimum temperature for the oil is around 375°F. At this temperature the ingredients are sealed quickly when dropped into the oil; then the heat gradually gets transmitted and cooks the center.

Very dense ingredients such as root vegetables are commonly double-fried. For the first pass the oil is kept at a temperature of around 350°F. The ingredients are removed from the oil after they are cooked through. The oil temperature is then cranked up to about 375°F before the ingredients are returned to the oil to crisp and brown the surface.

Ingredients that are deep-fried without a coating are always marinated first. Chicken or squab, for example, would be marinated in a soy sauce, wine, and sugar mixture before frying. The soy sauce and sugar enhance the color of the meat, which will brown beautifully when fried. Coated ingredients are generally not marinated first.

Fried foods are normally served with a simple dipping sauce or spiced salt on the side. If the coating is already flavorful, the dish may simply be served as is.

CRISPY CHICKEN
WITH FRIED GARLIC | 蒜香油淋雞
GUANGDONG

A favorite in many Cantonese restaurants, this chicken is full of flavor. The fried garlic and savory soy sauce contribute to the complex taste. Air-drying the chicken is the most important part in crisping the skin, so plan ahead when making this dish. | SERVES 4 OR MORE, AS A SIDE DISH

1 cup Shaoxing cooking wine

4 whole scallions

1 (2-inch-long) piece of fresh ginger

1 (3½- to 4-pound) whole chicken

4 quarts vegetable oil

1 head garlic, minced

COATING

1 tablespoon soy sauce

¼ cup maltose syrup or honey

1 tablespoon tapioca starch

SAUCE

2 tablespoons soy sauce

1 tablespoon vegetable oil

1 tablespoon Shaoxing cooking wine

1 tablespoon sugar

8 cilantro sprigs

In a large stockpot, combine 5 quarts water with the wine, scallions, and ginger and bring to a boil over medium heat. Boil gently for 10 minutes.

Put the chicken into the boiling water and return the water to a boil. Immediately turn the heat off and cover the pot. Let the chicken sit in the hot water for 1 hour.

(CONTINUES)

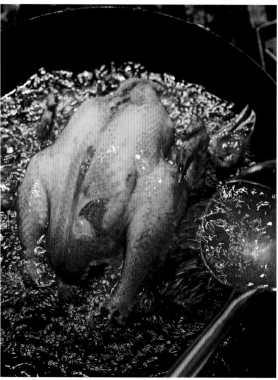

Drain the chicken and let it cool on a wire rack. When it is cool, put the chicken, uncovered, in the refrigerator to air-dry for at least 2 days and up to 3 days.

To make the fried garlic, heat 1 cup vegetable oil in a wok over medium heat until it begins to shimmer, about 350°F. Add the garlic to the wok and fry it until only lightly browned, about 2 minutes. Use a fine-mesh skimmer to remove the garlic from the oil and place it on a paper towel to drain. The garlic will continue to brown as it cools.

Thirty minutes before you plan to fry the chicken, remove it from the refrigerator and let it stand at room temperature.

To make the coating, combine the soy sauce and maltose syrup in a small bowl and mix well. Spread the mixture evenly over the entire chicken, then sprinkle the chicken with the tapioca starch.

Heat the remaining vegetable oil in a wok over high heat until it begins to shimmer, about 350°F. Fry the chicken in the hot oil for about 15 minutes or until the skin is crisp and browned. Be sure to turn the chicken every few minutes to ensure even frying. Drain the chicken thoroughly on paper towels.

Combine all the ingredients for the sauce in a small saucepan. Heat and stir until all the sugar has dissolved.

To serve the chicken, remove the wings and legs, and separate the breast meat from the bones. Cut the bird into serving pieces (see page 72), and reassemble on a serving platter into the shape of a chicken. Pour the sauce over the chicken and scatter the fried garlic evenly over the top. Garnish with the cilantro sprigs.

FRIED SQUAB WITH FIVE-SPICE SALT | 炸乳鴿

GUANGDONG

This was one of my favorite dishes as a child. We would always order crispy fried squab whenever we ate in a Cantonese restaurant. I remember a trip to Hong Kong as a teenager when the whole family traipsed to the outer reaches of Kowloon in search of the best fried squab. | SERVES 2 OR MORE, PAIRED WITH A VEGETABLE DISH

MARINADE

¼ cup rose-flavored rice wine or white rice wine

2 tablespoons soy sauce

3 thick slices fresh ginger

1 scallion, cut into 2-inch pieces

2 whole star anise

1 (1-inch) square of cassia bark

1 teaspoon sugar

2 (2-pound) whole squabs, cleaned

1 teaspoon five-spice powder

2 tablespoons salt

¼ cup maltose syrup or honey

1 teaspoon white rice vinegar

4 cups vegetable oil

Put all the ingredients for the marinade in a medium saucepan and bring the liquid to a boil. Cook the marinade for about 10 minutes and then let it cool. Pour into a large bowl.

Add the squabs to the cooled marinade and cover with plastic wrap. Marinate in the refrigerator for at least 8 hours or overnight.

Remove the squabs from the marinade and set the birds in the refrigerator, uncovered, to air-dry for 6 to 8 hours.

In a small bowl, mix the five-spice powder with the salt.

Mix the maltose syrup and vinegar in a small bowl and brush the mixture evenly over the air-dried squabs. Be sure to cover every part of the birds. Let the syrup dry for about 30 minutes and then apply another layer. Repeat this process three times.

Heat the vegetable oil in a wok over high heat until it begins to shimmer, about 350°F. Fry the squabs in the oil, turning them once, for 10 minutes or until golden brown. Remove from the oil and set on paper towels to drain the excess oil.

Cut the head and the neck off each squab if necessary, and then quarter the bodies. Arrange the pieces on a serving platter and serve with the five-spice salt on the side.

FRIED SESAME PORK TENDERLOIN | 芝麻里脊

GUANGDONG

A crunchy and fragrant sesame coating transforms ordinary pork tenderloin into a classic Cantonese dish that has become a favorite throughout China and overseas. For a little extra flavor, serve this with Sweet-and-Sour Dipping Sauce (page 54). | SERVES 2 OR MORE AS A MAIN DISH

MARINADE

1 tablespoon white rice wine

1 teaspoon soy sauce

1 tablespoon minced scallion whites

½ teaspoon salt

¼ teaspoon ground white pepper

8 ounces pork tenderloin, cut into ⅛-inch-thick slices

2 large eggs

2 tablespoons tapioca starch

½ cup white sesame seeds

¼ cup all-purpose flour

4 cups vegetable oil

4 cilantro sprigs

Combine all the marinade ingredients in a medium bowl and mix well. Add the pork slices, turn to coat, and let marinate for 20 minutes.

Beat the eggs in a small bowl and then add the tapioca starch. Blend well. Spread the sesame seeds on a plate. Sprinkle the flour on the pork slices and make sure each one is completely coated.

Heat the vegetable oil in a wok over high heat until it is just beginning to smoke, about 395°F. Fry in the pork in two batches: Working quickly, dip one pork slice at a time in the egg batter, then coat it with sesame seeds before dropping it into the hot oil. As the slices turn golden brown, after about 3 minutes, remove them from the oil and drain on a paper towel.

Serve garnished with the cilantro sprigs.

The term "steeping" is used here for lack of a more exact way of describing this technique. "Steeping" customarily means extracting flavor from an ingredient by soaking it in hot liquid, but here the term is used to indicate food that is dropped into hot oil and then left without further heating until it is completely cooked.

This unique way of deep-frying is very effective for cooking whole fish, as it allows the fish to retain its delicate texture. Critical to the success of this technique is to use fresh, clean oil and heat it to an extremely high temperature of about 395°F. Use a large pot or a wok to hold the oil, and never fill it more than one-third of the way. There should be sufficient space for the oil to bubble up when the fish is frying. Carefully lower the whole fish into the oil and then immediately turn the heat off. Let the fish cook for 5 to 8 minutes. Drain the fish thoroughly and then dress it with a sauce.

In order to ensure that the fish cooks completely, it is common to cut the meat away from the center bones while leaving it attached in the head and tail areas. This will promote heat transmission and cook the fish more easily. For flat-bodied fish, scoring the body with a tight crosshatch pattern will produce the same effect.

OIL-STEEPED SOON HOCK WITH SOY SAUCE | 油浸旬殼
GUANGDONG

Soon hock fish is also known as marble goby and is native to the rivers and lakes of Southeast Asia. The meat is sweet and tender, making it highly sought after. The soy sauce beautifully complements the fish, which should be just lightly crisp. | SERVES 2 OR MORE, PAIRED WITH A VEGETABLE DISH

1 (1½-pound) whole soon hock, butterflied and backbones removed (see page 73)
¼ cup tapioca starch

SAUCE
2 tablespoons soy sauce
2 tablespoons Shaoxing cooking wine
1 teaspoon sugar
½ teaspoon ground white pepper

4 cups vegetable oil
2 scallions, finely julienned
¼ cup finely julienned fresh ginger

Pat the fish dry and sprinkle it with the tapioca starch, making sure to cover the entire fish. Shake off any excess starch.

Combine all the sauce ingredients in a small saucepan and mix well. Heat the sauce and keep it warm.

Heat the vegetable oil in a wok over high heat until it is just beginning to smoke, about 395°F. Carefully put the fish in the oil, making sure the body is spread out so that the butterfly shape is retained while frying. Turn off the heat and let the fish sit for 10 minutes or until the meat in the middle is cooked through. (This butterfly shape is awkward to work with and it is sometimes impossible to submerge the entire fish. When this happens, use a ladle to pour hot oil over the exposed top part of the fish until it is completely cooked.)

Remove the fish with a skimmer and transfer it to a serving platter. Pour the hot sauce over the fish and garnish with the julienned scallions and ginger. With a ladle, scoop about 2 tablespoons of the hot oil from the wok and pour it on top of the sauce.

YIN-YANG FRYING | 陰陽油

The yin-yang frying technique is almost counter-intuitive. It calls for frying food in hot oil, then adding cold oil to lower the temperature before bringing it back up again to finish the frying. One would think that reducing the temperature of the oil after the food has been added would make it greasy and soggy. But on the contrary, the initial frying in hot oil seals the food immediately and then continues to cook the center of the food to perfect doneness before the oil becomes hot again and crisps the exterior.

Although most commonly used for snack foods or dim sum items, this technique is excellent for frying any food that is enclosed in a thin edible wrapper. Some examples include sausage meat rolled in tofu skin and shrimp paste rolls with seaweed.

FRESH WATER CHESTNUTS

FRIED TOFU SKIN ROLLS
閩南五香卷
FUJIAN

Growing up in a Fujian household in Singapore, we ate these five-spice fried meat rolls regularly; they are often referred to simply as ngo hiong, *or "five spice," in the Fujian dialect. This meat roll is appetizing and perfect as a snack, but it can also be elevated to a sophisticated banquet dish by enhancing it with seafood such as shrimp or crabmeat, as in this recipe.* | SERVES 4 AS AN APPETIZER, OR 2 OR MORE WHEN PAIRED WITH A VEGETABLE DISH

1 pound coarsely ground pork

4 ounces medium shrimp, shelled, deveined, and chopped

4 ounces water chestnuts, coarsely chopped

1 tablespoon minced scallion whites

2 teaspoons five-spice powder

2 tablespoons tapioca starch

1 egg white

1 teaspoon salt

¼ teaspoon ground white pepper

4 pieces tofu skin, each about 5 by 12 inches

8 cups vegetable oil

Sweet-and-Sour Dipping Sauce (page 54)

Combine the pork, shrimp, water chestnuts, scallion whites, five-spice powder, tapioca starch, egg white, salt, and pepper in a bowl and mix well.

Divide the pork mixture into four portions. Lay one sheet of the tofu skin flat on a cutting board. Shape one portion of the pork mixture into a log about 1 inch in diameter and about 9 inches long. Place this meat log lengthwise at one edge of the tofu skin and roll it up. Fold the extra tofu skin at either end under the log to keep it in place. Repeat with the remaining tofu skins and pork mixture.

Heat 6 cups vegetable oil in a wok over high heat until it begins to shimmer, about 350°F. Put all four meat rolls in the oil and let them fry for about 30 seconds. Add 1 cup of the remaining vegetable oil to the wok and let it heat up. Once the oil is bubbling again, let the meat rolls fry for 30 seconds. Add the remaining 1 cup vegetable oil to the wok and once again let the oil heat up until bubbles. Fry for 30 seconds or until the meat rolls are golden brown.

Remove the meat rolls from the oil and drain them on paper towels. Cut the rolls into ½-inch-thick wheels and arrange them on a plate. Serve with the sweet-and-sour dipping sauce on the side.

PAN-FRYING 煎

The single Chinese character *jian* (煎) represents basic pan-frying in a shallow pool of oil. It is similar to pan-frying techniques that we know from other parts of the world, where food is cooked in moderately hot oil until browned. The food ingredient is usually flipped over at the halfway point to make sure both sides are cooked thoroughly. Seasoning is added at the end, just before serving, or a spice salt or dipping sauce can be served on the side.

Even though this is one of the simplest techniques in Chinese cooking, correct cooking temperature and length of time are crucial in making sure that the ingredient browns and cooks through perfectly instead of burning. There should be no more than 1 inch of oil in the wok and it should be heated to about 350°F. This temperature should be kept as constant as possible. This means that the wok should not be crowded. Fry one medium whole fish at a time or arrange just enough pieces of ingredients to form a single layer at the bottom of the wok. Cook one side of the food completely before flipping to cook the other side.

Whole fish, as well as prawns in their shell, seafood paste, julienned potato, stuffed tofu, and other ingredients are regularly pan-fried. Whenever possible the ingredients being pan-fried are made as flat as can be for easy cooking.

PAN-FRIED POMPANO WITH GINGER AND SCALLION | 煎鯧魚

SHANDONG

Pompano is a flat fish with a diamond-shaped body and fine-textured meat. I often steam pompano, but pan-frying is a great alternative. The light egg coating is slightly crunchy and the sauce brings out the sweetness in the fresh fish. | SERVES 2 OR MORE, PAIRED WITH A VEGETABLE DISH

MARINADE

2 tablespoons white rice wine

¼ teaspoon salt

1 (1-pound) whole pompano, cleaned, body scored with crisscross cuts about ½ inch apart

SAUCE

¼ cup white rice wine

¼ ounce fresh ginger
(about three 1/16-inch-thick slices)

1 scallion, cut into 1½-inch pieces

½ teaspoon salt

¼ teaspoon ground white pepper

¼ cup all-purpose flour

1 tablespoon tapioca starch

1 egg

½ cup vegetable oil

4 cilantro sprigs

Combine the marinade ingredients in a small bowl and rub the mixture all over the pompano. Set the fish aside and let marinate for 15 minutes.

Combine all the sauce ingredients in another bowl and mix well.

Combine the flour and tapioca starch in a small bowl and mix well. Spread the flour mixture evenly on a plate. Lightly beat the egg in a bowl. Spread the egg into a thin layer on a second plate. Dredge the pompano on both sides in the flour mixture and then dip it in the egg. Be sure the fish is evenly coated with the egg on both sides.

Heat the vegetable oil in a wok over medium heat until it begins to shimmer, about 350°F. Fry the pompano in the oil until golden brown, about 4 minutes on each side. Remove the fish from the wok.

Remove all but 2 tablespoons of the vegetable oil from the wok. Pour the sauce mixture into the wok and return the fried pompano to the wok. Cook the fish for about 1 minute on each side or until the sauce has been completely absorbed by the fish.

Serve the pompano topped with any scallion and ginger pieces still left in the wok. Garnish with the cilantro sprigs.

PAN-FRIED SALT AND PEPPER WHOLE PRAWNS | 椒鹽對蝦

GUANGDONG

These pan-fried shrimp are crisp and full of flavor. The combination of black pepper and green chile gives this dish two kinds of spicy heat. The crunchy shrimp heads and the shells are the best tasting. I like eating the entire shrimp—head, shell, and all. | SERVES 2 OR MORE, PAIRED WITH A VEGETABLE DISH

12 ounces large shrimp with shell and head

MARINADE
2 tablespoons white rice wine
1 teaspoon minced fresh ginger
½ teaspoon salt

½ cup vegetable oil
3 tablespoons minced garlic
1 teaspoon ground black pepper
½ teaspoon salt
2 tablespoons tapioca starch
1 green longhorn chile, cut into ⅛-inch-thick slices

Cut off the shrimps' antennae and devein them by cutting open the shell along the back, but do not peel them. Pat the shrimp dry and put them in a bowl along with the marinade ingredients. Toss to coat and let marinate for 10 minutes.

Heat the vegetable oil in a wok over medium heat until it begins to shimmer, about 350°F. Add the garlic and stir-fry until it just turns light brown, about 3 minutes. Be sure not to overcook the garlic. Scoop the garlic out of the oil with a fine-mesh strainer and let it drain on a paper towel. Combine the drained fried garlic, black pepper, and salt in a small bowl and mix well.

Reheat the vegetable oil in the wok over high heat until it is just beginning to smoke, about 395°F. Sprinkle the shrimp with the tapioca starch to coat. Put the shrimp in the wok and pan-fry them, turning them over once, until golden brown, about 5 minutes. Remove the shrimp from the wok and set them on a paper towel to drain.

Arrange the shrimp on a plate and sprinkle the garlic pepper salt all over them. Garnish with the green chile slices.

PAN-FRIED BATTERED TOFU | 鍋塌豆腐

SHANDONG

Covering tofu with egg batter traps the moisture within and creates a succulent dish. This northern Chinese way of cooking tofu is very flexible. You could stuff the tofu with a little bit of seasoned raw ground pork before battering and pan-frying, or you might add sweet green and red peppers to the sauce. | SERVES 2 OR MORE, PAIRED WITH A VEGETABLE DISH

SAUCE

2 tablespoons white rice wine

1 tablespoon soy sauce

1 teaspoon sugar

1 teaspoon tapioca starch

BATTER

1 large egg

1 tablespoon tapioca starch

½ cup vegetable oil

12 ounces firm tofu, cut into 8 pieces, each 1 inch square and ½ inch thick

1 tablespoon minced scallion whites

1 tablespoon minced garlic

1 dried shiitake mushroom, rehydrated (see page 78) and cut into ¼-inch cubes

1 ounce fresh or canned bamboo shoots (drained if canned), cut into ¼-inch cubes

Combine all the sauce ingredients in a small bowl and mix well.

Combine all the batter ingredients in a small bowl and mix well.

Heat the vegetable oil in a wok over medium heat until it begins to shimmer, about 350°F. Dip the tofu squares in the batter and then pan-fry them, turning them over once, until just lightly browned, about 3 minutes. Remove the tofu from the oil and drain on a paper towel.

Remove all but 2 tablespoons of the vegetable oil from the wok. Add the scallion whites and garlic to the wok and stir-fry for about 30 seconds. Add the shiitake mushroom and bamboo shoots and continue to stir-fry for another 30 seconds. Add the sauce mixture to the wok and cook until it thickens, about 1 minute. Return the tofu pieces to the wok and let the sauce simmer with the tofu for another 30 seconds.

Remove the tofu from the wok and neatly arrange the pieces on a plate to form a large square. Pour the sauce all over the tofu.

CHAPTER NINE

Flavoring with Sauces

IN HER BOOK *THE FORTUNE COOKIE CHRONICLES*, JENNIFER 8. LEE PROPOSES AN APT ANALOGY BY COMPARING HOW AMERICAN CHINESE TAKEOUT RESTAURANTS ARE RUN TO HOW OPEN SOURCE TECHNOLOGY OPERATES. The open source code, in the case of the American Chinese restaurant, is the menu and the operation model. These restaurants offer similar menu items that customers can always rely on. From New York City to Kansas City, one can order Beef with Broccoli or General Tso's Chicken and get a similar dish, delivered within minutes with a fresh menu attached.

One thing this open source American Chinese restaurant community has clearly learned in their search for the most popular menu items is that crunchy, sweet, and gooey dishes are beloved by the American public. Let's face it: Who doesn't enjoy anything fried to a crisp, then doused with a flavorful sweet sauce? So it is not surprising that Sweet-and-Sour Pork was one of the earliest Chinese food sensations in the U.S. market. General Tso's Chicken followed in its footsteps and has become the iconic takeout food of America.

Called *liu* (熘), deep-frying flour-coated meat and then covering it with a thick sauce is as quintessentially Chinese as stir-frying. Although it has many distinct variations, the one unifying characteristic is that the finished dish and the sauce are always prepared separately. Pouring sauce over cooked ingredients is common in the Western cooking tradition, but this is the only technique in Chinese cooking that does this.

For the most part the main ingredients in this technique consist of tender meat such as chicken, pork, fish, and shellfish. But tofu and root vegetables are also used in vegetarian versions. Fish is often cooked whole, while chicken, pork, shellfish, and other ingredients are cut into bite-size cubes.

The variations of this technique are defined by the different ways of cooking the main ingredients and include deep-frying, poaching, and steaming. The deep-fried version is the most popular in American Chinese restaurants because of the crisp texture; it is most closely associated with southern Chinese cooking. Other variations, more common in the north, are subtler, resulting in a delicate silken texture dressed with a bright, flavorful sauce. There are also regional preferences for the sauce. Whereas the southern Chinese like using the sweet-and-sour flavor profile, the northern Chinese fancy wine and vinegar flavors in their sauces.

How Thick Should the Sauce Be?

One of the most common complaints about Chinese food is that the sauce accompanying the dishes is often cloyingly thick. Although there is a reason why some sauces should be thick, not all should, and many American restaurants fail to make a distinction. It is important to understand when a thick sauce is desirable and when it is not.

When pouring a sauce over crisp fried food, a thicker consistency is necessary to keep the crust from absorbing too much moisture and becoming soggy. The optimum thickness should be similar to that of ketchup. This is also true for dipping sauces that accompany fried dishes such as tofu skin rolls or wontons.

However, when dressing food that has been boiled or steamed, the sauce should have a smooth and velvety texture that is closer to a French demi-glace or reduced meat jus. It is in this situation that many cooks falter and create sauces that are too thick.

The best way to control the thickness of the sauce is to drizzle in the starch slurry progressively, rather than adding the starch into a sauce mix. You can better control the thickness as the slurry is added a little bit at a time and judge the thickness of the sauce accordingly.

A CLOSE RELATION CALLED PENG | 烹

Another technique, known as *peng* (烹), is closely related to *liu*. The difference is in the sauce. Instead of dressing the cooked food with a thickened sauce, a rich broth is drizzled over the cooked ingredient and is absorbed into the coating. What is interesting with this technique is that the outer layer maintains a slight crunch.

Two ways of precooking the main ingredients for *peng* include deep-frying and pan-frying, known as *qingpeng* (清烹) and *jianpeng* (煎烹) respectively. *Qingpeng* calls for the main ingredients to be either coated with a dry starch or covered in an egg batter and then deep-fried, and *jianpeng* simply calls for them to be lightly coated with starch and then pan-fried. It was at a Dongbei restaurant in the Flushing neighborhood of New York City that I first encountered a dish cooked using this technique: *jianpeng* pompano. I specifically remember enjoying the still slightly crisp pan-fried coating full of ginger and scallion aroma; it made a big impression on me.

The *peng* technique is common in northern China and is used with many different types of meat, including chicken, fish, and shellfish. Because southern cuisines rarely use this method, it was not brought to the United States by the early Cantonese immigrants. Only now, with the increase of northern Chinese immigrants to the United States, are dishes using the technique becoming more available.

SAUCING AFTER DEEP-FRYING | 焦熘

As one of the most successful early American Chinese dishes, Sweet-and-Sour Pork is perhaps the most famous of the *liu* dishes. The pork cubes are coated with starch, deep-fried until crisp, and finished with a tangy sweet sauce.

The coating should be thin and crunchy, never heavy or lumpy. Some recipes call for flour, but using a starch such as tapioca is the best way to keep the coating light. When deep-frying these nuggets, the oil should be kept at a high temperature, about 375°F. With the meat cut to about ¾-inch cubes, the hot oil will crisp them quickly and still keep the interior tender.

Once the meat is properly fried, you can turn your attention to the consistency and flavor of the sauce. The sauce should be thick but not cloyingly so, and the flavor should be balanced—neither too sweet nor too tart. The sauce should be thick enough to easily coat the fried pieces of meat. Too thin and the sauce will be absorbed and the coating will lose its crunchiness. I suggest thickening the sauce a little bit at a time so you can monitor the consistency.

Old-Fashioned Sweet-and-Sour Pork

The origin of Sweet-and-Sour Pork is a mystery that so far has not been solved by contemporary food historians. But there are plenty of legends and much speculation as to how this dish was invented and how the original recipe evolved into the current form.

The Chinese name for sweet-and-sour pork is *gulu pork* (咕嚕肉). The most commonly told story regarding the name is that this dish was so delicious that diners' stomachs would start to make a growling noise, like *gulu*, before the dish was served. Another legend suggests that the recipe is so old that it was originally known as "ancient pork," which in Chinese is *gulao* pork (古老肉).

No one, however, disputes the fact that the original recipe called for haw fruits as the main ingredient for the sauce. The ripened fruit of hawthorn trees, haw fruits resemble red crabapples with tiny brown spots. They are tart but have a pleasant quince-like flavor. The original sweet-and-sour sauce purportedly was made by cooking haw fruits into a paste, then adding sugar and stock before tossing in the crunchy pork nuggets.

The burning question is when and how did this recipe get transformed into the current ketchup-based version? One theory is that when early immigrants from China tried to reproduce this dish without haw fruits, they decided to substitute ketchup. Another theory suggests that the evolution happened earlier, in Hong Kong, where Western cooking influences prompted the local chefs to reach for the imported tomato sauce.

SWEET-AND-SOUR PORK | 咕嚕肉

GUANGDONG

I am willing to bet that anyone in the world who has ever eaten Chinese food knows what Sweet-and-Sour Pork is. This classic Cantonese dish is so iconic that it is practically synonymous with Chinese food outside of China. How this happened is a mystery to culinary historians. But I can report that the sweet-and-sour flavor is equally popular in China. | SERVES 2 OR MORE, AS A MAIN DISH

MARINADE

1 large egg white

2 tablespoons white rice wine

½ teaspoon salt

¼ teaspoon ground white pepper

1 pound boneless pork loin, cut into ¾-inch cubes

SAUCE

¼ cup pork stock (see page 89) or water

3 tablespoons white rice wine

3 tablespoons ketchup

2 tablespoons sugar

1 tablespoon white rice vinegar

2 teaspoons tapioca starch

4 cups vegetable oil

¾ cup tapioca starch

1 tablespoon minced garlic

1 small red bell pepper, cut into ¾-inch pieces

1 small green bell pepper, cut into ¾-inch pieces

½ cup canned pineapple chunks, drained

4 cilantro sprigs

Combine all the marinade ingredients in a bowl, add the pork cubes, and mix well. Let marinate for 20 minutes.

Combine all the sauce ingredients in another bowl and mix well.

Heat the vegetable oil in a wok over high heat until it is shimmering, about 375°F. Put the tapioca starch in a large bowl, then roll the marinated pork cubes in the starch. Be sure to coat each piece generously. Fry the pork cubes in the hot oil in two batches until they are golden brown, about 4 minutes. Drain the pork cubes and set them aside on two layers of paper towel.

Remove all but 2 tablespoons of the vegetable oil from the wok. Add the garlic to the wok and stir-fry for about 30 seconds. Add the red and green pepper pieces and stir-fry for 1 minute. Add the pineapple chunks. Give the sauce a quick stir and pour it into the wok. Cook until the sauce thickens, about 1 minute.

Return the pork cubes to the wok and stir-fry until all the pieces are coated with the sauce, about 30 seconds. Garnish with the cilantro sprigs.

CARP WITH PINE NUTS | 松子魚

ZHEJIANG

This sweet-and-sour vinegar sauce with pine nuts is one of my favorite ways to dress crispy fried fish. The tartness contrasts well with the nutty toasted pine nuts. Any whole fish with a firm texture, such as branzino or striped bass, works well in this recipe. | SERVES 2 OR MORE, AS A MAIN DISH

1 (2-pound) whole small carp, cleaned

½ teaspoon salt

¼ cup tapioca starch

SAUCE

½ cup chicken stock (see page 88) or water

¼ cup Shaoxing cooking wine

1 tablespoon soy sauce

1 tablespoon Chinkiang black vinegar

2 teaspoons sugar

½ teaspoon salt

¼ teaspoon ground white pepper

2 teaspoons tapioca starch

8 cups vegetable oil

1 tablespoon minced garlic

1 tablespoon minced fresh ginger

½ ounce dried shiitake mushroom, rehydrated (see page 78) and cut into ¼-inch cubes

1 ounce fresh or canned bamboo shoots (drained if canned), cut into ¼-inch cubes

¼ cup pine nuts, toasted

Score the fish on both sides with bias cuts spaced about ½ inch apart. Sprinkle the salt over the fish and then dredge it thoroughly in the tapioca starch, covering it from head to tail.

In a bowl, mix together all the sauce ingredients except the tapioca starch. Separately, mix the tapioca with 2 tablespoons water to make a slurry.

Heat the vegetable oil in a wok over high heat until it is just beginning to smoke, about 395°F. Deep-fry the carp in the hot oil for about 5 minutes on one side; then turn it over and continue to fry for 3 minutes on the other side. Insert a fork at the thickest part of the fish to make sure the meat flakes off the bones easily. Drain thoroughly and put the fish on paper towels to absorb any excess oil.

Remove all but 2 tablespoons vegetable oil from the wok. Add the garlic and ginger to the wok and stir-fry for about 30 seconds. Add the shiitake mushroom and bamboo shoots and stir-fry for another 30 seconds. Pour the sauce mixture into the wok and cook for 1 minute. Add the starch slurry and cook until the sauce has thickened, about 1 minute. Turn the heat off and add the pine nuts.

Put the fried fish on a serving platter and pour the sauce evenly over the fish.

CHEF PENG CHANG-KUEI: INVENTOR OF GENERAL TSO'S CHICKEN

In 1953, Admiral Arthur W. Radford, chairman of the U.S. Joint Chiefs of Staff, visited Taiwan for talks with President Chiang Kai-Shek of the Republic of China (Taiwan). The official presidential palace chef, Peng Chang-Kuei (彭長貴), was asked to create a banquet to entertain the illustrious guest. After planning some traditional dishes, he decided to come up with a few new ones, too. One of them was General Tso's Chicken, which was named after a distinguished Qing dynasty general, Zuo Zongtang (左宗棠), from chef Peng's home province of Hunan, whom he admired.

Wanting to know more about the history of this famous chicken dish and the background of the chef, I visited Chef Peng's family in Taiwan. The story, recounted by his son, Chuck Peng, begins in a small village in Hunan not far from Changsha (長沙), the capital. Chef Peng was born there but left his family when he was thirteen years old. He went to Changsha to work for the private chef of the family of Tan Yankai (譚延闓), former premier of the Republic of China. There he apprenticed under the tutelage of Chef Cao Jingchen (曹藎臣), who was at that time renowned in China. Using the connections of his employer, he worked for many important political figures of the government of the Republic of China during the chaos of the 1930s and 1940s. After the defeat of the Nationalist government, Chef Peng followed his patron to Taiwan and settled there to become the de facto presidential palace chef. He eventually opened his own restaurant in Taipei, serving his version of modern Hunan cuisine.

But how General Tso's Chicken was introduced to the United States is rather murky. It is generally accepted that chef Peng was not the first to bring the dish to the United States. Around 1971 two New York City Hunan restaurants, opened by Chef T. T. Wang and restaurateur David Keh, included General Tso's chicken on their menus after sampling the dish at Chef Peng's restaurant in Taipei. They introduced their own version, adjusting the flavors to appeal to local diners. When Peng moved to New York City a year later and opened his own restaurant, Peng Yuan, ironically he was considered a latecomer and his original General Tso's Chicken ended up being considered a second-rate copy.

Chef Peng's version of General Tso's Chicken has a lighter batter coating and more tartness in the sauce. The garlic and vinegar flavors are more pronounced and overall the dish has more spicy heat. But it is the version by Chef T. T. Wang at his Hunan restaurant, with its heavier, crunchier crust and sweeter sauce, that ended up becoming the one beloved by Americans.

Still, Chef Peng found success through the patronage of Taiwanese diplomats working at the United Nations, which was near his restaurant on 44th Street and Second Avenue. Not long after the restaurant's opening, Henry Kissinger was introduced to Peng Yuan by the architect I. M. Pei, and his visit generated great curiosity among many New Yorkers. Word spread that Peng's restaurant was offering a new and exciting Chinese cuisine never seen before. But it wasn't until 1974, when the local ABC station in New York broadcast a segment filmed at the restaurant with Chef Peng demonstrating the making of General Tso's Chicken, that the dish finally reached the level of acclaim it now has. Fifteen hundred requests for the recipe were received by the station within a few days of the broadcast.

General Tso's Chicken is not the only well-known creation of Chef Peng. One signature dish in his Taipei restaurant is Double Fortune Squares (富貴雙方), which are made up of Chinese ham and crisp tofu skin served in a steamed bun sandwich. Peng Family Tofu (彭家豆腐) and Quail Soup in Bamboo (竹節鴿盅) are two other favorites created in the 1960s. While in New York he created Stir-Fried Shrimp Served in a Lettuce Bowl (生菜蝦鬆). All these dishes have become classics that are widely copied in many restaurants throughout Asia. Chef Peng's creations are not what one would call authentic Hunan cooking; rather they reflect an innovative use of ingredients and techniques while staying true to the flavors of Hunan cuisine. Therein lies his brilliance.

GENERAL TSO'S CHICKEN | 左宗棠雞

HUNAN

This version of General Tso's Chicken resembles the original created by Peng Chang-Kuei in Taiwan. Strictly speaking it is not a traditional Hunan dish, but the technique and flavors are inspired by the chef's Hunan background. It is not as sweet as the standard American version, and is laced with lots of garlic. | SERVES 2 OR MORE, AS A MAIN DISH

MARINADE

2 tablespoons Shaoxing cooking wine

1 large egg white

½ teaspoon salt

¼ teaspoon ground white pepper

1 pound boneless, skinless chicken thighs, cut into ¾-inch cubes

SAUCE

¾ cup chicken stock (see page 88) or water

¼ cup Shaoxing cooking wine

2 tablespoons Chinkiang black vinegar

1 tablespoon soy sauce

1 teaspoon hoisin sauce

2 tablespoons tapioca starch

1 tablespoon sugar

4 cups vegetable oil

¾ cup tapioca starch

3 tablespoons minced garlic

1 tablespoon minced fresh ginger

¼ cup dried red chiles

1 tablespoon toasted sesame oil

1 teaspoon sesame seeds, toasted

2 tablespoons thinly sliced scallion greens

Combine all the marinade ingredients in a bowl and mix well. Add the chicken cubes and stir well. Let marinate for 20 minutes.

Combine all the sauce ingredients in another bowl and mix well.

Heat the vegetable oil in a wok over high heat until it is shimmering, about 375°F. Put the tapioca starch in a large bowl and roll the marinated chicken cubes in the starch. Be sure to coat each piece generously. Fry the chicken cubes in the hot oil in two batches until they are golden brown, about 4 minutes. Drain the chicken cubes and set them aside on a double layer of paper towels.

Remove all but 2 tablespoons of the vegetable oil from the wok. Add the garlic and ginger to the wok and stir-fry for about 30 seconds. Add the chiles and stir-fry for another 30 seconds. Stir the sauce mixture so the starch is blended completely and pour it into the wok. Cook until the sauce thickens, about 1 minute. Return the chicken to the wok and quickly toss the pieces in the sauce. Add the sesame oil and stir it into the chicken.

Garnish with the toasted sesame seeds and sliced scallion greens.

CRISP FRIED RED SNAPPER
WITH SPICY SWEET-AND-SOUR SAUCE | 香辣糖醋魚
HOME-STYLE

Sweet-and-sour sauce is a classic way to dress a crisp fried fish. But I've pushed this recipe up a notch by spicing the sauce and covering the fish with lots of fresh herbs. Any fresh firm whole fish will work well with this recipe. | SERVES 2 OR MORE, AS A MAIN DISH

½ carrot, julienned

1 (2-pound) whole red snapper, cleaned

½ teaspoon salt

¼ cup tapioca starch

SWEET-AND-SOUR SAUCE

¼ cup ketchup

¼ cup chicken stock (see page 88) or water

2 tablespoons white rice wine

1 tablespoon white rice vinegar

1 tablespoon soy sauce

1 tablespoon chopped pickled red chiles

1 tablespoon sugar

1 teaspoon tapioca starch

8 cups vegetable oil

1 teaspoon minced garlic

1 teaspoon minced fresh ginger

½ cucumber, seeded and julienned

6 cilantro sprigs

6 basil sprigs

6 mint sprigs

Bring 2 cups water to a boil in a saucepan, add the julienned carrot, and parboil over medium heat for 5 minutes. Drain the carrot and set aside.

Score the fish on both sides with bias cuts spaced about ½ inch apart. Sprinkle the salt over the fish and then dredge it thoroughly in the tapioca starch, covering it from head to tail.

In a bowl, mix together all the sauce ingredients except the tapioca starch. Separately, mix the tapioca with 2 tablespoons water to make a slurry.

Heat the vegetable oil in a wok over high heat until it is just beginning to smoke, about 395°F. Deep-fry the carp in the hot oil for about 5 minutes on one side; then turn it over and continue to fry for 3 minutes on the other side. Insert a fork at the thickest part of the fish to make sure the meat flakes off the bones easily. Drain thoroughly and put the fish on paper towels to absorb any excess oil.

Remove all but 2 tablespoons vegetable oil from the wok. Add the garlic and ginger to the wok and stir-fry for about 30 seconds. Pour the sauce mixture into the wok and cook for 1 minute. Add the starch slurry and cook until the sauce has thickened, about 1 minute.

Put the fried fish on a serving platter and scatter the julienned carrot and cucumber on top of the fish. Pour the sauce evenly over the fish. Serve garnished with the cilantro, basil, and mint sprigs.

SAUCING AFTER OIL POACHING | 滑熘

Similar to the pass-through technique for stir-frying (see page 99), oil poaching very quickly cooks meat and fish that has been covered in a velveting mixture in moderately hot oil. Unlike stir-frying, where seasoning and flavoring is incorporated during the cooking process, a separate sauce is prepared that smothers the meat after it is cooked.

Tender proteins such as chicken breast, flounder, and sea bass are excellent choices for this technique. The meat is usually thinly sliced. If a whole fish is used, it should be butterflied (see page 73) and cooked upright in the wok during oil poaching. Butterflying the fish allows easy heat transfer when cooking.

Two factors will ensure the tender texture of the meat: the cooking temperature and the velveting sauce. Maintaining the pass-through temperature at around 350°F is important to cooking the meat through while not crisping the coating. You should use enough oil to prevent overcrowding, which would result in a quick drop in temperature. A moist velveting mixture of egg white and starch will ensure that the meat is covered with a smooth coating.

Wine-flavored sauces created from wine lees are the classic choice to pair with oil-poached meat and fish. There are many varieties of rice wine lees in China, including red wine lees from the southern coastal region and white wine lees from the north.

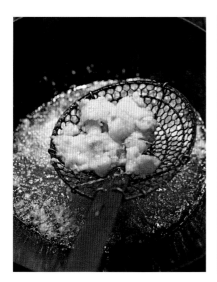  

OIL-POACHED FLOUNDER WITH RICE WINE SAUCE | 酒釀熘魚片

SHANGHAI

White wine lees is a distinctly Shanghai ingredient that is used in both savory and sweet dishes. Whether bought in a market or fermented at home, this sweet-smelling ingredient will liven up your cooking with its intoxicating aroma. | SERVES 2 OR MORE, AS A MAIN DISH

VELVETING MIXTURE

1 large egg white

1 tablespoon Shaoxing cooking wine

1 tablespoon tapioca starch

½ teaspoon salt

12 ounces flounder fillet, cut into ¼-inch-thick slices

SAUCE

¼ cup Shaoxing cooking wine

2 tablespoons White Wine Lees, homemade (see page 52) or store-bought

½ teaspoon salt

¼ teaspoon ground white pepper

2 teaspoons tapioca starch

2 cups vegetable oil

6 thin slices fresh ginger

¼ cup shelled edamame

⅛ ounce dried wood ear mushroom, rehydrated (see page 78), root end trimmed

Combine all the velveting mixture ingredients in a medium bowl and mix well. Add the flounder slices and coat well. Let marinate for 20 minutes.

In a bowl, mix together all the sauce ingredients except the tapioca starch. Separately, mix the tapioca with 2 tablespoons water to make a slurry.

Heat the vegetable oil in a wok over medium heat until it begins to shimmer, about 350°F. Gently drop the fish slices into the oil and use a spatula to separate them and move them around. Fry them for about 1 minute, until the fish is cooked through, then remove them from the oil with a spider strainer. Put the fish on a serving plate.

Remove all but 2 tablespoons vegetable oil from the wok. Add the ginger slices to the wok and stir-fry until fragrant, about 30 seconds. Pour the sauce mixture into the wok and bring to a boil. Add the edamame and wood ear and cook for 1 minute. Add the tapioca slurry and cook until the sauce has thickened, about 1 minute.

Pour the sauce over the fish and serve.

SAUCING AFTER BOILING OR STEAMING | 軟熘

Of all the *liu* techniques, precooking by boiling or steaming is the gentlest way of cooking the main ingredient, making this a great way to prepare tender ingredients such as chicken breast, trout, flounder, shrimp, and scallops. Whole fish can be used also, but it should be butterflied to allow it to cook easily.

When boiling is the method for precooking, the meat or seafood should first be thinly sliced and a velveting mixture applied. The silky coating protects the meat and keeps the flavorful juices from leaching into the cooking water. Make sure to use enough water so the slices can cook without crowding and sticking to one another.

Some degree of disagreement has emerged when considering how to precook meat or seafood by steaming. When steaming fish, some chefs recommend deep-frying it very quickly first to seal the meat and prevent it from falling apart during steaming. Others insist that the silky-smooth texture that is prized in the *liu* technique is lost with deep-frying. Another consideration when steaming is what to do with the liquid that accumulates in the steaming container. Some people feel that this liquid is mostly condensation and should be discarded, whereas others feel that it can bring extra flavor if added to the sauce.

The important thing to remember is that this technique is for cooking tender ingredients that should be handled with utmost care. The finished dish should have the smooth texture that is the hallmark of *liu* cooking.

WEST LAKE VINEGAR TILAPIA
西湖醋魚

ZHEJIANG

West Lake, which abuts the city of Hangzhou, used to be full of fish and was a food source for the local residents. After years of overfishing, the catch has now dwindled, but the natives' ways of cooking lake fish are still beloved across China. This vinegar-sauced fish is one example. | SERVES 2 OR MORE, AS A MAIN DISH

SAUCE

¼ cup chicken stock (see page 88) or water

2 tablespoons Shaoxing cooking wine

2 tablespoons soy sauce

2 tablespoons Chinkiang black vinegar

1 tablespoon sugar

½ teaspoon tapioca starch

1 (2-pound) whole tilapia, cleaned and butterflied (see page 73)

2 tablespoons vegetable oil

1 tablespoon minced fresh ginger

In a bowl, mix together all the sauce ingredients except the tapioca starch. Separately, mix the tapioca with 2 tablespoons water to make a slurry.

Bring 2 quarts water to a boil in a wok over high heat. Using a spider strainer, gently lower the fish into the boiling water; the strainer will keep the fish slightly suspended, preventing the skin from sticking to the bottom of the wok. Boil the fish until the meat flakes easily when a fork is inserted, about 5 minutes. Remove the fish from the wok and drain it thoroughly. Put the fish on a serving platter.

Remove all the water from the wok and wipe it dry. Heat the wok over high heat until a droplet of water sizzles and evaporates immediately upon contact. Swirl the vegetable oil around the bottom and sides of the wok to coat it evenly. Add the ginger to the wok and stir-fry until fragrant, about 30 seconds. Add the sauce mixture and cook for about 1 minute. Add the starch slurry and cook until the sauce has thickened, about 1 minute.

Pour the sauce over the fish and serve.

STEAMED SHRIMP PASTE WITH CLEAR SAUCE | 軟熘蝦滑

HOME-STYLE

You can use 12 ounces ready-made shrimp paste or fish paste from Chinatown fishmongers for this recipe, but I've included the instructions for preparing shrimp paste at home in case you want to make it yourself. I have to say that freshly made shrimp paste is just absolutely heavenly and definitely worth the effort. | SERVES 2 OR MORE, AS A MAIN DISH

SHRIMP PASTE

12 ounces medium shrimp, shelled and deveined

2 tablespoons tapioca starch

1 teaspoon salt

½ teaspoon ground white pepper

1 large egg white

1 ice cube

SAUCE

¼ cup chicken stock (see page 88) or water

2 tablespoons white rice wine

½ teaspoon salt

¼ teaspoon ground white pepper

2 teaspoons tapioca starch

2 tablespoons vegetable oil

1 tablespoon minced fresh ginger

1 medium cucumber, peeled, quartered lengthwise, seeded, and cut on the diagonal into ½-inch-thick pieces

To make the shrimp paste, put the shrimp, tapioca starch, salt, and pepper in a food processor and blend until the mixture forms a paste. Add the egg white and blend for another 30 seconds. Add the ice cube and pulse until it is completely blended into the shrimp paste. Remove the paste from the food processor and spread it over an oiled pie plate so it is about an inch thick.

Bring 6 cups water to a boil in a wok over high heat. Place a steaming rack in the wok and set the pie plate on the rack. Cover and steam until the shrimp paste is cooked through, about 15 minutes.

Remove the shrimp paste from the pie plate and let it cool on a cutting board. Make two parallel cuts in the cooled round cake and create three blocks of equal width. Cut the blocks crosswise into ¼-inch-thick slices.

In a bowl, mix together all the sauce ingredients except the tapioca starch. Separately, mix the tapioca starch with 2 tablespoons water to make a slurry.

Heat a wok over high heat until a droplet of water sizzles and evaporates immediately upon contact. Swirl the vegetable oil around the bottom and sides of the wok to coat it evenly. Add the ginger to the wok and stir-fry until fragrant, about 30 seconds. Add the cucumber and the sauce mixture and cook for 2 minutes. Add the tapioca slurry and cook until the sauce has thickened, about 1 minute. Add the shrimp paste slices and toss them around to coat them evenly with the sauce.

Closely related to the *liu* technique is the *peng* technique, which is most common in northern China. The first variation of this technique is to deep-fry the meat before flavoring it with a simple broth. The meat is either simply coated with starch or covered in an egg batter. It is then fried to a crisp before a seasoned broth is drizzled over it; the broth is then absorbed by the coating. If done properly, the coating will retain a slight crispness yet be extremely flavorful.

Common choices for the main ingredient include any sturdy white fish, shrimp, shellfish, and chicken, cut into bite-size pieces to facilitate quick crisping when frying. They should be fried in hot oil, about 395°F.

FRAGRANT DEEP-FRIED PRAWNS
炸烹大蝦

BEIJING

Be sure to use large prawns for this recipe: the texture of the meat will be a great contrast to the light, crisp batter. Serve the dish immediately; the batter will absorb the sauce and if left too long tends to get a bit soggy. | SERVES 2 OR MORE, AS A MAIN DISH

BATTER

2 large eggs

⅓ cup tapioca starch

SAUCE

2 tablespoons white rice wine

1 tablespoon soy sauce

2 teaspoons sugar

1 teaspoon white rice vinegar

4 cups vegetable oil

10 large prawns (12 ounces), shelled and deveined but tails left on

2 tablespoons julienned scallion whites

2 tablespoons julienned fresh ginger

1 tablespoon toasted sesame oil

To make the batter, whisk together the egg and tapioca starch in a bowl.

Combine all the sauce ingredients in another bowl and mix well.

Heat the vegetable oil in a wok over high heat until it is just beginning to smoke, about 395°F. Dip the prawns in the batter and then drop them into the hot oil. Deep-fry the prawns, stirring to prevent them from sticking to one another, until golden brown, about 5 minutes. Drain them thoroughly on paper towels.

Remove all but 2 tablespoons vegetable oil from the wok. Add the scallion whites and ginger to the wok and stir-fry for about 15 seconds. Return the fried prawns to the wok and toss the prawns around for about 15 seconds to coat them evenly with the sauce. Drizzle the sesame oil evenly over the prawns and serve.

WUXI CRISPY EEL | 無錫脆鱔

JIANGSU

Named after the city of Wuxi in Jiangsu province, this crispy eel is sometimes called Liangxi Crispy Eel for the river that flows through the center of the city. The eel's skin crisps up without any starch coating and the sweet sauce complements the tender meat beautifully.
SERVES 4 AS AN APPETIZER, OR 2 AS A MAIN DISH WHEN PAIRED WITH A VEGETABLE DISH

SAUCE

2 tablespoons Shaoxing cooking wine

1 tablespoon soy sauce

1 tablespoon sugar

¼ teaspoon salt

¼ teaspoon ground white pepper

4 cups vegetable oil

2 pounds Asian swamp eel, cleaned, deboned (see page 78), and cut into strips 2 inches long and about ⅛ inch thick

1 tablespoon minced scallion whites

1 tablespoon minced fresh ginger, plus 2 tablespoons julienned fresh ginger

1 tablespoon toasted sesame oil

1 teaspoon sesame seeds, toasted

Combine all the sauce ingredients in a small bowl and mix well.

Heat the vegetable oil in a wok over high heat until it is just beginning to smoke, about 395°F. Gently put the eel strips in the oil and fry for about 1 minute, stirring continuously to make sure the pieces do not stick together. Use a spider strainer to remove all the eel strips from the oil. Bring the temperature of the oil back up to 395°F. Once again submerge the eel strips in the hot oil. Fry them, stirring, for another minute. Remove them from the oil again and turn down the heat to medium. Bring the oil temperature to about 350°F and return the eel strips to the oil. Deep-fry the eel for another minute, until the strips are lightly crisp but not too brown. Remove the eel from the wok and place it in a skimmer set over a bowl to drain off the excess oil.

Remove all but 2 tablespoons vegetable oil from the wok. Add the scallion whites and minced ginger to the wok and stir-fry for about 30 seconds. Pour the sauce mixture into the wok and bring it to a boil. Cook the sauce for about 1 minute or until it has reduced to a slightly syrupy consistency. Return the eel to the wok and quickly toss it in the sauce. Drizzle the sesame oil evenly over the eel.

Garnish with the julienned ginger and sesame seeds.

BROTH FLAVORING AFTER PAN-FRYING | 煎烹

Pan-frying allows the main ingredients to be cooked with minimal oil and yet produces the same crispness that is characteristic of deep-frying. My favorite pan-fried *peng* dish is a crisp pompano infused with a soy sauce and ginger broth.

Many other types of meat, such as chicken, pork, and shellfish, can be successfully cooked this way as well, but they should be cut into thin slices for easy cooking in the shallow oil—unless the ingredient itself is already flat, such as fish. The main ingredient can also be ground to a paste and mixed with aromatics to form flat cakes, which can then be coated with starch before pan-frying.

Coating the meat should also be done very sparingly. It should be just enough to produce a thin, crisp film but not so thick that it becomes nubby. Controlling the amount of the aromatic broth is crucial to maintaining the crispness. Be sure that the broth is already seasoned before sprinkling it over the meat, and use it sparingly.

GINGER SCALLION PAN-FRIED SOFT-SHELL CRAB | 煎烹軟殼蟹
GUANGDONG

Soft-shell crab is an American delicacy that is perfect for pan-frying. This version is served with a Canton-style ginger and scallion–flavored broth. It is simple yet flavorful. | SERVES 4 AS AN APPETIZER, OR 2 AS A MAIN COURSE WHEN PAIRED WITH A VEGETABLE DISH

4 (about 1 pound) soft-shell crabs

BATTER
2 large egg whites
¼ cup tapioca starch

SAUCE
3 tablespoons Shaoxing cooking wine
1 tablespoon white rice vinegar
1 teaspoon salt
1 teaspoon sugar

¼ cup vegetable oil
2 tablespoons julienned scallion whites
2 tablespoons julienned fresh ginger
1 tablespoon toasted sesame oil

To clean the soft-shell crabs, use a pair of kitchen shears to first cut across the face of the crab. Then turn the crab so the bottom is facing up. Lift and cut off the tail, revealing the gills, and then cut off the gills. Finally, cut the entire crab bilaterally in half.

To make the batter, whisk the egg whites and starch together in a bowl.

Combine all the sauce ingredients in another bowl and mix well.

Heat the vegetable oil in a wok over high heat until it is shimmering, about 375°F. Dip each crab half in the batter, then put it in the oil. Fry all the pieces in one layer, moving them around so they brown evenly, for about 5 minutes. Carefully flip them over and fry the other side for about 3 minutes or until browned. Drain them thoroughly on paper towels.

Add the scallion whites, ginger, and the sauce to the wok. Cook for 1 minute. Arrange the crab pieces on a serving plate and pour the aromatic broth over them. Drizzle the sesame oil evenly over the crab pieces.

CHAPTER TEN

The Virtues of Slow Cooking

ARCHEOLOGICAL RECORDS REVEAL THAT AROUND THE TIME THAT THE PRODUCTION OF BRONZE VESSELS WAS FIRST DEVELOPED IN CHINA, A COOKING METHOD KNOWN AS *GENG* (羹) WAS USED TO COOK FOOD IN THEM. No one can really be certain what a *geng* dish was like at that time, but it is assumed that it resembled a soupy stew since it was cooked in a cauldron-like object called a *fu* (釜) over a fire. Traced back to the Western Zhou period more than three thousand years ago, this was the first recorded cooking method that utilized a vessel; before that, cooking in China was done by roasting over an open fire or searing on a heated stone.

Scholars speculate that the term *geng* was most likely used as a universal description for boiling food in liquid—probably for boiling tough game meats over a long period of time until tender. As cooking became more sophisticated, spices and seasonings were added to make the stews more appetizing. Eventually this method evolved into the many variants of the braising technique that we know in modern Chinese cooking. Hence it is possible to attribute the numerous Chinese slow-cooking techniques to this single ancestor known as *geng*. In fact the term *geng* is still used to describe a way of making thickened soups that is described in Chapter 13.

The singular term "braise" in Western cooking is inadequate for describing the distinctions the Chinese make in cooking temperature, length of cooking time, and flavorings added to the sauce. For each variant of slow cooking there is a specific Chinese term and a distinct cooking process. These include red cooking (紅燒), *men* (燜) braising, *dun* (燉) braising, *wei* (煨) braising, and flavor potting (滷).

Undeniably red cooking has to be one of the most important techniques in Chinese cooking. It is used so extensively that casual home cooks think of it as the only slow-cooking technique. The central idea with red cooking is to braise cut-up pieces of meat in an aromatic soy sauce–based liquid for an extended period of time and to thicken the braising liquid at the end, either naturally or by adding starch. While red cooking uses only soy sauce, the other techniques use many different flavoring agents in the braising liquid.

Collectively known as the "slow heat techniques" (火功菜), the three methods called *men*, *dun*, and *wei* are all similar, with subtle differences between them. The *men* technique is used to cook ingredients that require a slightly shorter cooking time than the *dun* and *wei* techniques, whose ingredients are usually tough cuts of meat that will become tender only after cooking for hours. The *dun* technique uses a relatively larger amount of liquid than the *wei* technique, resulting in a final dish that is almost a soup. (Slow-braising soup techniques, which use the most liquid, are covered in detail in Chapter 13.)

Another important but unusual slow-cooking technique—one that has no equivalent in other culinary cultures—is known as "flavor potting." This is virtually the same as other braising methods except that the braising liquid is not discarded after use. Instead it is reused repeatedly, making the braising liquid richer and more concentrated over time. In fact there are restaurants in China that claim to have used the same braising liquid for years. Whether this is true or not, it offers an interesting take on enriching the flavor of braised meat.

Regardless of the slight differences, all braising techniques ultimately center around breaking down tough cuts of meat and infusing them with flavor. Maintaining a steady temperature for cooking over a long period of time is instrumental to the success of braising, and as such clay pots are recommended for their preparation (see page 37). The pots transmit heat evenly to cook the meat gently over time.

Whole vs. Ground Spices

Spices, in addition to aromatics, are used liberally in many Chinese braised dishes. In order to produce a smooth, clean sauce at the end, whole spices are recommended. Using ground spices results in a gritty and unappealing sauce. The whole spices are normally not removed before serving at home. However, in professional restaurant kitchens, the chefs sometimes wrap the spices and the aromatics in cheesecloth for easy removal. Personally, I like leaving the spices in the dish for a rustic presentation.

WHY PARBOIL THE MEAT?

When I first started cooking Chinese food many years ago, my aunt Hong, who is the most formidable cook among my relatives, told me that it is important to parboil meat that is intended for braising or soup making. At first I thought this step was cumbersome and redundant, so I skipped it. But then I realized that the resulting sauce was almost always muddied with residue and looked somewhat unappetizing. Since then I've been parboiling all meat intended for slow cooking.

Unlike the Western cooking tradition where meat is seared until browned before being braised or stewed, in Chinese cooking techniques it is always parboiled. As such the impurities from the curdling protein can be removed before the actual slow cooking begins. The reduced sauce from this slow-cooking method always turns out smooth, clear, and visually appealing. Parboiling is recommended for all slow-cooking techniques including stock making, soup making, and braising.

How thoroughly cooked the meat should be after parboiling is an important issue. I recommend that it be cooked through but still retain its structural integrity. For 1-inch cubes this means boiling for about 10 minutes. For larger pieces of meat, such as a whole pork picnic shoulder, the cooking time should be adjusted so the meat is cooked through. Insert a metal skewer all the way into the center of the meat and make sure the juices run clear.

Whether to use or discard the parboiling liquid is another often-asked question. Traditionalists would insist that the parboiling liquid be discarded, but I would allow an exception to that. If the liquid is strained through a very-fine-mesh sieve so that it is clear, it can be excellent for enhancing the flavor of the final dish when used in place of water in the braising liquid.

THE CROCK-POT AND CHINESE BRAISING

Irving Naxon was a prolific inventor who had filed more than two hundred patents by the time he died in 1989. Among the most important of his inventions is the electric slow cooker, which was inspired by stories his mother, Tamara Kaslovski Nachumsohn, told him when he was a boy. Tamara grew up in a shtetl in Lithuania with her Jewish family. As part of their observation of the Jewish Sabbath, the family was not allowed to work or cook from sundown Friday until Saturday evening. Irving's grandmother would prepare a pot of uncooked meat and beans for a stew known as cholent on Friday afternoon; then she would ask young Tamara to bring the pot to the village bakery to be put in their oven. As the oven cooled after being turned off for the Sabbath, the stew cooked slowly overnight and was ready for dinner the next evening. Naxon would later imitate this slow-heating process when he created a metal pot with an electrical heating element that operates at just about the simmering temperature. He called it the Naxon Beanery and successfully marketed it during the 1960s.

Naxon's operation was sold to the Rival Company in 1970, and the slow cooker was redesigned with a removable glazed ceramic pot and cover. The new design was then marketed under the brand name Crock-Pot and became popular during the 1970s. Many kitchen appliance companies now market their own versions of the slow cooker.

This concept of slow cooking in moist heat is pretty much the same as Chinese braising techniques. As such an electric slow cooker is perfect for cooking Chinese braised dishes. The ceramic pot in the slow cooker acts just like Chinese clay pots, which distribute heat evenly and gently throughout the dish. I find that multiple or variable heat settings in the modern slow cooker are useful in controlling the cooking temperature. For red cooking, flavor potting, and *men* and *dun* braising, a medium temperature setting of 250°F is ideal. For *wei* braising, a lower temperature setting of 200°F is more suitable.

RED COOKING 紅燒

Despite the fact that the Chinese language is very precise, there is no character to describe the color brown. Instead, the names of common items are used to evoke a mental image of "brown." The Chinese commonly use two characters to describe the color. One of them is *zong* (棕), a character for "palm tree" that conjures up the reddish brown color of palm tree husk, and the other is *he* (褐), the character for "hemp cloth," which is often used to represent a grayish brown color. The ancient Chinese were likely faced with a dilemma when describing the brown-colored gravy that results from braising with soy sauce. The auspicious color red was chosen over the other two characters, thus resulting in the technique becoming known as *hongshao* (紅燒), or red cooking.

This slow-cooking technique is the basis of numerous braised dishes in China. It is so versatile that just about anything can be red cooked, from red meats such as beef and lamb to fish, chicken, and even vegetarian items like tofu and mushrooms. The main ingredient is cooked in a liquid of soy sauce, cooking wine, sugar, aromatic ingredients such as scallions, ginger, and garlic, and spices including star anise, Sichuan peppercorns, fennel, and cassia bark. The aromatics and spices are adjusted to complement the main ingredient.

Successful red cooking depends on properly controlling both the temperature and the time. The technique in general is excellent for tough cuts of meat, and in order to perfectly cook and gently infuse maximum flavor into them, it is crucial to cook over low heat. A steady simmer—a slow, constant bubbling of the liquid—is ideal. Too low a temperature will not properly infuse the flavor into the meat, and too high will simply burn the meat on the bottom of the pot without evenly cooking it.

Proper timing depends on the type of meat. For pork belly, 1½ hours should suffice, whereas beef tendon will need 2 to 3 hours of cooking. What is important is to ensure that the braising liquid is not depleted. When cooking for a long period of time, liquid should be added regularly. When the meat is done, it can be removed from the pot and the sauce reduced separately. In dishes where the meat contains a high amount of collagen, the sauce naturally thickens and can be served as is. Otherwise the reduced sauce is often thickened with a starch slurry before serving.

When red cooking tender ingredients like fish or tofu, the cooking time should be shortened. Red cooking fish, for example, should take less than 20 minutes. Any longer will overcook the fish and change the texture. For tofu or root vegetables such as taro, braising for about 30 minutes is ideal.

THE LEGENDARY RED-COOKED PORK

Red-cooked pork was served at least once a week at home when I was growing up in Singapore. But on special occasions when we entertained guests, I remember that red-cooked pork was served sandwich-style in steamed buns shaped like half-moons that opened like hot dog buns. As kids my brother and I used to pile as many of the buns as possible on our plates.

This dish is iconic of Chinese traditional comfort food, akin to beef stew in American homes, and so I've always wondered why red-cooked pork is not better known in the United States. Very few American Chinese restaurants serve it. Perhaps it is because pork belly, the cut of pork used for making this dish, was alien to many Americans until recently.

Is there a best way to make red-cooked pork? Many families have their own special recipe and keep it secret, passing it down through generations but rarely sharing it outside the home. Some red-cooked pork aficionados insist on the merits of caramelizing the sugar with the pork, but others do it separately. Some purists insist that star anise has no place in scenting the braising liquid, while others think it essential. Still others debate whether the sauce should be thickened with starch. As you practice making this dish and understand the entire cooking process better, you can come to your own conclusions. Ultimately personal preferences should be the deciding factors in determining how to make the best red-cooked pork.

THE MEAT

It was not more than ten years ago that I would host a Chinese dinner, serve red-cooked pork, and watch my non-Chinese guests politely remove the skin and fat before picking out and eating only the lean meat of the pork belly. I would cringe but be resigned to the fact that pork belly is an acquired taste. Little did I know how times would change. Chef David Chang, of Momofuku fame, put pork belly on the American gourmet radar in his restaurant. Now it seems almost impossible to go to a fine-dining restaurant without seeing pork belly prominently listed on the menu. And my dinner guests, regardless of ethnicity, seek out pieces with thick layers of skin and fat and eat them wholeheartedly.

Traditionally, pork belly is the cut of choice for red-cooked pork. The combination of tender skin, springy fat tissue, delicate lean meat, and mild pork taste makes it the most suitable cut. Similar cuts such as pork picnic shoulder and pig's feet, which contain a good balance of lean meat, fat, and skin, also make excellent choices. Lean cuts of pork such as the loin are not appropriate and should be avoided.

If you're concerned about the amount of fat in this dish, make it a day ahead, separate the meat from the sauce, and refrigerate them overnight in different containers. The next day the fat that has solidified on top of the sauce can be easily discarded before the sauce is combined with the meat for reheating.

CARAMELIZING

A unique step in making red-cooked pork—a step that is not usually followed when red cooking other types of meat—is caramelizing the sugar. While traditionalists insist upon using rock sugar and caramelizing it while browning the meat, others suggest that granulated sugar is an acceptable substitute and prefer to caramelize it apart from the meat. For the most part I embrace the traditional approach, but I also appreciate the fact that there are times when substitutions and adjustments are unavoidable. I am a flexible traditionalist.

Rock sugar, according to many experienced Chinese cooks, creates a sauce that is silky-smooth in texture, yet I have achieved excellent results using granulated sugar. What's critical is to make sure to cook the sugar without burning it. My suggestion is to dissolve the sugar, rock or granulated, in a small amount of water and cook it over medium heat until the syrup just begins to turn yellow. Immediately add the pork pieces to the golden syrup. The moisture from the pork will slightly dilute the syrup and evenly coat the meat. Continue to cook the pork belly over medium heat while the sugar slowly caramelizes. At this point be aware that the fat starts to render and often splatters; you may want to use a splatter guard to reduce the chance of accidental burns.

THE SAUCE

While the sauces of most red-cooked dishes are thickened with starch, the sauce for red-cooked pork is naturally thickened by the gelatin produced from the skin, and can be reduced to varying degrees depending on personal preference. I like the unctuous texture similar to a demi-glace in French cooking. The sauce should hold together in a thick layer when poured on a plate. But if you plan to serve the red-cooked pork with rice, then a thinner sauce is ideal. Remove the meat after it has cooked to the desired doneness and reduce the sauce separately.

RED-COOKED PORK | 紅燒肉
HOME-STYLE

A good red-cooked pork recipe is a family treasure and this one is no exception. I learned to make this dish from my aunt Hong, and her recipe is the foundation for mine, which has evolved over the years after much experimentation with parboiling and caramelizing, aromatic ingredients, and spices. Serve it with rice or in steamed buns, topped with julienned scallions and some cilantro sprigs. | SERVES 4 AS AN APPETIZER WITH STEAMED BUNS, 2 AS A MAIN COURSE WHEN PAIRED WITH A VEGETABLE DISH

1½ **pounds pork belly**

2 **tablespoons sugar**

3 **garlic cloves**

2 **scallions, cut into 2-inch pieces**

3 **whole star anise**

2 **tablespoons dark soy sauce**

1 **tablespoon soy sauce**

¼ **cup Shaoxing cooking wine**

1½ **cups pork stock (see page 89), the liquid from the parboiling, or water, plus more as needed**

Put the entire pork belly in a stockpot and add enough water to cover the meat completely. Bring the water to a boil, then turn down the heat to medium. Parboil the pork belly, uncovered, for 20 minutes, continuously skimming off the scum that forms on the surface. Drain, and let the pork belly cool. Then cut it into pieces about 1½ inches square.

Combine the sugar with 3 tablespoons water in a wok over medium heat. Continue heating until the sugar syrup just begins to turn yellow. Add the cubed pork belly to the wok and brown it with the caramelized sugar, stirring the meat regularly to prevent burning. If you like, cover the wok with a splatter guard to prevent the fat from splattering.

Add the garlic, scallions, star anise, both soy sauces, wine, and stock to the wok. Bring the liquid to a boil, then transfer the contents to a clay pot or Dutch oven. (Alternatively, this dish can be cooked in a slow cooker.) Simmer, covered, over low heat, stirring the meat every 15 minutes to prevent scorching the pork on the bottom, for 1 hour or until the meat is tender when pierced with a knife.

Remove the meat and put it in a bowl. Reduce the sauce over medium-high heat until it reaches the desired consistency. Return the meat to the pot and reheat before serving.

RED-COOKED BEEF | 紅燒牛肉

HOME-STYLE

Red-cooked beef is a versatile dish that can be the star of a dinner or, with extra stock, the base of a noodle soup. Use cuts of beef that are highly marbleized; they will remain moist when cooked. | SERVES 2 OR MORE, PAIRED WITH A VEGETABLE DISH

1 pound stew beef or chuck, cut into 1-inch cubes

4 cups beef stock (see page 89), the liquid from the parboiling, or water, plus more as needed

½ cup Shaoxing cooking wine

2 tablespoons dark soy sauce

1 tablespoon soy sauce

1 (1-inch-long) piece of fresh ginger, crushed with the flat side of a knife

1 tablespoon sugar

BRAISING SPICES

3 whole star anise

1 (2-inch) square of cassia bark

1 (2-inch) square of dried tangerine peel

1 teaspoon Sichuan peppercorns

1 teaspoon fennel seeds

4 dried red chiles (optional)

1 medium carrot, cut into 1-inch pieces

1 medium daikon radish, cut into 1-inch pieces

1 tablespoon chopped scallions

1 tablespoon chopped cilantro

Put the beef in a medium saucepan and add enough water to cover the meat completely. Bring the water to a boil and parboil the beef over medium heat for about 10 minutes, continuously skimming off any scum that forms on the surface. Drain the meat thoroughly.

Put the beef, stock, wine, both soy sauces, ginger, and sugar in a large clay pot or Dutch oven with a cover. (Alternatively, this dish can be cooked in a slow cooker.) Add all the braising spices. (For easy removal later, tie the spices up in cheesecloth.) Bring the liquid to a boil, then reduce the heat to low and gently simmer the beef, covered, for 2 hours or until the meat is tender when pierced with a knife. During that time, replenish the liquid as needed to prevent scorching.

Add the carrot and daikon radish, mixing well so the root vegetables are fully immersed in the liquid. Continue to cook over medium heat until the vegetables are tender, about 10 minutes.

Serve garnished with the chopped scallions and cilantro.

Red Cooking Another Way: Dry Braising	乾燒

Although the dry braising, or *ganshao*, technique is considered to be a variation of red cooking, the result is quite different. The most important difference is that in dry braising the cooking liquid is reduced to the point of becoming a sauce that coats the main ingredient.

In different regions of China, variations exist where special local flavorings, such as bean paste and chile, are added to the basic soy sauce braising broth. Dry braising completely changes the flavors of a traditional red-cooked dish in that the sauce is richer and more complex.

RED-COOKED LAMB | 紅燒羊肉
HOME-STYLE

The Chinese use lots of different spices to neutralize the gaminess of lamb. Here cassia bark, tangerine peel, and Sichuan peppercorns are added to spice up this red-cooked dish. It is one of the most common ways to cook lamb at home. | SERVES 2 OR MORE, PAIRED WITH A VEGETABLE DISH

1 pound boneless lamb shoulder or leg meat, cut into 1-inch cubes

5 cups lamb stock (see page 89), the liquid from the parboiling, or water, plus more as needed

½ cup Shaoxing cooking wine

2 tablespoons dark soy sauce

1 tablespoon soy sauce

1 (1-inch-long) piece of fresh ginger, crushed with the flat side of a knife

1 tablespoon sugar

BRAISING SPICES

3 whole star anise

1 (2-inch) square of cassia bark

1 (2-inch) square of dried tangerine peel

1 teaspoon Sichuan peppercorns

4 dried red chiles (optional)

1 medium carrot, cut into 1-inch pieces

1 medium daikon radish, cut into 1-inch pieces

1 tablespoon chopped scallions

1 tablespoon chopped cilantro

Put the lamb in a medium saucepan and add enough water to cover the meat completely. Bring the water to a boil and parboil the lamb over medium heat for about 10 minutes, continuously skimming off any scum that forms the surface. Drain the meat thoroughly.

Put the lamb, stock, wine, both soy sauces, ginger, and sugar in a large clay pot or Dutch oven with a cover. (Alternatively, this dish can be cooked in a slow cooker.) Add all the braising spices. (For easy removal later, tie the spices up in cheesecloth.) Bring the liquid to a boil, then reduce the heat to low and gently simmer the lamb, covered, for 2 hours or until the meat is tender when pierced with a knife. During that time, replenish the liquid as needed to prevent scorching.

Add the carrot and daikon radish, mixing well so the root vegetables are fully immersed in the liquid. Continue to cook over medium heat until the vegetables are tender, about 10 minutes.

Serve garnished with the chopped scallions and cilantro.

RED-COOKED LION'S HEAD | 紅燒獅子頭

This is a classic Shanghai dish that gets its name from the large meatballs that are supposed to remind diners of large lions' heads. Done well, the meatballs remain juicy and tender while the sauce imparts a sweet and aromatic soy flavor typical of red-cooked dishes. | SERVES 2 OR MORE, PAIRED WITH A VEGETABLE DISH

MEATBALLS

1 (½-inch-long) piece of fresh ginger, cut into ¼-inch cubes

2 scallions, cut into 1-inch pieces

1 pound ground pork (80% lean)

4 ounces fresh or canned water chestnuts (drained if canned), peeled and cut into ⅛-inch cubes

2 tablespoons tapioca starch

1 large egg white

1 teaspoon salt

¼ teaspoon ground white pepper

4 cups vegetable oil

SAUCE

3 cups chicken stock (see page 88) or water

3 tablespoons Shaoxing cooking wine

2 tablespoons dark soy sauce

1 garlic clove

1 teaspoon sugar

1 tablespoon tapioca starch

4 ounces baby bok choy, halved lengthwise

To make the meatballs, combine the ginger, scallions, and ½ cup water in a blender and puree until smooth. Strain the liquid through a fine-mesh strainer into a medium bowl and discard the solids. Add the pork, water chestnuts, tapioca starch, egg white, salt, and pepper to the bowl and mix well. The mixture will be very moist.

Heat the vegetable oil in a wok over high heat until it is shimmering, about 375°F. Divide the pork mixture into six portions. Wet your hands with water, pick up one portion of the pork mixture, and toss the meatball back and forth between your two hands until it is round and smooth. Immediately but carefully drop the meatball into the hot oil. Repeat with the other portions. Fry the meatballs for about 3 minutes, until browned. Remove the meatballs from the oil and drain them on a paper towel. The meatballs will still be raw in the center; they will cook through when braised.

In a medium clay pot or Dutch oven with a cover, combine all the sauce ingredients except the tapioca starch. (Alternatively, this dish can be cooked in a slow cooker.) Arrange the meatballs in the clay pot, bring the liquid to a boil, and braise them, covered, over low heat until the braising flavor is infused into the meatballs, about 40 minutes.

In a small bowl, mix the tapioca starch with 2 tablespoons water to make a slurry. Stir it into the braising broth and cook until the broth has thickened, about 1 minute. Arrange the baby bok choy around the meatballs, cover the clay pot, and cook for about 3 minutes, until the bok choy is just tender.

RED-COOKED CHICKEN WITH CHESTNUTS | 紅燒栗子雞
HOME-STYLE

This is one of the most beloved home-style braised chicken dishes anywhere in China. The combination of tender chicken and sweet chestnuts makes for classic Chinese comfort food. | SERVES 2 OR MORE, PAIRED WITH A VEGETABLE DISH

1½ pounds broiler chicken parts, cut into 1-inch-thick pieces

8 ounces peeled fresh chestnuts (from 12 ounces in the shell), or 3 ounces dried chestnuts, rehydrated (see page 78)

¼ cup Shaoxing cooking wine

1 tablespoon dark soy sauce

1 tablespoon soy sauce

1 (1-inch-long) piece of fresh ginger

1 teaspoon sugar

Put the chicken in a medium saucepan and add enough water to cover the meat completely. Bring the water to a boil and parboil the chicken over medium heat for about 10 minutes, continuously skimming off any scum that forms on the surface. Drain the meat thoroughly.

Put the chicken, chestnuts, 1½ cups water, wine, both soy sauces, ginger, and sugar in a large clay pot or Dutch oven with a cover. (Alternatively, this dish can be cooked in a slow cooker.) Bring the liquid to a boil, then reduce the heat to low and gently simmer the chicken, covered, for 45 minutes or until the meat is tender when pierced with a knife. During that time, replenish the liquid as needed to prevent scorching.

RED-COOKED FISH | 紅燒魚
HOME-STYLE

Unlike red-cooked meat, red-cooked fish cooks in a relatively short time, making it perfect for a quick weeknight meal. Use any flaky white fish, either whole or cut into steaks. | SERVES 2 OR MORE, PAIRED WITH A VEGETABLE DISH

3 cups vegetable oil

1½ pounds grouper or sea bass steaks

1 tablespoon tapioca starch

3 garlic cloves

6 thin slices fresh ginger

½ cup chicken stock (see page 88)

1 tablespoon dark soy sauce

1 tablespoon soy sauce

¼ cup Shaoxing cooking wine

1 teaspoon sugar

1 tablespoon julienned scallions

4 cilantro sprigs

Heat the vegetable oil in a wok over high heat until it is beginning to shimmer, about 350°F. Deep-fry the fish in the hot oil for about 3 minutes on each side, until golden brown. Remove the fish from the wok and transfer it to a plate. Remove all but 2 tablespoons of the vegetable oil from the wok.

In a small bowl, mix the tapioca starch with 2 tablespoons water to make a slurry.

Put the garlic and ginger in the wok and stir-fry for about 1 minute. Add the chicken stock, both soy sauces, wine, and sugar. Simmer the sauce for 3 minutes, then return the fish to the wok. Simmer for another 3 minutes or until the fish is saturated with the sauce. Stir in the tapioca slurry and cook until the sauce has thickened, about 1 minute.

Serve garnished with the scallions and cilantro.

BRAISED SEA CUCUMBER WITH SCALLION | 蔥燒海參

SHANDONG

The Shandong coast produces an abundance of sea cucumbers. One of my favorite ways to cook them is to braise them in soy sauce with scallions. The highly prized spiky variety of sea cucumbers is often used to make this dish. | SERVES 2 OR MORE, PAIRED WITH A VEGETABLE DISH

2 tablespoons vegetable oil

2 scallions, cut into 2-inch pieces

6 thin slices fresh ginger

4 ounces small or medium dried sea cucumbers, rehydrated, cleaned (see page 80), and cut into 1½-inch squares

¼ cup Shaoxing cooking wine

½ cup chicken stock (see page 88) or water

1 tablespoon dark soy sauce

2 tablespoons soy sauce

2 teaspoons sugar

¼ teaspoon ground white pepper

1 tablespoon tapioca starch

Heat a wok over high heat until a droplet of water sizzles and evaporates immediately upon contact. Swirl the vegetable oil around the bottom and sides of the wok to coat it evenly. Add the scallions and ginger to the wok and stir-fry until fragrant, about 30 seconds. Add the sea cucumbers and continue to stir-fry for 1 minute. Add the wine, stock, both soy sauces, sugar, and pepper and bring to a boil.

Transfer the ingredients to a large clay pot or Dutch oven with a cover. (Alternatively, this dish can be cooked in a slow cooker.) Simmer, covered, over low heat for 1 hour or until the sea cucumber is tender.

In a small bowl, mix the tapioca starch with 2 tablespoons water to make a slurry. Stir the slurry into the pot and cook until the sauce has thickened, about 1 minute.

RED-COOKED TOFU | 紅燒豆腐
HOME-STYLE

This red-cooked tofu is another Chinese comfort dish that is served in many homes. It is made with a little bit of ground pork, which can be eliminated to turn it into a vegetarian dish. | SERVES 2 OR MORE, PAIRED WITH A SEAFOOD OR VEGETABLE DISH

1 pound firm tofu

2 cups vegetable oil

2 garlic cloves, thinly sliced

2 ounces ground pork (optional)

½ ounce dried shiitake mushrooms, rehydrated (see page 78), stemmed, and halved

¼ cup thinly sliced fresh or canned bamboo shoots (drained if canned)

¼ cup Shaoxing cooking wine

1 tablespoon dark soy sauce

1 teaspoon soy sauce

1 teaspoon sugar

¼ teaspoon ground white pepper

1 teaspoon tapioca starch

1 scallion, julienned

Cut the tofu blocks into 1-inch squares that are ½ inch thick. Pat dry with a paper towel.

Heat the vegetable oil in a wok over high heat until it is just beginning to smoke, about 395°F. In two batches, deep-fry the tofu pieces until a brown skin forms on the outside, about 5 minutes. Use a skimmer to transfer the tofu to a paper-towel-lined plate.

Remove all but 2 tablespoons of the vegetable oil from the wok. Add the garlic to the wok and stir-fry until it is fragrant, about 30 seconds. Add the pork and continue to stir-fry for another 30 seconds or until it is completely cooked.

Add the shiitake mushrooms, bamboo shoots, 1½ cups water, the wine, both soy sauces, sugar, and pepper to the wok and bring the liquid to a boil.

Put the tofu in a saucepan and pour the contents of the wok over the tofu. Bring the liquid to a boil, then cover and braise the tofu over medium heat for about 10 minutes, until the tofu has absorbed the flavor.

In a small bowl, mix the tapioca starch with 2 tablespoons water to make a slurry. Stir this into the braising broth and cook until the broth has thickened, about 1 minute.

Serve the tofu garnished with the julienned scallion.

DRY-BRAISED FISH HEAD | 乾燒魚頭
SICHUAN

Dry-braised fish head is a classic Sichuan dish that can be made with a whole fish as well. It is traditionally spicy, but you can adjust the amount of chile to suit your liking. Sichuan ya cai, *which is now found in Chinatown markets, adds authenticity here, but it can be omitted if it is not available.* | SERVES 2 OR MORE, PAIRED WITH A VEGETABLE DISH

½ large carp head (about 2½ pounds), or
1 (2-pound) whole small carp, cleaned

¼ cup tapioca starch

4 cups vegetable oil

1 tablespoon minced garlic

1 tablespoon minced fresh ginger

2 ounces ground pork

1 tablespoon chopped fresh red chile

2 tablespoons minced *ya cai*
(Sichuan pickled greens; optional)

2 tablespoons Sichuan chile bean paste

2 tablespoons white wine lees, homemade
(see page 52) or store-bought (optional)

1½ cups chicken stock (see page 88) or water

3 tablespoons Shaoxing cooking wine

1 teaspoon soy sauce

1 teaspoon Chinkiang black vinegar

1 teaspoon sugar

¼ cup chopped scallion greens

If using a whole fish, score the fish on both sides with bias cuts placed about ½ inch apart. Dredge the fish or the head thoroughly in the tapioca starch, coating both sides.

Heat the vegetable oil in a wok over high heat until it is beginning to shimmer, about 350°F. Deep-fry the fish in the hot oil for about 3 minutes on each side, until golden brown. Remove the fish from the wok and transfer it to a plate.

Remove all but about 2 tablespoons of the vegetable oil from the wok. Add the garlic and ginger to the wok and stir-fry for about 1 minute. Add the pork and stir-fry for 2 minutes, until cooked through. Add the red chile and *ya cai* and continue to stir-fry for 1 minute. Return the fish to the wok and add the chile bean paste, wine lees, chicken stock, wine, soy sauce, vinegar, and sugar. Bring the liquid to a boil and simmer, turning the fish over once, for 10 minutes or until the braising liquid has reduced to a thick sauce.

Serve garnished with the scallion greens.

MEN BRAISING | 燜

Men braising is very similar to red cooking. The main difference is that this method is used for meats or vegetables that do not require an extremely long cooking time. A secondary difference is that the braising liquid in the *men* technique may contain ingredients beyond those in the soy-based brown sauce common to red cooking. Fermented tofu, bean paste, and wine sauce are some examples.

The basic steps for *men* are similar to other slow-cooking techniques. The meat is parboiled, then drained of all the liquid. After that it is transferred to a covered clay pot for further slow cooking. In certain recipes, the ingredients are quickly fried in hot oil before braising. This variation of the *men* technique is known as oil *men* braising (油燜), and is perfect for braising root vegetables, bamboo shoots, and shrimp.

Another characteristic of the *men* technique is that the braising liquid is cooked down until it becomes a thick sauce. The amount of liquid at the beginning should be just sufficient to cook the meat and is not replenished during braising. Too little liquid and the meat will scorch; too much and the sauce will be weak and watery. Unlike red cooking, the sauce is not normally thickened with starch.

Successful *men* braising should be done at a low simmering temperature. Bring the liquid to a boil at the beginning, then immediately reduce the heat to low to continue cooking. Any accompanying vegetables for the dish should be added at the midpoint or toward the end to ensure that they are not overcooked.

BRAISED CHICKEN WITH RED WINE LEES | 紅糟燜雞
HAKKA

Red wine lees is a classic Hakka cooking ingredient, especially when braising chicken. Just about every Hakka family has a special recipe for making this dish. | SERVES 2 OR MORE, PAIRED WITH A VEGETABLE DISH

1½ pounds chicken thighs or legs, each cut into 2 pieces

2 tablespoons red wine lees, homemade (see page 52) or store-bought

2 tablespoons white rice wine

2 tablespoons soy sauce

1 teaspoon sugar

6 thin slices fresh ginger

1 tablespoon julienned scallion greens

Put the chicken pieces in a large saucepan and add enough water to cover the meat completely. Bring the water slowly to a simmer, skimming off any scum that forms on the surface. Simmer the chicken for 10 minutes. Drain the chicken and discard the water.

Transfer the chicken to a clay pot or Dutch oven with a cover. (Alternatively, this dish can be cooked in a slow cooker.) Add 2 cups water, the red wine lees, wine, soy sauce, sugar, and ginger. Bring the liquid to a boil, then turn down the heat to medium and simmer the chicken, covered, for about 40 minutes or until it is cooked through and the liquid has reduced to a thick sauce.

Serve garnished with the scallion greens.

THREE CUP CHICKEN | 三杯雞

TAIWAN

This traditional Taiwanese dish, made with chicken in a soy sauce braising liquid, gets its name from the original recipe, which calls for cooking the chicken in one cup each of soy sauce, cooking wine, and toasted sesame oil. Thai basil added at the end gives this dish a distinctly local flavor that has become a hallmark of Taiwanese cuisine. Use dark meat on the bones for best results. | SERVES 2 OR MORE, PAIRED WITH A VEGETABLE DISH

1½ pounds chicken thighs or legs, each cut into 2 pieces

2 tablespoons vegetable oil

6 thin slices fresh ginger

¼ cup plus 2 tablespoons white rice wine

2 tablespoons soy sauce

¼ cup toasted sesame oil

Leaves from 1 medium bunch (2 ounces) Thai basil

Put the chicken pieces in a large saucepan and add enough water to cover the meat completely. Bring the water slowly to a simmer, skimming off any scum that forms on the surface. Simmer for 10 minutes. Drain the chicken and discard the water.

Heat a wok over high heat until a droplet of water sizzles and evaporates immediately upon contact. Swirl the vegetable oil around the bottom and sides of the wok to coat it evenly. Add the ginger to the wok and stir-fry until it is fragrant, about 30 seconds. Add the chicken and stir-fry for about 30 seconds. Add the 2 tablespoons rice wine and 1 tablespoon soy sauce. Continue to stir-fry for another 2 minutes or until the chicken is browned.

Transfer the chicken to a clay pot or Dutch oven with a cover. (Alternatively, this dish can be cooked in a slow cooker.) Add the remaining ¼ cup rice wine, the remaining 1 tablespoon soy sauce, and the sesame oil. Cover the pot and simmer the chicken over medium heat for 30 minutes, until it is tender and the liquid has reduced to a thick sauce.

Just before serving, stir in the basil leaves.

BRAISED CHICKEN WINGS WITH SHIITAKE MUSHROOMS | 黃燜雞翅
HOME-STYLE

The Chinese love chicken wings for their flavorful meat as well as their skin and cartilage. This dish is a common part of a simple home-cooked dinner, yet it is so savory, thanks to the shiitake mushrooms and Shaoxing cooking wine, that it is often served in neighborhood restaurants in southern China. | SERVES 2 OR MORE, AS A MAIN DISH

1 pound chicken wings (drumettes or wingettes)

1 tablespoon vegetable oil

6 thin slices fresh ginger

1 ounce dried shiitake mushrooms, rehydrated (see page 78), stemmed, and halved

1 teaspoon soy sauce

¼ cup Shaoxing cooking wine

1 cup chicken stock (see page 88) or water

1 teaspoon sugar

½ teaspoon salt

¼ teaspoon ground white pepper

1 tablespoon toasted sesame oil

2 tablespoons chopped scallion greens

Put the chicken in a large saucepan and add enough water to cover the meat completely. Bring the water slowly to a simmer, skimming off any scum that forms on the surface. Simmer the chicken for 10 minutes. Drain the chicken and discard the water.

In a medium clay pot or Dutch oven with a cover, heat the vegetable oil and ginger over medium heat until the ginger is just about to turn brown, 2 minutes. Add the chicken wings, shiitake mushrooms, soy sauce, wine, stock, sugar, salt, and pepper. Bring the liquid to a boil, then lower the heat to medium, cover the pot, and braise the chicken at a gentle boil for about 30 minutes, until it is cooked through and the liquid has reduced to a sauce. (Alternatively, this dish can be cooked in a slow cooker.)

Add the sesame oil and garnish with the chopped scallion greens.

BRAISED LAMB WITH JUJUBES | 黃燜羊肉

SHANDONG

Although lamb dishes are more common in the western part of China, they are also widely consumed in the north. Bursting with five-spice flavor, this braised lamb is more typical of Han cuisine than the Muslim cooking in Xinjiang. Jujubes, wine, cassia bark, and star anise supply a subtle, fragrant flavor to this dish. | SERVES 2 OR MORE, PAIRED WITH A VEGETABLE DISH

1 pound boneless lamb shoulder or leg meat, cut into 1-inch cubes

2 cups lamb stock (see page 89) or water

½ cup white rice wine

1 (1-inch-long) piece of fresh ginger, smashed with the flat side of a knife

12 jujubes

1 (2-inch) square of cassia bark

4 whole star anise

2 tablespoons soy sauce

1 teaspoon sugar

¼ teaspoon ground white pepper

1 teaspoon tapioca starch

Put the lamb in a large saucepan and add enough water to cover the meat completely. Bring the water slowly to a simmer, skimming off any scum that forms on the surface. Simmer the lamb for 10 minutes. Drain the lamb and discard the water.

Put the lamb, stock, wine, ginger, jujubes, cassia bark, star anise, soy sauce, sugar, and pepper in a medium clay pot or Dutch oven with a cover. (Alternatively, this dish can be cooked in a slow cooker.) Bring the liquid to a boil, then turn the heat to low and simmer, covered, for about 1½ hours or until the meat is tender when pierced with a knife.

In a small bowl, mix the tapioca starch with 2 tablespoons water to make a slurry. Stir this into the braising broth and cook until the broth has thickened, about 1 minute.

The Ultimate in Chinese Braising: The *Pa* Technique	扒

Considered to be the most refined way of making a braised dish, the *pa* technique involves cooking a large piece of meat with exotic and luxurious ingredients. The main meat ingredient is either a whole bird, such as a duck, or an entire side of meat, such as a pork picnic ham. The meat is deboned, braised with multiple complementary ingredients, and then served on a large platter so that the meat covers the other ingredients. Diners cut through the meat to discover the multitude of exotic foods hidden underneath. Truly a decadent dish.

MAPO TOFU | 麻婆豆腐

SICHUAN

This searingly spicy tofu dish is quintessentially Sichuan with its mala *(spicy hot and numbing) flavors. This recipe is a very spicy version of the dish, close to the original, but the heat level can be adjusted downward by reducing the amount of red chile powder.* | SERVES 2 OR MORE, PAIRED WITH A VEGETABLE DISH

1 pound firm tofu, cut into ½-inch cubes

Pinch of salt

1 tablespoon vegetable oil

4 ounces lean ground beef

CHILE BEAN PASTE OIL

¼ cup vegetable oil

1 tablespoon minced scallion whites

1 tablespoon minced fresh ginger

1 tablespoon Chinese red chile powder

½ teaspoon Sichuan peppercorn powder

2 tablespoons Sichuan chile bean paste

1 tablespoon fermented black beans, coarsely chopped

SAUCE

¾ cup chicken stock (see page 88) or water

2 tablespoons Shaoxing cooking wine

1 tablespoon soy sauce

2 teaspoons tapioca starch

2 Chinese leeks, cut crosswise on the diagonal into ½-inch-thick slices

Put the tofu in a medium saucepan and add 5 cups water and the salt. Bring the water to a boil and then cook gently over medium heat for 5 minutes, until the tofu is soft. Turn the heat off and let the tofu sit in the water.

Heat a wok over high heat until a droplet of water sizzles and evaporates immediately upon contact. Swirl the vegetable oil around the bottom and sides of the wok to coat it evenly. Add the ground beef to the wok and stir-fry for about 3 minutes or until the beef has browned slightly. Remove the beef from the wok and transfer it to a bowl.

To make the chile bean paste oil, heat the vegetable oil in the wok over medium heat until it is just starting to shimmer, about 350°F. Add the scallion whites and ginger to the wok and stir-fry for about 30 seconds. Add the chile powder and Sichuan peppercorn powder and stir-fry for about 30 seconds or until the oil has turned red. Add the chile bean paste and fermented black beans and stir-fry for another 30 seconds.

Drain the tofu and add it to the wok. Return the cooked ground beef to the wok. Stir in all the sauce ingredients. Cover the wok and simmer over medium heat for about 3 minutes, until the tofu has absorbed the flavors.

In a small bowl, mix the tapioca starch with 2 tablespoons water to make a slurry. Stir it into the broth and cook until the broth has thickened, about 1 minute. Add the leek slices and simmer for 30 seconds, until they just turn bright green.

BRAISED WHOLE DUCK WITH EIGHT TREASURES | 八珍扒鴨

GUANGDONG

This braised duck is one of the most elegant dishes found at a Cantonese banquet. The eight treasures hidden underneath usually include luxurious ingredients such as sea cucumber, abalone, fish maw, and dried scallops. It is always fun to cut up the duck and reveal which eight treasures the host has chosen to include. | SERVES 6 OR MORE, ACCOMPANIED BY A SEAFOOD DISH AND A VEGETABLE DISH

1 (4- to 5-pound) whole duck

4 tablespoons dark soy sauce

2 tablespoons honey

4 cups vegetable oil

6 thin slices fresh ginger

2 scallions, cut into 2-inch pieces

4 cups chicken stock (see page 88) or water

½ cup white rice wine

4 whole star anise

1 (2-inch) square of cassia bark

1 tablespoon soy sauce

1 tablespoon sugar

½ teaspoon ground white pepper

1 small dried sea cucumber, rehydrated (see page 80), cleaned, and cut into ½-inch-thick slices

1 medium dried abalone, rehydrated (see page 80) and cut into ¼-inch-thick slices

4 small dried scallops, rehydrated (see page 80)

1 ounce dried fish maw, rehydrated (see page 80) and cut into ½-inch cubes

2 ounces dry-cured Virginia ham, cut into ¼-inch cubes

2 ounces dried shiitake mushrooms, rehydrated (see page 78) and cut into ¼-inch squares

4 ounces fresh or canned bamboo shoots (drained if canned), cut into ⅛-inch-thick slices

4 ounces medium shrimp, shelled and deveined

2 tablespoons tapioca starch

4 ounces baby bok choy, halved lengthwise

Put the duck in a stockpot and add enough water to completely cover the bird. Bring the water to a boil and then turn the heat down to medium. Gently parboil the duck for 20 minutes, skimming off any scum that forms on the surface. Drain the duck and discard the water.

In a small bowl, mix together 2 tablespoons dark soy sauce and the honey. Paint the mixture evenly all over the skin of the duck.

Heat the vegetable oil in a wok until it is just beginning to shimmer, about 350°F. Fry the duck in the oil, turning it occasionally, until evenly browned, about 10 minutes. Remove from the oil and let it cool just until you can handle it.

Debone the duck breast while keeping the legs and wings attached to the meat: Cut a slit down the center of the duck breast from the neck to the cavity and carefully spread the breast meat apart while exposing the joints connecting the rib cage to the legs and wings. Using a sharp knife, separate the legs and wings from the rib cage and continue to remove the carcass from the meat. Reserve the carcass for another purpose, such as making stock.

Remove all but 2 tablespoons of the vegetable oil from the wok. Add the ginger and scallions to the wok and stir-fry until they are fragrant, about 30 seconds. Add the stock, wine, star anise, cassia bark, remaining 2 tablespoons dark soy sauce, the soy sauce, sugar, and pepper to the wok and bring to a boil. Spread the duck, meat-side down with legs and wings arranged on the sides, in the wok and reduce the heat to low. Cover the wok and simmer the duck until the meat is tender, about 1 hour. Check the liquid level occasionally and replenish with water if necessary.

Remove the duck and set it aside on a platter. Strain the braising broth and discard all the aromatics and spices; there should be about 2 cups strained broth. Return the liquid to the wok and add the sea cucumber, abalone, scallops, fish maw, ham, shiitake mushrooms, and bamboo shoots. Bring the liquid to a boil and then reduce the heat to low. Simmer the ingredients for about 30 minutes, until they are

tender. Add the shrimp. Continue to simmer for 5 minutes, until the shrimp are cooked through.

In a small bowl, mix the tapioca starch with 2 tablespoons water to make a slurry. Stir it into the braising liquid and cook until the broth has thickened, about 1 minute.

Bring 3 cups water to a boil in a saucepan, add the bok choy, and boil for 1 minute, until the color turns bright green. Drain the bok choy.

Put the eight treasure ingredients, without the sauce, in the middle of a large platter. Set the duck over the eight treasures, covering them. Pour the sauce over the duck. Arrange the baby bok choy around the duck.

POCKMARKED CHEN'S WORLD-RENOWNED TOFU

Little is known of the woman whose smallpox-riddled complexion led to her being dubbed Pockmarked Chen, or *Chen Mapo* in Chinese. But her tofu is legendary. During the late Qing Dynasty in the 1860s, Chen operated a small restaurant north of Chengdu, near the old Wanfu Bridge (萬福橋) that crosses the Jinjiang River (錦江). She catered to the local workers who toiled for merchants along the river. Legend has it that the workers often brought beef and tofu to her restaurant and asked Chen to cook it for them. She created a spicy and numbing dish adored by the workers, who started calling it the Chen Mapo Tofu (陳麻婆豆腐). Other guests started ordering this new tofu dish and it became a sensation.

Journals and city guides of the time listed Chen's restaurant as one of the top dining venues. A contemporary poet named Feng Jiaji (馮家吉)

even wrote a poem in praise of the dish. As it was imitated by other chefs in the city, the name of the dish was shortened to simply Mapo Tofu (麻婆豆腐). It was introduced to the American dining public when the first Sichuan restaurants opened in New York City during the 1970s, although the spiciness of that version was drastically modified to meet the taste of American diners.

Amazingly, it is still possible to sample the real Mapo Tofu at Chen's original restaurant in Chengdu. It has weathered all the political turmoil from the overthrow of the Qing Dynasty through the Cultural Revolution of Mao Tse-tung. Chen Mapo Tofu Restaurant has prospered since the economic reforms of the 1980s, and now operates a few branches in downtown Chengdu in addition to marketing its own line of Sichuan sauces.

OIL-BRAISED SPRING BAMBOO SHOOTS | 油燜春筍

SHANGHAI

One of the highly anticipated crops in China is the spring bamboo shoot. The tender young shoot of southern bamboo, it offers a crisp, succulent texture and sweet flavor that is much appreciated by devotees. This oil-braised dish enhances that flavor yet maintains the crunch of the shoots beautifully. Canned spring bamboo shoots are available year-round when fresh ones are not in season. | SERVES 2 OR MORE, PAIRED WITH A VEGETABLE DISH

2 pounds fresh spring bamboo shoots, or 1 pound canned (drained if canned)

1 cup vegetable oil

1 teaspoon Sichuan peppercorns

1 tablespoon sugar

2 tablespoons dark soy sauce

¼ cup Shaoxing cooking wine

½ cup vegetarian stock (see page 89) or water

Finely chopped scallions

If using fresh spring bamboo shoots, follow the instructions on page 82 to prep them. Use the rolling cut to slice them into small irregular pieces about 1 inch wide.

Heat the vegetable oil in a wok over high heat until it is beginning to shimmer, about 350°F. Deep-fry the bamboo shoots for 5 minutes or until the edges begin to brown. Drain the bamboo shoots on paper towels.

Remove all but 2 tablespoons of the vegetable oil from the wok. Add the Sichuan peppercorns and cook over medium heat for about 3 minutes to infuse their flavor into the oil. Remove and discard the peppercorns. Return the bamboo shoots to the wok and add the sugar, soy sauce, wine, and stock.

Transfer the ingredients in the wok to a clay pot or Dutch oven with a cover. (Alternatively, this dish can be cooked in a slow cooker.) Braise, covered, over low heat for about 20 minutes, until the shoots have absorbed the flavor. Uncover and continue to cook until the sauce has reduced to the point that it just coats all the bamboo shoots.

Serve garnished with chopped scallions.

DUN BRAISING | 燉

While a large number of Chinese braised dishes use soy sauce or other flavored pastes to fortify the sauce, a technique known as *dun* (燉) is different. Instead of featuring a heavily flavored sauce, *dun* braising, sometimes known as white braising, relies on a broth infused with herbs or spices, sometimes including exotic medicinal herbs such as ginseng, caterpillar fungus (蟲草), or Chinese angelica (當歸). These dishes are often featured at elegant multi-course banquets, and they also appear on home tables. The herbal ingredients are used to compensate for seasonal changes, balance internal energies, and improve a person's well-being.

White braising follows the same basic steps as other Chinese braising techniques. Meat is first parboiled, then slow cooked in an aromatic liquid, which in this case consists of simply water, wine, herbs, spices, and other aromatic ingredients. The end result is a dish with a fragrant, rich broth that is paler in color than soy sauce–based braises but no less delicious.

The white braising technique is also used for making soup. Extra liquid is put into the pot at the beginning of cooking so more remains at the end. Braising soup is covered in more detail in Chapter 13.

BRAISED FROG WITH WISCONSIN GINSENG | 洋參燉田雞
HOME-STYLE

Like chicken, frog meat has a mild flavor that pairs well with other mild-flavored ingredients. In addition to being rich and savory, this braised dish provides the benefits from ginseng, a perfect companion in a white-braised dish. The ginseng purportedly helps regulate blood sugar for diabetics as well as easing the side effects of cancer and cancer treatment. | SERVES 4 OR MORE, ACCOMPANIED BY A MEAT OR SEAFOOD DISH AND A VEGETABLE DISH

3 large frogs (about 1 pound), cut into 1-inch-thick pieces

½ cup Shaoxing cooking wine

1 (½-inch-long) piece of dried Wisconsin ginseng

2 tablespoons dried lily bulb sections

1 tablespoon goji berries

8 thin slices fresh ginger

1 tablespoon chopped scallion greens

Put the frogs in a large saucepan and add enough water to cover them completely. Bring the water to a boil and then turn the heat down to medium. Gently parboil the frogs for 10 minutes, skimming off any scum that forms on the surface. Drain the frogs and discard the water.

Put the frogs, 2 cups water, the wine, ginseng, lily bulb, goji berries, and ginger in a medium clay pot or Dutch oven with a cover. (Alternatively, this dish can be cooked in a slow cooker.) Bring the liquid to a boil and then turn the heat down to low. Simmer, covered, for about 45 minutes, until the frogs are tender.

Serve garnished with the chopped scallion greens.

BUDDHA JUMPING OVER THE WALL | 佛跳牆

FUJIAN

Created toward the end of the Qing dynasty, this most luxurious of braised dishes was originally a decadent way of serving shark fins, but I omit them here in order to help save the shark from extinction caused by overfishing. With all the meat and exotic seafood, the broth of this dish is so rich and savory that the shark fin will not be missed. | SERVES 6 OR MORE, AS PART OF A MULTI-COURSE BANQUET

½ chicken (1½ pounds), cut into 6 pieces

½ duck (2 pounds), cut into 6 pieces

8 ounces country-style pork ribs, cut into 6 pieces

1 cup *laojiu* cooking wine

4 ounces dry-cured Virginia ham, cut into 4 pieces

3 whole star anise

1 (2-inch) square of cassia bark

1 (3-inch-long) piece of fresh ginger, crushed with the flat side of a knife and cut in half

3 small dried sea cucumbers (2 ounces), rehydrated (see page 80), cleaned, and kept whole

6 small dried abalones (3 ounces), rehydrated (see page 80)

6 small dried scallops (2 ounces), rehydrated (see page 80)

2 ounces dried fish maw, rehydrated (see page 80) and cut into 6 pieces

12 quail eggs, hard-boiled and peeled

6 small dried shiitake mushrooms, rehydrated (see page 78) and stemmed

½ cup thinly sliced fresh or canned bamboo shoots (drained if canned)

2 teaspoons salt

½ teaspoon ground white pepper

Put the chicken, duck, and pork ribs in a large pot and add enough water to cover them completely. Bring the water to a boil, then turn the heat down to medium. Gently parboil the meats for 10 minutes, skimming off any scum that forms on the surface. Drain the meats and discard the water.

Return the meats to the stockpot and add 4 quarts water, the wine, ham, star anise, cassia bark, and ginger. Bring the liquid to a boil, then reduce the heat to low. Simmer uncovered for 1½ hours.

Meanwhile, put a wire rack in a wok, add about 5 cups water, and bring to a boil. Put the sea cucumbers, abalones, scallops, and fish maw in separate heatproof bowls. Working in batches, steam the sea cucumbers, scallops, and fish maw for 20 minutes, and the abalone for 40 minutes, until they are all tender.

Now assemble all the ingredients in a large Chinese soup tureen: Put the chicken, duck, pork ribs, and ham on the bottom of the tureen. Then decoratively layer the sea cucumbers, abalones, scallops, fish maw, quail eggs, shiitake mushrooms, and bamboo shoots over the meats. Strain the stock to remove the ginger and spices, then pour it into the tureen. Sprinkle with the salt and pepper and cover the tureen.

Put a metal steaming rack on the bottom of a large stockpot and set the tureen on the rack. Add about 4 cups water to cover the steaming rack. Cover the pot and steam the soup over medium heat, replenishing the water as it evaporates, for 2 hours or until all the ingredients are tender.

Serve the dish directly from the tureen.

BRAISED BEEF WITH MOUNTAIN YAM | 山藥燉牛肉
HOME-STYLE

Mountain yam is known as nagaimo *in Japanese and is a very popular ingredient in northern Asian countries. In China, mountain yam has been used for millennia as an herbal medicine to fortify one's internal energy, or qi. Since both beef and mountain yam are considered neutral in terms of heating and cooling, this is a hearty dish as well as an excellent way of enhancing your qi without upsetting your temperature balance.* | SERVES 4 OR MORE, ACCOMPANIED BY A SEAFOOD DISH AND A VEGETABLE DISH

1 pound beef stew meat, cut into 1½-inch cubes

½ cup white rice wine

6 thin slices fresh ginger

3 whole star anise

1 (2-inch) square of cassia bark

2 bay leaves

1 teaspoon salt

¼ teaspoon ground white pepper

8 ounces mountain yam, peeled and roll-cut into 1-inch-thick pieces

4 cilantro sprigs

Put the beef in a large saucepan and add enough water to cover the meat completely. Bring the water to a boil, then turn the heat down to medium. Gently parboil the beef for 10 minutes, skimming off any scum that forms on the surface. Drain the beef and discard the water.

Put the beef, wine, ginger, star anise, cassia bark, bay leaves, salt, and pepper in a medium clay pot or Dutch oven with a cover. (Alternatively, this dish can be cooked in a slow cooker.) Bring the liquid to a boil, then turn down the heat to low and simmer, covered, for about 50 minutes or until the beef is tender. Add the mountain yam to the pot and continue to braise, covered, for another 10 minutes, until the mountain yam is cooked through.

Remove from the heat and serve hot in the clay pot, garnished with the cilantro sprigs.

This third member of the "slow heat techniques" trio is an extension of *dun*, or white braising. Called *wei* (煨), it has the longest cooking time and is reserved for preparing the toughest cuts of meat or offal, such as tendon or stomach. The process is similar to other braising methods except that it uses a relatively large amount of liquid and the heat is extremely low. The idea is to keep the level of moisture high while slowly breaking down the meat, leaving it flavorful and tender. Once the meat is ready, there should still be enough braising liquid for a thick, rich broth.

A clay pot is ideal for maintaining a steady, gentle heat for the long cooking process. But it is worth mentioning that an electric slow cooker or Dutch oven are also perfect for this method.

BRAISED PIG'S FEET WITH
PEANUTS | 花生煨豬手
FUJIAN

This dish of pig's feet and peanuts has its culinary roots in the Fujian province on mainland China but has become more closely identified with the cooking across the strait in Taiwan. On a visit there I met the celebrity chef Zeng YanJi (鄭衍基), better known as Master A-Ji (阿基師) to his many television fans. One thing that truly impressed me was his advice to keep Taiwanese cooking plain and simple. He insisted that no spices should be used with this dish: The natural flavor of the pig's feet and peanuts should be savored unadorned. | SERVES 2 OR MORE, PAIRED WITH A VEGETABLE DISH

2 pounds pig's feet, cut into 2-inch-thick pieces (ask your butcher to do this)

3 cups pork stock (see page 89) or water

1 cup shelled raw peanuts (6 ounces), skinned

1 (1-inch-long) piece of fresh ginger, smashed with the flat side of a knife

½ cup *laojiu* cooking wine

2 teaspoons salt

1 teaspoon sugar

½ teaspoon ground white pepper

Put the pig's feet in a large saucepan and add enough water to cover them completely. Bring the water to a boil, then turn the heat down to medium. Gently parboil the pig's feet for 20 minutes, skimming off any scum that forms on the surface. Drain the pig's feet completely and discard the water.

Put the pig's feet, stock, peanuts, ginger, wine, salt, sugar, and pepper in a medium clay pot or Dutch oven with a cover. Bring the liquid to a boil, then turn the heat down to low. Gently simmer the pig's feet, covered, for 2 hours, replenishing the liquid with water if necessary, until the meat is tender. (Alternatively, you can bake the pig's feet in a 3- to 4-quart clay pot or Dutch oven in a regular oven at 200°F.)

Serve the pig's feet in the clay pot.

OVEN-BRAISED OXTAIL WITH CHINESE ANGELICA | 當歸炖牛尾

HOME-STYLE

Chinese angelica, known as dang gui *in Chinese, can be found in a Chinese herbal pharmacy. It is often known as "female ginseng" because of its supposedly beneficial properties for women's health. It is believed to cure mild anemia and to reduce high blood pressure, among other benefits. This herbal-flavored braised oxtail is a delectable way to consume this medicinal ingredient. Men are not discouraged from enjoying it, too.* | SERVES 2 OR MORE, PAIRED WITH A VEGETABLE DISH

1½ pounds oxtail

4 slices (½ ounce) *dang gui* (Chinese angelica)

10 jujubes

6 thin slices fresh ginger

½ cup Shaoxing cooking wine

1 teaspoon soy sauce

½ teaspoon salt

¼ teaspoon ground white pepper

1 small daikon radish, roll-cut into 1-inch-thick pieces

Preheat the oven to 300°F.

Put the oxtail in a large saucepan and add enough water to cover it completely. Bring the water to a boil, then turn the heat down to medium. Gently parboil the oxtail for 10 minutes, skimming off any scum that forms on the surface. Drain the oxtail and discard the water.

Put the oxtail, 3 cups water, the *dang gui*, jujubes, ginger, wine, soy sauce, salt, and pepper in a clay pot or a small Dutch oven with a cover. (Alternatively, this dish can be cooked in a slow cooker.) Cover the pot, put it in the oven, and braise for 2 hours or until the oxtail is tender.

Remove the pot from the oven and stir in the daikon so all the pieces are submerged in the liquid. Cover the pot, return it to the oven, and cook for 1 hour or until the daikon is tender.

Clay Urn Oven for *Wei* Braising

In Western cooking, braising usually means baking in a covered pot in the oven. In some areas of China the virtues of braising in an oven have been embraced. But instead of a regular oven they use a very large clay urn, about 5 feet high, with a wood-burning brazier inside. Soup pots are placed on racks along the wall of the urn. Then the top of the urn is covered and the food is cooked.

FLAVOR POTTING | 滷

On a side street in the Flushing neighborhood of New York City, a takeout food vendor sells a very special type of Chinese food out of a postage-stamp storefront. A row of refrigerated display cases lines one side of the store, in which mounds of dark-colored, fragrant meat are showcased. They have all been slow cooked in an aromatic braising broth for many hours to break down the meat's tough connective tissue and to infuse it with the broth's flavors. This is a shop that sells what the Chinese call flavor-potted meat.

Flavor potting, known as *lu* (滷) in Chinese, is a special braising technique that possibly exists only in China. In it the braising broth, also known as the master sauce, is saved and continuously reused in future cooking. Fresh spices and herbs are added every time the liquid is reused. Repeated cooking in the same liquid enhances the flavor over time.

In Asia flavor-potted meat is usually offered for sale in retail outlets by chefs who've mastered the technique. The braising broth is reused daily and ultimately becomes a rich and flavorful broth that would be difficult to replicate in a home kitchen. Famous flavor-potting shops pride themselves on the age of their braising broth, cooking with a "century-old broth" (百年老滷) that has been passed down for generations in their family kitchen. Many families in China do the same at home. The key is to make sure that flavor-potted meat is prepared regularly so the broth remains fresh.

Flavor-potted dishes are normally served cold or at room temperature. They are often served as cold appetizers, or as a meat dish accompanying noodles or congee. The most common ingredients cooked this way include tough cuts of meat such as pork or beef shank, pig's feet, beef tendon, and chicken or duck feet. Innards such as pork intestine and stomach, beef tripe, and chicken or duck gizzards are also used.

Whole chicken, duck, and goose are other options. Although meat is the most common ingredient for flavor potting, certain vegetables, tofu, peanuts, and kelp are also cooked this way.

THE BRAISING BROTH

As the key ingredient in flavor potting, the braising broth requires special attention. There are two main types of braising broth: red (紅滷) and white (白滷). Red broth contains soy sauce, which turns the cooked meat brown. White broth flavor potting is more common in northern China and produces a pale-colored meat that can be very attractive and just as flavorful.

Spices used in the broth are matched to the meat being braised. The gamier the meat, the more complex the spice mix. Commonly used spices include star anise, Sichuan peppercorns, cloves, cassia bark, fennel, bay leaf, black cardamom, green cardamom, licorice, coriander seed, and tangerine peel. Ginger and scallions are almost always added to the broth as aromatics.

Whereas other braising techniques simply start cooking the meat in a liquid along with the herbs and spices, with flavor potting the initial broth is often made with bones and water. This is an attempt to give the initial broth an "old broth" taste right from the start. In the recipes that follow, however, I suggest using meat stock instead to fortify the broth's flavor.

To start the flavor-potting process and create your broth, make one recipe of the braising broth. Remove all the aromatics and spices from the broth, and then braise the meat. Save the broth after cooking. The next time, prepare another recipe of the braising broth, remove the aromatic and spices, add the leftover liquid from the first batch, and then braise the meat. By doing so the braising broth becomes richer every time. Note that the amount of broth may not continue to increase because some liquid evaporates during cooking and some is used as a sauce when serving the meat.

RETAINING AND STORING THE BRAISING BROTH

Since the braising broth is reused repeatedly, it is important to preserve it properly. To ensure freshness, the broth should be strained through a very-fine-mesh sieve to remove all solid particles. Once the broth is cool, remove all the fat floating on top of the liquid as it solidifies. These precautions will ensure that the broth is clear of any impurities and also maintain the fragrance of the spices during refrigeration.

In a professional kitchen the broth is used daily. Once cool, it is covered and stored in a refrigerator overnight for use again the next day. The home cook should keep in mind that refrigerated broth will stay fresh for only about a week. For longer storage it should be frozen; if used regularly, say once every month, just a minimum loss of flavor will occur. The broth may start acquiring off flavors from freezer burn if frozen without being reused for longer periods.

CHAOZHOU FLAVOR-POTTED TOFU | 潮州滷豆腐
CHAOZHOU

Tofu is often braised in the same pot as Chaozhou flavor-potted goose. To do this, add the tofu to the goose halfway through its cooking time. If you're interested in serving this tofu as a vegetarian dish, follow the directions here. | SERVES 4 OR MORE, AS AN APPETIZER

3 cups vegetable oil

12 ounces firm tofu, quartered and patted dry

Braising broth from Chaozhou Flavor-Potted Goose (page 226), made with water or vegetable stock

Leftover vegetarian broth from a previous batch, if available

Heat the vegetable oil in a wok over high heat until it is just beginning to smoke, about 395°F. Put the tofu in the oil and deep-fry until a brown skin forms on the outside, about 5 minutes. Remove the tofu from the oil and drain it on paper towels.

Put the braising broth, along with any leftover broth, in a saucepan and add the tofu. Set the heat to low and simmer the tofu, covered, for 30 minutes or until it has absorbed the flavors.

Remove the pot from the heat and let it cool completely. Take the tofu out of the pot and store it, submerged in the broth, in a covered container in the refrigerator.

Cut the tofu into ¼-inch-thick slices, pour a little bit of the braising broth over the slices, and serve at room temperature.

FLAVOR-POTTED SQUAB | 滷水鴿

GUANGDONG

Squab is very popular in the south of China, especially among the Cantonese. Commonly crisp-fried, this fowl is also frequently flavor potted. | SERVES 4 OR MORE, AS AN APPETIZER

BRAISING BROTH

6 cups chicken broth (see page 88) or water

½ cup soy sauce

¼ cup white rice wine

2 tablespoons sugar

1 (2-inch-long) piece of fresh ginger

2 scallions, cut into 2-inch-long pieces

4 whole star anise

1 (2-inch) square of cassia bark

1 tablespoon whole cloves

1 black cardamom pod

2 slices dried licorice

5 bay leaves

1 (2-inch) square of dried tangerine peel

2 whole squabs (about 2 pounds total), cleaned, feet removed

Leftover broth from a previous batch, if available

Combine all the ingredients for the braising broth in a pot and bring the liquid to a boil. Turn the heat to low and simmer the broth for about 30 minutes. Filter the braising broth through a fine-mesh sieve to remove all the aromatics and spices.

Put the squabs in a medium pot and add enough water to cover them completely. Bring the water to a boil, then turn the heat down to medium. Gently boil the squabs for 10 minutes, skimming off any scum that forms on the surface. Drain the squabs and discard the water.

Put the squabs in the braising broth (along with any leftover broth from a previous batch of squab) and set the heat to low. Simmer the squabs, covered, for 40 minutes, until the squabs are tender when pierced with a knife, checking every 20 minutes or so to make sure there is enough liquid to completely cover the birds. Add water if the broth has reduced too much.

Remove the pot from the heat and let it cool completely. Take the squabs out of the pot and store them, submerged in the broth, in a covered container in the refrigerator.

When ready to serve, cut the squabs into quarters and arrange them on a plate. Pour a few tablespoons of the broth over the squabs and serve at room temperature. Reserve the remaining broth for next time.

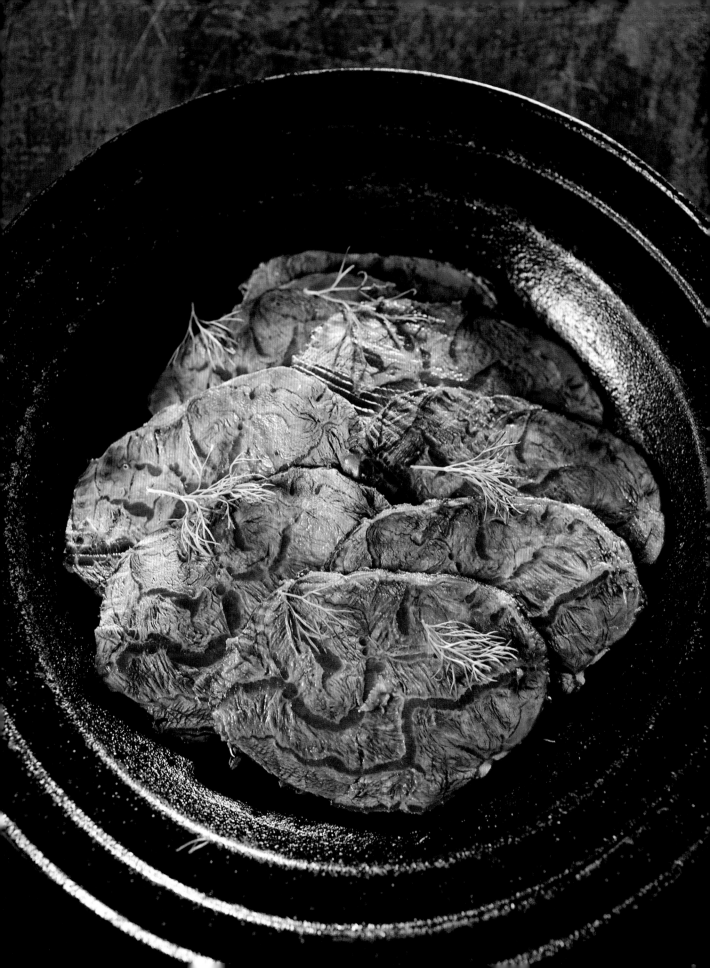

FLAVOR-POTTED BEEF SHANK | 滷牛腱

HOME-STYLE

Beef shank is tough and sinewy but makes an excellent cut for slow cooking. Flavor potting is a great way of infusing flavors into the meat. This recipe is a common household favorite since the beef can be cooked ahead and stored in the refrigerator for the week ahead. | SERVES 6 OR MORE, AS AN APPETIZER

BRAISING BROTH

5 cups beef broth (see page 89) or water

½ cup Shaoxing cooking wine

⅓ cup dark soy sauce

3 tablespoons soy sauce

¼ cup sugar

1 (2-inch-long) piece of fresh ginger

3 scallions, cut into 2-inch pieces

1 (2-inch) square of cassia bark

4 whole star anise

2 black cardamom pods

1 tablespoon Sichuan peppercorns

1 tablespoon fennel seeds

2 bay leaves

2 pounds boneless beef shank

Leftover broth from a previous batch, if available

Chopped cilantro

Combine all the ingredients for the braising broth in a pot and bring the liquid to a boil. Turn the heat to low and simmer the broth for about 30 minutes. Filter the braising broth through a fine-mesh sieve to remove all the aromatics and spices.

Put the beef in a medium pot and add enough water to cover it completely. Bring the water to a boil, then turn the heat down to medium. Gently boil the beef for 20 minutes, skimming off any scum that forms on the surface. Drain the beef and discard the water.

Put the beef in the braising broth (along with any leftover broth from a previous batch of beef) and set the heat to low. Simmer the beef, covered, for 3 hours or until it is tender when pierced with a knife; check the pot every 30 minutes or so to make sure there is enough liquid to completely cover the meat. Add water if the broth has reduced too much.

Remove the pot from the heat and let it cool completely. Then take the beef out of the pot and store it, submerged in the broth, in a covered container in the refrigerator.

When ready to serve, cut the beef against the grain into thin slices, about 1/16 inch thick, and arrange them on a plate. Pour a few tablespoons of the broth over the beef and garnish with the chopped cilantro. Serve at room temperature. Reserve the remaining broth for next time.

CHAOZHOU FLAVOR-POTTED GOOSE | 潮州滷水鵝

CHAOZHOU

Chaozhou flavor potting is well known throughout China, with goose a particular local specialty, often accompanied by tofu (see page 222). | SERVES 6 OR MORE, AS AN APPETIZER

BRAISING BROTH

2 tablespoons vegetable oil

1 (2-inch-long) piece of fresh ginger

2 scallions (white, green, or both white and green parts), cut into 2-inch-long pieces

4 garlic cloves

1 lemongrass stalk, cut into 1-inch pieces

10 cups chicken broth (see page 88) or water

1 cup Shaoxing cooking wine

½ cup soy sauce

¼ cup white rice wine

¼ cup sugar

4 whole star anise

1 (2-inch) square of cassia bark

1 tablespoon whole cloves

1 tablespoon coriander seeds

1 black cardamom pod

2 slices dried licorice

5 bay leaves

1 (2-inch) square of dried tangerine peel

1 whole goose (about 5 pounds)

Leftover broth from a previous batch, if available

DIPPING SAUCE

¼ cup white rice vinegar

3 tablespoons minced garlic

1 tablespoon minced fresh red chile

3 tablespoons toasted sesame oil

To make the braising broth, put the vegetable oil, ginger, scallions, garlic, and lemongrass in a stockpot and fry over high heat until lightly browned, about 3 minutes. Add the rest of the braising broth ingredients and bring the liquid to a boil. Turn the heat down to low and simmer for 1 hour. Strain the braising broth through a fine-mesh sieve into a large pot, discarding all the aromatics and spices.

Put the goose in a large pot and add enough water to cover it completely. Bring the water to a boil, then turn the heat down to medium. Gently boil the goose for 20 minutes, skimming off any scum that forms on the surface. Drain the goose and discard the water.

Put the goose in the strained braising broth (along with any leftover broth from a previous batch of goose). Bring the liquid to a boil, then turn the heat down to low. Simmer the goose, covered, for 60 minutes or until it is tender when pierced with a knife, checking every 30 minutes or so to make sure there is enough liquid to completely cover the meat. Add water if the broth has reduced too much.

Remove the pot from the heat and let it cool completely. Take the goose out of the pot and store it, submerged in the broth, in a covered container in the refrigerator.

Combine all the ingredients for the dipping sauce in a small bowl.

Cut up the goose, following the instructions for cutting up a whole fowl (see page 72). Arrange the meat on a plate and pour a few tablespoons of the braising broth and the sesame oil over the goose. Reserve the remaining broth for next time.

Serve the goose at room temperature, accompanied by a small bowl of the dipping sauce.

COLD BRAISED CARP | 五香酥魚

BEIJING

Flavor potting fish uses the same basic process of first making the braising broth and then cooking the fish. But the braising broth is not reused from batch to batch. Instead, it is reduced and used as a sauce. This flavor-potted fish is popular in Beijing and is served regularly as a cold appetizer in the city's restaurants. It is excellent with a cup of hot rice wine on chilly days. | SERVES 4 AS AN APPETIZER

4 cups vegetable oil

4 (8-ounce) whole small carp or perch, cleaned and scaled

BRAISING BROTH

1 scallion, cut into 1-inch pieces

2 garlic cloves

4 thin slices fresh ginger

1 (2-inch) square of cassia bark

2 whole star anise

½ cup Shaoxing cooking wine

¼ cup soy sauce

½ cup Chinkiang black vinegar

1 teaspoon salt

2 tablespoons sugar

6 large napa cabbage leaves

2 tablespoons toasted sesame oil

2 tablespoons chopped scallion greens

Heat the vegetable oil in a wok over high heat until it is beginning to shimmer, about 350°F. Add the fish and fry until lightly browned, about 5 minutes. Remove the fish and drain them on a paper towel.

Remove all but 2 tablespoons of the vegetable oil from the wok. Turn the heat to high and add the scallion, garlic, and ginger. Stir-fry until fragrant, about 1 minute. Add the cassia bark and star anise and stir-fry for another 30 seconds. Add the wine, soy sauce, vinegar, salt, sugar, and 4 cups water. Bring the liquid to a boil. Turn the heat down to low and simmer for 30 minutes. Remove all the solid ingredients with a fine skimmer and discard.

Turn off the heat and line the bottom of a wok with two layers of cabbage leaves. Then arrange the fried fish side by side on top of the cabbage. Simmer the fish, covered, over low heat for 5 hours, checking the liquid every 30 minutes or so and adding water as needed to keep the fish submerged.

After 5 hours, turn the heat up and boil the liquid until it has reduced and just covers the cabbage. Turn the heat off. Gently remove the fish from the wok and arrange it neatly in a container. Remove and discard the cabbage. Pour the reduced braising liquid and the sesame oil over the fish. Let cool completely, then cover and refrigerate overnight or for up to 5 days.

Serve the whole fish cold, on a plate garnished with the scallions. Pour a little of the braising liquid over the fish for added flavor.

MARBLED TEA EGG | 茶葉蛋
HOME-STYLE

Found in just about every corner convenience store all over China, this tea egg is a popular snack food that is also commonly served as an appetizer at formal banquets. Any Chinese red or green tea works well with this recipe, but do not use black tea, as it can make the eggs too bitter. | SERVES 4 OR MORE, AS AN APPETIZER

BRAISING BROTH

¼ cup Shaoxing cooking wine

1 tablespoon dark soy sauce

2 tablespoons soy sauce

3 tablespoons Chinese green or red tea leaves

1 (2-inch) square of dried tangerine peel

1 (2-inch) square of cassia bark

2 whole star anise

1 teaspoon sugar

6 large eggs

Put all the braising broth ingredients in a pot with 4 cups water and bring to a boil. Turn the heat to low and simmer the broth for about 30 minutes. Filter the braising broth through a fine-mesh sieve into another pot and discard all the aromatics and spices.

Put the eggs in a separate pot and add enough water to cover them completely. Slowly bring the water to a simmer and then cook for about 10 minutes. Drain the eggs and crack the shells but do not peel them.

Put the eggs in the strained braising broth and simmer for 40 minutes. Remove the pot from the heat and let them cool completely. Transfer the cooled eggs along with the broth to a covered container and store the eggs, submerged in the broth, in the refrigerator.

Peel each egg and cut them into 6 wedges each. Pour a little bit of the braising broth over the eggs, and serve cold.

CHAPTER ELEVEN

The Intricacy of Boiling

THERE ARE MANY FAMOUS BOILED DISHES IN COUNTRIES AROUND THE WORLD. France's *pot-au-feu* is a traditional dish using beef, oxtail, and marrowbones with vegetables like carrots, turnips, celery, and onions. The Iberian dish known as *cozido* in Portugal and *cocido* in Spain includes ingredients such as beef, sausages, pork, chicken, carrots, turnips, and cabbage. And in the United States, the New England boiled dinner, featuring corned beef and cabbage as the main ingredients, is a famously hearty meal that can fend off the region's winter chill. In China, boiled lamb pieces served with a dipping soy sauce and blanched asparagus dressed in a gingery sauce are popular dishes enjoyed by all. From simple long and slow boiling of meats to quick blanching of paper-thin slices of beef and pork, the Chinese have found ways to exploit the boiling technique.

One of the most practical uses of boiling is to cook tough cuts of meat over a long period of time. Unlike braising, where herbs and spices infuse flavor into the meat while it cooks, boiling meat does not generally flavor it very much. Simple aromatic ingredients are added only to cut the gaminess of the meat. Otherwise boiling is ideal for showcasing the natural flavor of the meat.

Certain types of meat, such as chicken, require gentle handling when boiling. Steeping, a variation, utilizes gentle heat to cook delicate meat and is similar to the oil steeping described in Chapter 8. The cooking liquid, in this case water, is brought to a boil before the meat is plunged into it. After being brought back to a boil, the heat is turned off and the meat left to cook in the residual heat. This method produces a delicate, tender texture for certain types of meat.

Blanching is a common technique used by many Chinese cooks to prepare tender greens as well as delicate shellfish. Ingredients are dipped in hot boiling water, sometimes only for seconds, and drained. Then a simple sauce, usually made from soy sauce and some oil, is all that's needed to finish the dish.

Finally there is the ultimate Chinese boiled dish known as the hot pot, a fun participatory meal not unlike a Swiss fondue. A specially designed charcoal-fueled pot with a chimney in the center is placed in the middle of the dining table. Thin slices of meat, pieces of seafood, dumplings, and cut-up vegetables are arranged on plates around the pot. Diners cook these ingredients by dipping them in the boiling liquid for a few seconds before dabbing them in a sauce. This is the best cold-weather meal imaginable.

BOILING 白煮

The most fundamental way of boiling food is simply to cook tough cuts of meat in water for an extended period of time. In fact boiling meat is one of the earliest methods of cooking recorded in China and can be traced back to the Zhou Dynasty during the 10th century BCE, when it was known by the term *geng* (羹).

Just about every region has its own variation of boiled meat. The difference is usually in the sauces used to flavor the cooked meat. In the northern part of China, a sauce made from garlic and black vinegar is most common; in the western region of Xinjiang, cumin-flavored sauces predominate; while in Sichuan, numbing and peppery hot sauces are standard.

In just about every region, though, the boiling process is similar. Water for boiling is frequently infused with some kind of aromatic ingredients and basic spices, such as ginger, scallions, star anise, and Sichuan peppercorns. Cooking wine is also added to help neutralize some of the gaminess in certain cuts of meat. But only minimal quantities of these ingredients are added so as not to overwhelm the natural flavor of the meat.

While a long period of boiling is suitable for cooking meat, it is never appropriate for cooking vegetables. Cooked too long, vegetables disintegrate and their appeal—and nutritional value—is lost.

BOILED PORK BELLY WITH SPICY GARLIC DRESSING | 蒜泥白肉

SICHUAN

Pork belly is beloved by the Chinese. This is the dish that truly serves up the natural fresh taste of pork— except in Sichuan they just can't help but add a garlic and chile sauce to kick up the taste and heat! | SERVES 4 OR MORE, ACCOMPANIED BY A SEAFOOD DISH AND A VEGETABLE DISH

1 pound pork belly

½ cup Shaoxing cooking wine

1 (2-inch-long) piece of fresh ginger

SAUCE

¼ cup Sichuan Spiced Chile Oil, homemade (see page 59) or store-bought

2 tablespoons soy sauce

1 tablespoon toasted sesame oil

3 tablespoons minced garlic

1 teaspoon salt

1 teaspoon sugar

1 hothouse cucumber, cut lengthwise into long, thin slices

Put the pork belly in a pot and add 2 quarts water, the wine, and the ginger. Bring the liquid to a boil, then turn the heat down to medium and gently boil the pork belly for 40 minutes, until tender.

Combine all the sauce ingredients in a small bowl and mix well.

Drain the pork belly and let it cool. When it has cooled somewhat but is still warm to the touch, cut it lengthwise into long 1/16-inch-thick strips. Arrange alternating and overlapping slices of pork and cucumber on a serving plate. Pour the sauce all over the pork and cucumber, and serve while still warm or at room temperature.

BOILED LEG OF LAMB | 白煮羊肉

XINJIANG

Lamb is a staple in the Muslim communities that dominate northwestern China. Although grilling lamb is the standard in Xinjiang, boiling is common as well—another way to appreciate this slightly gamy yet succulent meat. The vinegar, garlic, and chile sauce, which would overwhelm other meats, enhances the lamb's flavor. | SERVES 2 OR MORE, PAIRED WITH A VEGETABLE DISH

1 pound boneless leg of lamb, cut into 2-inch cubes

½ cup white rice wine

2 tablespoons Sichuan peppercorns

4 whole star anise

3 scallions, cut into 2-inch pieces

6 thin slices fresh ginger

DIPPING SAUCE

¼ cup Chinkiang black vinegar

1 tablespoon soy sauce

1 tablespoon toasted sesame oil

3 tablespoons minced garlic

1 tablespoon sliced fresh red chiles

1 teaspoon sugar

2 tablespoons chopped cilantro

Put the lamb in a pot and add enough water to cover it completely. Bring the water to a boil, then turn the heat down to medium. Boil the lamb gently for 20 minutes, skimming off any scum that forms on the surface. Drain the lamb and discard the water.

Return the lamb to the pot and add 4 cups water, the wine, Sichuan peppercorns, star anise, scallions, and ginger. Bring the liquid to a boil, then turn the heat to medium and gently boil the lamb until tender, about 1 hour.

Drain the lamb cubes thoroughly, discarding the spices and aromatics, and put the lamb in a serving bowl. In a small bowl, combine all the ingredients for the dipping sauce and mix well. Garnish the sauce with the chopped cilantro. Serve the lamb with the dipping sauce on the side.

STEEPING 浸

Not all types of meat require a long boiling time. Overcooked chicken becomes dry or, conversely, mushy, and fish will fall apart. For delicate meats, there is another method, called steeping. The meat, which is usually cooked whole, is plunged into boiling liquid and then the liquid is brought back to a boil. After that the heat is turned off and the meat continues to cook as the liquid cools down. Using this technique will guarantee that the meat is not overcooked.

Many cooks steep meat in plain water, while others turn the water into an aromatic broth before steeping. The broth does not have to be highly flavored, but rather it should subtly infuse the meat. This light broth may not be flavorful enough to use as cooking stock, but it can be used for making a soup to accompany the meat by adding a few pieces of vegetable.

One way to ensure that the meat is cooked through during steeping is to make certain that it is not too cold when it is first placed in the boiling liquid. In Asia freshly slaughtered chicken or just-caught fish is usually used immediately for steeping. In the United States meat is very likely to be refrigerated or frozen. Frozen meat must be completely thawed before steeping, and I would even suggest that refrigerated meat be left at room temperature for up to an hour, depending upon its size, before steeping. Bring the liquid to a gentle boil, then add the meat. Let the liquid come back to a gentle boil and then turn off the heat. Cover the pot and steep until the liquid's temperature drops to about 160°F.

The steeping time is generally between 30 and 45 minutes, depending on the size of the piece of meat. It is important to make sure that the center is fully cooked through. The best way to test for doneness is to use a meat thermometer: Remove the meat from the liquid and insert a meat thermometer to check the temperature. For chicken and rabbit the internal temperature should be about 160°F. If the meat fails to reach the appropriate internal temperature, then repeat the process of bringing the liquid to a boil and turning off the heat. Steeping whole fish should require much less time: For a 2-pound fish, the steeping time should be only around 15 minutes. In general the fish is fully cooked if the thickest part of the meat flakes easily.

In southern China, steeped meat is usually allowed to cool to room temperature before it is served. The result is a dish that is neither cold nor piping hot. This is the main difference between steeping in water and oil steeping: While they both generally use the same procedure to cook the meat, oil-steeped dishes are served hot. Because of this difference, and the cooking medium of oil versus water, they are considered two separate techniques. Cantonese white cooked chicken and Hainan chicken rice are two southern favorites that use this water steeping method.

An Alternative Steeping Process

A variation of the steeping method used by many restaurant kitchens is to dip and remove the meat several times as it cooks. The procedure is to bring the liquid to a gentle boil, then drop the meat into the liquid and turn the heat off. Let the meat steep for about 15 minutes, and then remove it from the liquid. Let it rest for about 5 minutes while the broth is reheated, and then repeat the process another two times. Professional chefs claim that dipping the meat three times lets them better assess the doneness of the meat, adjust the steeping time accordingly, and complete the process more quickly.

MOUTHWATERING RABBIT | 口水兔

SICHUAN

"Mouthwatering" flavor is a classic Sichuan chile oil–based sauce that is slightly tart, numbing, and spicy hot. More commonly associated with chicken, this sauce also works well with rabbit. | SERVES 4 AS AN APPETIZER, 2 WHEN PAIRED WITH A VEGETABLE DISH

1 whole rabbit (about 2 pounds)

½ cup Shaoxing cooking wine

1 (1-inch-long) piece of fresh ginger

2 scallions, cut into 2-inch pieces

4 whole star anise

CHILE OIL SAUCE

1 tablespoon Chinkiang black vinegar

1 tablespoon Chinese toasted sesame paste

1 teaspoon salt

1 tablespoon sugar

1 teaspoon minced fresh ginger

½ teaspoon Sichuan peppercorn powder

1 teaspoon chopped pickled red chiles (optional)

¾ cup Sichuan Spiced Chile Oil, homemade (see page 59) or store-bought

3 tablespoons coarsely chopped peanuts

2 tablespoons mixed black and white sesame seeds, toasted

2 tablespoons chopped scallions

2 tablespoons chopped cilantro

Let the rabbit sit at room temperature for 20 minutes before cooking.

Combine 3 quarts water, the wine, ginger, scallions, and star anise in a stockpot and bring to a boil. Submerge the rabbit in the boiling liquid and bring the liquid to a boil again. Immediately turn the heat off and cover the pot. Let the rabbit steep in the hot liquid for about 30 minutes.

Meanwhile, combine all the sauce ingredients in a bowl and mix well.

Remove the rabbit from the stockpot and drain it well. Test for doneness by using a meat thermometer to check the internal temperature of the thickest part of the rabbit. It should read 160°F when done. If it does not, heat the liquid to a boil and steep the rabbit again for another 10 minutes or so before retesting.

Let the rabbit rest until it is cool enough to handle but still warm. Cut the rabbit into pieces about ½ inch thick and arrange them on a serving plate. Pour the sauce all over the rabbit and drizzle the chile oil over it as well. Garnish with the chopped peanuts, sesame seeds, scallions, and cilantro. Serve warm.

WHITE COOKED CHICKEN | 白切雞

GUANGDONG

Steeped chicken is a classic technique used in the
southern provinces of Guangdong, Fujian, and Hainan.
The meat is always perfectly cooked and tender.
Varieties of dipping sauces can include ginger soy sauce,
chile sauce, and galangal sauce. | SERVES 4 OR MORE,
PAIRED WITH A VEGETABLE DISH

1 whole chicken (3 to 4 pounds)

½ cup white rice wine

1 (2-inch-long) piece of fresh ginger

2 scallions, cut into 2-inch pieces

DIPPING SAUCE

¼ cup vegetable oil

1 teaspoon toasted sesame oil

3 tablespoons minced garlic

3 tablespoons minced fresh ginger

1 teaspoon salt

3 tablespoons vegetable oil

2 tablespoons toasted sesame oil

Let the chicken sit at room temperature for
20 minutes before cooking.

Combine 3 quarts water, the wine, ginger, and
scallions in a stockpot and bring to a boil. Submerge
the chicken in the boiling liquid and let the liquid
return to a boil. Immediately turn the heat off and
cover the pot. Let the chicken steep in the hot liquid
for about 30 minutes.

Meanwhile, combine all the dipping sauce
ingredients in a bowl and mix well.

Remove the chicken from the stockpot and drain
it well. Test for doneness by inserting a fork through
the thickest part of the chicken near the thigh. The
chicken is done if the juice flowing out is clear and
not pink. You can also use a meat thermometer to
check the internal temperature of the thigh. It should
read 160°F when done. If the chicken is not done,
heat the liquid to a boil and steep the chicken again
for another 10 minutes or so before retesting.

Let the chicken rest until it is cool enough
to handle but still warm. Cut up the chicken by
separating the legs and wings from the body first.
Separate the thighs, drumsticks, drumettes, and
wings, then cut the thighs and drumsticks in half;
arrange them on a serving plate. Remove the breast
meat from the bones and cut it into ½-inch-thick
strips. Add the breast meat to the serving plate as
well. (The bones can be returned to the stockpot to
make chicken stock by simmering them for an hour or
so in the broth.)

Combine the vegetable oil and sesame oil in a
small bowl and drizzle this all over the chicken. Serve
the chicken warm, with the dipping sauce on the side.

STEEPED WHOLE TILAPIA | 水浸鯽魚
HOME-STYLE

Steeping a fish in boiling water is a healthy alternative to frying. This dish exemplifies typical home-style cooking. The result is very similar to steamed fish but the meat is even more moist. All kinds of small whole fish, including striped bass and carp, can be used for this dish. | SERVES 2 OR MORE, PAIRED WITH A VEGETABLE DISH

½ cup Shaoxing cooking wine

4 thin slices fresh ginger

1 whole tilapia (about 2 pounds), cleaned and butterflied according to one of the methods on page 73

SAUCE

3 tablespoons soy sauce

2 tablespoons Shaoxing cooking wine

1 tablespoon sugar

¼ cup julienned fresh ginger

¼ cup julienned scallions

¼ cup vegetable oil

Combine 4 cups water with the wine and ginger in a wok and bring the liquid to a boil. Gently submerge the fish in the boiling liquid and cover the wok. Turn the heat off and let the fish steep in the liquid for 5 minutes. Carefully turn the fish over and bring the liquid to a boil again. Turn the heat off and cover the wok. Steep the fish for another 5 minutes or until the thickest part of the meat flakes readily.

Meanwhile, in a small saucepan, combine all the sauce ingredients and heat until just boiling. Keep warm.

Drain the fish with a large spider strainer and put it on a serving plate. Garnish the fish with the julienned ginger and scallions, then pour the sauce evenly over the fish.

Discard all the liquid in the wok and wipe the wok dry. Heat the vegetable oil in the wok until it is just about to shimmer. Pour the hot oil all over the fish and serve the dish hot.

BLANCHING | 白灼

For ingredients that are simply too delicate to withstand prolonged cooking, blanching is the answer. This technique is used for vegetables and shellfish that cook in a very short period of time. The process for blanching is fundamentally the same as steeping, but instead of holding the food in hot water for an extended period, it is cooked in gently boiling water for minutes, or seconds, instead.

Ingredients for blanching are usually vegetables such as Chinese broccoli, asparagus, and celtuce, or shellfish such as shrimp, fresh abalone, conch, and squid. For blanching vegetables, a small quantity of vegetable oil is added to the boiling liquid so the ingredient is coated with a little bit of fat when scooped out. For shellfish, ginger and scallions, as well as some wine, flavor the water.

BLANCHED ASPARAGUS WITH GINGER SOY SAUCE | 白灼薑汁蘆筍
GUANGDONG

For me, one of the best parts about spring is the availability of tender young asparagus, which I like to blanch quickly and then season with an aromatic ginger soy sauce. I prefer pencil-thin tender asparagus, but if the large thick variety is being used, be sure to peel the bottom end to remove the fibrous outer skin, and adjust the blanching time if needed. | SERVES 2 OR MORE, PAIRED WITH A MEAT OR SEAFOOD DISH

1 pound asparagus

¼ cup vegetable oil

SAUCE

2 tablespoons soy sauce

2 tablespoons Shaoxing cooking wine

1 teaspoon sugar

2 tablespoons vegetable oil

2 tablespoons minced fresh ginger

Sliced fresh red chile (optional)

Snap off the tough bottom part of the asparagus stalks and peel the outer skin if necessary. Bring 2 quarts water to a boil in a saucepan. Add the vegetable oil to the water. Blanch the asparagus in the boiling water for about 1 minute or until the color just turns bright green. Drain the water and arrange the spears on a plate.

To make the sauce, in a small bowl, combine the soy sauce, wine, and sugar and mix well. Heat the vegetable oil in a wok over high heat for about 30 seconds. Add the ginger to the oil and stir-fry until fragrant, about 30 seconds. Add the soy sauce mixture and let simmer for 15 seconds.

Pour the sauce over the asparagus and garnish with the red chile.

BLANCHED CONCH WITH SOY SAUCE | 白灼響螺

FUJIAN

Seafood is abundant along the Fujian coast. This is one of the most common and delicious ways the residents cook it. | SERVES 2 OR MORE, PAIRED WITH A VEGETABLE DISH

BLANCHING LIQUID

½ cup *laojiu* cooking wine

2 scallions (white, green, or both white and green parts), cut into 2-inch pieces

6 thin slices fresh ginger

SAUCE

2 tablespoons vegetable oil

2 tablespoons soy sauce

2 tablespoons *laojiu* cooking wine

1 teaspoon sugar

3 thin slices fresh ginger

1 scallion (white, green, or both white and green parts), cut on the diagonal into ⅛-inch pieces

12 ounces conch, thinly sliced

1 fresh red chile, thinly sliced on the diagonal

Put 6 cups water and all the blanching liquid ingredients in a pot and bring to a boil. Turn the heat down to low and simmer for 5 minutes.

To make the sauce, combine the vegetable oil, soy sauce, wine, and sugar in a small saucepan, mix well, and bring to a simmer. Add the ginger and scallion and cook for 1 minute. Turn the heat down to the lowest setting to keep the sauce warm.

Bring the blanching liquid back to a boil and add the conch slices to the pot. Stir to make sure the slices are separated. Blanch for 5 seconds, until the slices begin to curl, then drain thoroughly.

Put the conch slices in a deep plate and pour the sauce over them. Garnish with the chile slices.

BLANCHED SHRIMP WITH GINGER SOY SAUCE | 白灼明蝦

GUANGDONG

This is one of the easiest ways to serve fresh shrimp. Try to find shrimp with their heads and shells on—these tend to be freshest and most flavorful. When eating, pull off the shrimp heads and suck out the juice. | SERVES 2 OR MORE, PAIRED WITH A VEGETABLE DISH

½ cup white rice wine

6 thin slices fresh ginger

2 scallions, cut into 2-inch pieces

SAUCE

¼ cup vegetable oil

¼ cup soy sauce

2 tablespoons white rice wine

2 tablespoons minced fresh ginger

½ teaspoon sugar

1 pound medium shrimp

In a saucepan, combine 6 cups water, the wine, ginger, and scallions and bring to a boil.

Combine all the sauce ingredients in a small bowl and mix well.

Drop the shrimp into the boiling liquid and turn the heat down to medium. Gently cook the shrimp for about 3 minutes, until they have turned pink. Drain the shrimp by scooping them up with a spider strainer.

Arrange the shrimp on a plate and serve hot, with the sauce on the side.

HOT POT 涮

When I was growing up in Singapore in the 1960s, it was a developing country and much of the infrastructure was still quite basic. Air-conditioning was a luxury, so a majority of the buildings were constructed with large floor-to-ceiling French doors opening to outdoor spaces. This was especially true in many Chinese restaurants. One particularly beloved dining experience of my youth was to go to a hot pot meal at a seaside restaurant with such an open dining area.

A hot pot (火鍋) meal (more commonly known as a steamboat meal in Singapore) is a kind of DIY dining experience that revolves around a specially designed pot in the middle of the table. The pot has a chimney in the center, acting as the flue for the charcoal burning underneath. A doughnut-shaped trough full of boiling aromatic broth surrounds the chimney. Paper-thin slices of uncooked meat, seafood, and cut-up vegetables are ordered and brought to the table, where diners cook their food in the pot. The act of quickly cooking these extremely thin slices of meat in boiling liquid is known as *shuan* (涮) in Chinese. A variety of condiments, sauces, and flavored oils are also offered for creating personalized dipping sauces. As more food is cooked in the broth, it becomes richer. At the end of the meal, noodles of different types are brought out and eaten with the flavorful broth. Given the year-round hot weather of Singapore, one wonders why hot pot meals are so popular there. The only explanation is that it is a Chinese culinary tradition so cherished that even sweating and panting from the heat does not deter the craving!

Naturally, hot pot meals are more common during the winter months in mainland China, when friends and family huddle around the warm pot. In Beijing the Mongolian population of northern China cooks a lamb hot pot to ward off the bitter cold in the winter. In Sichuan a numbing and peppery stock known as *mala* stock (麻辣湯) has been popular for many years. During the past thirty years a pot with a divider in the middle was created, making it possible to serve a simple mild stock on one side with a *mala* stock on the other. Serving two stocks together has become so ubiquitous that it is now called *yuanyang* (鴛鴦) pot, named after Mandarin ducks, who mate for life and are inseparable.

For a good hot pot meal, the initial stock is undoubtedly the most important aspect. Although plain water could be used and will take on flavor as meat and vegetables are cooked in it, a good stock will enhance the dining experience exponentially. And with the *mala* stock, the entire flavor of the meal is carried to a different level.

As modern climate control has become the norm in Asia, the hot pot itself has evolved. The charcoal-fueled pot has largely been replaced with a butane or electric stove. In restaurants that specialize in serving hot pot meals, the stove is often built into the dining table, while at home portable stoves are customary. The pot has lost the center flue and is now just a single large bowl or one divided into two half-round compartments.

INGREDIENTS FOR HOT POT

Anything that can be cooked quickly is a fitting candidate for a hot pot meal; tender meat, seafood, soy products, and vegetables are all good choices.

Meats should be sliced very thin so they can be cooked quickly in the boiling liquid. The best way to do this is to partially freeze the meat, then cut it with a slicer. If you don't have access to a slicer, use a very sharp knife and cut the partially frozen meat as thin as possible. It is also possible to buy presliced meat specifically for a hot pot from Asian markets in major American cities.

Certain offal meat such as pig's or cow's stomach and intestine should be precooked before being sliced very thin. Others like liver and duck intestine can be thinly sliced and cooked entirely at the table.

When selecting fish, be sure to use firm-fleshed fish to minimize disintegration when cooking. Small mollusks and crustaceans can be cooked whole in the shell, whereas larger shellfish such as abalone or conch should be shelled and thinly sliced. Lobster should be cut up into small pieces, leaving the meat still attached to the shell; diners can dip each piece individually into the stock before prying the meat away from the shell.

Dumplings are also popular items for hot pot cooking, but only small, easily cooked dumplings are suitable. Examples include wonton, Cantonese *shui jiao* (small pork dumplings, or 水餃), and pork-filled egg dumplings (dumplings with an egg batter wrapper, or 蛋餃). They are all readily available in Chinatown markets.

For soybean products and vegetables, the list is endless. Tofu, tofu skin, and tofu puffs are all suitable. To add variety, frozen tofu or fried tofu can be used. Frozen tofu and tofu puffs have a spongy texture that absorbs the broth when cooked, rendering them extremely flavorful.

Mushrooms and root vegetables are also very desirable. All kinds of mushrooms can be served and they enrich the stock beautifully with their earthy flavors. Root vegetables should be cut into thin slices to make it easier to cook them through.

The chart at right is a list of some common foods typically offered in a hot pot meal.

Meat and Offal

Pork tenderloin	Beef liver
Pork liver	Beef tripe
Pig's blood curd	Lamb
Pig's intestine	Lamb tripe
Pig's stomach	Chicken breast
Beef tenderloin	Duck intestine

Seafood

Flounder	Squid
Tilapia	Clams
Carp	Mussels
Grouper	Abalone
Shrimp	Sea cucumber
Lobster	

Dumplings and Pastes

Pork dumplings	Shrimp paste
Shrimp dumplings	Shrimp balls
Egg dumplings with pork filling	Cuttlefish paste
	Cuttlefish balls
Fish paste	Pork meatballs
Fish balls	Beef meatballs

Soy Products

Tofu	Tofu puffs
Frozen tofu	Tofu skin

Vegetables

Napa cabbage	Oyster mushrooms
Spinach	Beech mushrooms
Chrysanthemum greens	Daikon
	Mountain yam
Shiitake mushrooms	Cilantro
Enoki mushrooms	

Noodles

Egg noodles	Bean noodles (glass noodles)
Rice noodles	

SAUCES FOR HOT POT

Once boiled, the cooked food is dipped in a sauce blended together by the diners themselves, using different types of condiments and sauces, which can vary by region. However, in modern China most items are available nationwide so the choice of sauces has become very large. There is no standard combination of sauce ingredients—it all depends on each diner's personal preference. The following is a list of commonly served condiments:

Chinese toasted sesame paste	Chinkiang black vinegar
Fermented tofu	Chile oil
Garlic chive blossom paste	Chile sauce
Soy sauce	Crisp-fried garlic
Fish sauce	Minced garlic
Sesame oil	Minced fresh ginger
Shaoxing cooking wine	Chopped scallions
	Sesame seeds
	Ground peanuts

STOCK FOR HOT POT

Traditionally, hot pot meals involved simply cooking in plain boiling water, but nowadays a flavorful stock is usually expected. Many restaurants in Asia have developed signature stocks from neighboring countries. Hot and sour Thai *tom yam*–style stock, Korean ginseng stock, and Japanese miso stock are just a few of the examples. But the two standard stocks available everywhere are plain chicken or pork stock and Sichuan *mala* stock.

For the plain stock simply make a chicken stock, pork stock, beef stock, or a compound stock (see page 90), then add slices of ginger, a few jujubes, and a tablespoon of goji berries. Replenish the hot pot with more stock as the meal progresses. Be adventurous and create unusual flavored stocks as you wish.

SICHUAN *MALA* HOT POT STOCK
麻辣火鍋底湯
SICHUAN

Mala *hot pot is found everywhere in China. It is a classic Sichuan dish served by both street vendors and fancy restaurants. The spicy hot and numbing sensation is sought after by many connoisseurs of Sichuan cooking. This* mala *stock is versatile and can be used as a soup base to cook other Sichuan dishes, such as pig's blood curd, fish balls, and other seafood.* | SERVES 6 OR MORE, ALONG WITH HOT POT INGREDIENTS

½ cup vegetable oil

2 ounces dried chiles

1 tablespoon Sichuan peppercorns

3 whole star anise

1 (2-inch) square of cassia bark

2 black cardamom pods

1 (2-inch-long) piece of fresh ginger

2 scallions, cut into 2-inch pieces

4 quarts Chicken and Pork Stock (page 90)

¼ cup chile oil

¼ cup Sichuan chile soybean paste

Put the vegetable oil, dried chile, Sichuan peppercorns, star anise, cassia bark, cardamom, ginger, and scallions in a medium saucepan and simmer over very low heat for 15 minutes, until the flavor has infused into the oil. Remove from the heat and let cool for about 15 minutes.

Pour enough of the stock into the hot pot to fill it two-thirds full. Add the vegetable oil, including the aromatics and spices, the chile oil, and the chile soybean paste and bring the stock to a boil. Cooking table-side can start immediately. Replenish the liquid with the remaining hot stock as it cooks down.

CHRYSANTHEMUM TEA HOT POT STOCK | 菊花火鍋底湯
GUANGDONG

For a simple flavorful hot pot soup base, this chrysanthemum tea stock is perfect. The chrysanthemum fragrance is subtle and will not overwhelm the natural flavors of the other ingredients. | SERVES 6 OR MORE, ALONG WITH HOT POT INGREDIENTS

4 quarts Chicken and Pork Stock (page 90)

1 (1-inch-long) piece of fresh ginger

10 dried chrysanthemum blossoms (chrysanthemum tea)

1 tablespoon goji berries

Pour enough of the stock into the hot pot to fill it three-quarters full. Add the rest of the ingredients and bring the stock to a boil. Cooking tableside can start immediately. Replenish the liquid with the remaining hot stock as it cooks down.

LAMB HOT POT STOCK
涮羊肉鍋底湯
MONGOLIAN

Traditionally, Mongolian-style lamb hot pot is basic, comprising sliced lamb meat, soybean products, mushrooms, and other vegetables. Dipping sauce options reflect northern Chinese taste and include sesame paste, garlic chive blossom paste, and lots of minced garlic. Many people nowadays bring out a whole lot of other items, but if a classic lamb hot pot meal is your goal, then that's it. | SERVES 6 OR MORE, ALONG WITH HOT POT INGREDIENTS

4 quarts lamb stock (see page 89)

1 (1-inch-long) piece of fresh ginger, cut into ¼-inch-thick slices

8 jujubes

1 tablespoon goji berries

3 large dried shiitake mushrooms, rehydrated (see page 78) and stemmed

DIPPING SAUCE OPTIONS

Chinese toasted sesame paste

Garlic chive blossom paste

Shaoxing cooking wine

Soy sauce

Fish sauce

Sesame oil

Chile oil

Minced garlic

Minced fresh ginger

Chopped scallions

Pour enough of the stock into the hot pot to fill it three-quarters full. Add the rest of the ingredients and bring the stock to a boil. Cooking tableside can start immediately. Serve the dipping sauce items of your choice alongside. Replenish the liquid with the remaining hot stock as it cooks down.

CHAPTER TWELVE

The Power of Steam

IN *LIJI*（禮記）, OR THE *BOOK OF RITES*, WHICH DATES BACK TO THE 1ST CENTURY, THERE IS A DESCRIPTION OF COOKING IN A VESSEL KNOWN AS A *YAN*（甗）. The bottom part of the *yan* was a three-legged cauldron with balloon legs called *li*（鬲）. Fitted on top of the cauldron was a vessel called a *zeng*（甑）, which had cross-shaped slits or openings at the bottom. Although not many covers were found at the excavation sites, it is believed that either wooden or bamboo covers were used with the *zeng*. This was the primitive vessel that early Chinese used to steam their food.

The actual cooking process has remained entirely unchanged; the only improvement is in the steaming utensils themselves. Bamboo steamers, and later perforated stainless steel steamers, were developed for use on the stovetop. In modern cooking, steaming has been formalized and can be classified into two main categories: simple steaming and flavored steaming.

Simple steaming is the basic steaming method. Fresh ingredients are suspended in a perforated vessel set over boiling water in a closed pot and cooked by the steam the water produces. They are then either served as is or dressed in a light sauce. Flavored steaming, on the other hand, is a lot more elaborate. The ingredients are marinated, then either covered with a spiced coating, wrapped in fragrant leaves, or submerged in an aromatic liquid before steaming. The results of these two steaming processes are dramatically different. One showcases the natural flavors of the main ingredients while the other highlights the combination and interplay of complex flavors.

Steamed dishes have developed their own characteristics in various regions. Many coastal areas are known for steaming seafood, whereas meat steaming is, naturally, more prevalent in the interior provinces. Southern steamed dishes are generally light and showcase the natural flavors of the ingredients, while regions that prefer stronger flavors kick their dishes up with local spices.

SIMPLE STEAMING | 清蒸

The eastern end of the strait between Hong Kong Island and mainland Kowloon is known as Lei Yue Mun, which translates as "Carp Gate." The villages on the Kowloon side of this entrance to Hong Kong harbor have become host to a row of fishmongers and restaurants along either side of the main alley that winds along the shore. Diners can choose fresh seafood from the vendors whose wall-to-wall aquarium tanks line one side of the alley and bring it to a restaurant on the other side to be cooked. It was here on a family trip in the 1970s that I came to appreciate the magnificence of simple steamed fresh seafood.

During the early part of the 20th century, Lei Yue Mun was populated by squatters who worked at a nearby quarry. As the population of these villages grew, fishing boats started docking near the waterfront to sell their daily catch. After the Second World War a few restaurants were established to serve the local community. As these restaurants became increasingly popular during the 1960s, the city planners formally developed the area into a seafood village and heavily promoted it. Lei Yue Mun is now a bustling dining destination for locals as well as tourists. Thankfully, the seafood remains fresh and delicious.

With simple steaming, ingredients are lightly seasoned and then cooked over hot steam without further adornment. A simple sauce is poured over the food just before serving. The advantage to this technique is that the natural essence of the ingredients comes through as the central flavor. Although used mostly for cooking fresh seafood, simple steaming can be applied to many other delicate ingredients such as tofu, chicken, and vegetables, which are sometimes seasoned with simple sauces before being steamed. It is a forgiving technique that results in perfectly cooked ingredients that taste like themselves.

STEAMED STRIPED BASS | 清蒸鱸魚

GUANGDONG

Steamed fish is the signature dish that epitomizes the Cantonese art of coaxing natural flavors from fresh ingredients. The ideal fish should have delicate, tender meat; good choices are bass, flounder, and grouper. | SERVES 2 OR MORE, PAIRED WITH A VEGETABLE DISH

1 whole striped bass (about 2 pounds), cleaned

2 tablespoons white rice wine

3 thin slices fresh ginger

SAUCE

2 tablespoons soy sauce

2 tablespoons white rice wine

1 teaspoon sugar

½ teaspoon ground white pepper

3 tablespoons vegetable oil

2 tablespoons julienned fresh ginger

2 tablespoons julienned scallion whites

4 cilantro sprigs

Slash the body of the fish diagonally at three places, spaced an inch apart, on both sides. Put the fish on an oval plate. Sprinkle the wine over the fish and arrange the ginger slices evenly on top.

Put a wire rack in a wok, add about 5 cups water, and bring it to a boil. (Alternatively, you can use a large pot filled with an inch of water or a traditional steamer.) Put the plate of fish on the rack. Cover the wok and steam for about 12 minutes or until the flesh on the thickest part of the fish separates easily from the bone.

While the fish is steaming, combine the sauce ingredients in a small saucepan, bring to a boil, and then keep warm over low heat.

Heat the vegetable oil in a small saucepan until it is just beginning to smoke, about 395°F.

When the fish is done, carefully remove the plate from the wok. Pour the sauce evenly over the fish, then pour the hot oil on top. (Be very careful when you pour the hot oil, as it will splatter.)

Garnish the fish with the julienned ginger, scallion whites, and cilantro sprigs.

STEAMED OYSTERS WITH FERMENTED BLACK BEAN SAUCE | 清蒸生蠔
GUANGDONG

One of the best ways to showcase the fresh briny taste of oysters is to steam them and then dress them with a simple fermented black bean sauce. Use plump fresh oysters, and be sure not to overcook them. | SERVES 2 OR MORE, PAIRED WITH A VEGETABLE DISH

24 oysters, such as Blue Point

SAUCE

¼ cup white rice wine

2 tablespoons soy sauce

2 tablespoons vegetable oil

1 tablespoon fermented black beans, coarsely chopped

1 tablespoon minced fresh ginger

1 teaspoon sugar

2 tablespoons finely chopped scallions

1 fresh red chile, finely chopped (optional)

Clean and shuck the oysters, retaining as much of the oyster liquor in the bottom shell as possible. Arrange them, on the half shell, on a round platter that can fit into a steamer. Keep the oysters refrigerated until ready to steam.

Combine the sauce ingredients in a small saucepan. Bring the sauce to a boil and then keep it warm over low heat.

Put a wire rack in a wok, add about 5 cups water, and bring it to a boil. (Alternatively, you can use a large pot filled with an inch of water or a traditional steamer.) Put the plate of oysters on the rack. Cover the wok and steam for about 3 minutes or until the oysters have shriveled slightly.

To serve, cover each oyster with a teaspoon of the warm fermented black bean sauce. Garnish with the chopped scallions and the chile if desired.

STEAMED CHICKEN LEGS WITH GOJI BERRIES | 清蒸雞腿
GUANGDONG

This is a simple and healthy dish that can be made at the last minute for a daily meal. The meat is tender and the skin is silky-smooth. The flavor is unassuming but savory, making it excellent for pairing with stronger-flavored vegetables such as bitter melon or chrysanthemum greens. | SERVES 2 OR MORE, PAIRED WITH A VEGETABLE DISH

1½ pounds chicken legs, cut crosswise into 1-inch-thick pieces

¼ cup white rice wine

6 thin slices fresh ginger

1 tablespoon goji berries

1 tablespoon soy sauce

½ teaspoon salt

¼ teaspoon ground white pepper

2 tablespoons sliced scallions

Put the chicken pieces in a medium saucepan and add enough water to cover the meat completely. Bring the water to a boil and parboil the chicken for 10 minutes. Drain the chicken and discard the water.

Put a wire rack in a wok, add about 5 cups water, and bring it to a boil. (Alternatively, you can use a large pot filled with an inch of water or a traditional steamer.) Put the chicken in a mixing bowl. Add the rice wine, ginger, goji berries, soy sauce, salt, and pepper and mix well. Transfer everything to a shallow bowl that will fit in the wok.

Put the bowl of chicken on the steamer rack, cover the wok, and steam the chicken for 20 minutes or until the meat is cooked through. (Prick the largest chicken piece with a fork to make sure the juices run clear.) Serve garnished with the scallions.

STEAMED CHICKEN LEGS
WITH GOGI BERRIES

STEAMED STUFFED TOFU | 蒸釀豆腐

HAKKA

According to Linda Lau Anusasananan, author of
The Hakka Cookbook, *this stuffed tofu dish is a
product of immigrants yearning to re-create familiar
food from home. When the Hakka people fled northern
China for the relative safety of the south, they could no
longer grow wheat in their new semitropical home, so
they began to stuff tofu with the meat filling they had
traditionally put inside dumplings. The result is this
now legendary Hakka dish.* | SERVES 2 OR MORE,
PAIRED WITH A SEAFOOD OR VEGETABLE DISH

STUFFING

4 ounces ground pork

4 ounces raw shrimp, coarsely chopped

3 large dried shiitake mushrooms, rehydrated
(see page 78) and minced

1 teaspoon tapioca starch

¼ teaspoon salt

¼ teaspoon ground white pepper

1 pound firm tofu, cut into 12 (1-inch) cubes
and patted dry

SAUCE

¼ cup Shaoxing cooking wine

¼ cup chicken stock (see page 88)

2 tablespoons vegetable oil

2 tablespoons soy sauce

1 teaspoon sugar

1 tablespoon chopped scallions

1 tablespoon chopped cilantro

1 teaspoon chopped fresh red chile (optional)

Put a wire rack in a wok, add about 5 cups water,
and bring it to a boil. (Alternatively, you can use a
large pot filled with an inch of water or a traditional
steamer.)

Meanwhile, mix all the stuffing ingredients
together in a bowl and divide the mixture into
12 portions. Use a teaspoon to scoop out a small
portion of the tofu from the middle of the top of a
tofu cube. Then insert a portion of the meat stuffing
into the cavity, forming a small lump on the top. Do
this for each of the tofu pieces.

Arrange the stuffed tofu pieces on a plate with the
stuffing upward. Put the plate on the steamer rack,
cover the wok, and steam the tofu for 12 minutes or
until the stuffing is cooked through.

While the tofu is steaming, combine all the sauce
ingredients in a small saucepan, bring to a boil, then
turn off the heat.

When the tofu is ready, remove the plate from the
steamer and pour the sauce over the top. Garnish the
dish with the chopped scallions and cilantro, adding
the red chiles if you choose.

FLAVORED STEAMING | 粉蒸

On the opposite end of the steaming spectrum is flavored steaming, which heavily alters the flavor of the star ingredient. The technique calls for marinating the main ingredient with spices and sauces, coating it with spice-blended cracked rice, or submerging it in a spiced liquid while steaming. This is an excellent cooking method for sturdier-textured and stronger-flavored meats such as beef, pork belly, and pork ribs.

Unlike simple steaming, the final dish is considerably complex. The spices and sauces often completely overpower the natural taste of the main ingredient. However, this does not make the dish any less delicious.

One specific flavored-steaming technique is called *kou* (扣) and is used for pork belly. The meat is sliced thin and arranged decoratively at the bottom of a bowl. Then preserved mustard greens or blocks of taro are piled on top of the meat. An aromatic liquid is poured into the bowl, and the contents are steamed. At the end of cooking, the sauce is drained and thickened. To serve the final dish, the bowl is flipped over a deep plate and served upside down so that the decorative pork belly is beautifully displayed on the top. Finally, the thickened sauce is poured over the meat.

STEAMED PORK MEAT PATTY
WITH SALTED FISH | 鹹魚蒸肉餅
GUANGDONG

A staple at Cantonese home dinner, steamed pork meat patty is simple yet delicious. The basic recipe calls for mixing ground pork with chopped salted fish, and a salted duck egg is often cracked on top and steamed. The finished meat patty ends up full of umami. | SERVES 2 OR MORE, PAIRED WITH A VEGETABLE DISH

1 pound lean ground pork

1 ounce salted fish, such as croaker or carp, minced

3 ounces fresh or canned water chestnuts (drained if canned), coarsely chopped

1 tablespoon minced fresh ginger

2 tablespoons tapioca starch

¼ cup white rice wine

¼ teaspoon salt

¼ teaspoon ground white pepper

1 uncooked salted duck egg (optional)

1 tablespoon finely chopped scallions

Put a wire rack in a wok, add about 5 cups water, and bring it to a boil. (Alternatively, you can use a large pot filled with an inch of water or a traditional steamer.)

Meanwhile, combine the pork, salted fish, water chestnuts, ginger, tapioca starch, wine, salt, and pepper in a bowl and mix well with a wooden spoon, stirring vigorously until smooth. Spread the pork mixture evenly on a round plate, forming it into a ½-inch-thick patty. Make a slight depression in the middle of the cake and crack the egg into the depression, if using.

Put the plate on the rack, cover the wok, and steam for about 10 minutes or until the meat is cooked through. (Check by piercing a knife through the patty and lifting a small piece.)

Remove the plate from the steaming rack and garnish with the chopped scallions.

STEAMED RED SNAPPER WITH SALTED PLUM | 鹹梅蒸紅鯛魚

CHAOZHOU

Salted plum in brine is almost never eaten by itself; it is usually added as a condiment to flavor a dish. This red snapper dish is based on a Chaozhou region recipe for steamed carp. The slightly spicy sweet-and-sour flavor perfectly complements the mild taste and slightly flaky flesh of the fish. | SERVES 2 OR MORE, PAIRED WITH A VEGETABLE DISH

1 whole red snapper (about 2 pounds), cleaned

¼ cup white rice wine

6 salted plums in brine, pitted and coarsely chopped

1 fresh red chile, seeded and coarsely chopped

1 teaspoon sugar

¼ teaspoon ground white pepper

3 thin slices fresh ginger, plus 2 tablespoons julienned fresh ginger

¼ cup vegetable oil

1 scallion white, julienned

Slash the body of the fish diagonally at three places, spaced an inch apart, on both sides. Put the fish on an oval plate.

Combine the wine, salted plum, chile, sugar, and pepper in a bowl and mix well. Spread the mixture all over the entire fish, and arrange the ginger slices evenly on top. Let stand for about 15 minutes.

Meanwhile, put a wire rack in a wok, add about 5 cups water, and bring to a boil. (Alternatively, you can use a large pot filled with an inch of water or a traditional steamer.)

Put the plate of fish on the rack, cover the wok, and steam for about 12 minutes or until the flesh on the thickest part of the fish separates easily from the bone.

Heat the vegetable oil in a saucepan until it is just beginning to smoke, about 395°F. Remove the plate from the wok and discard the sliced ginger. Pour the hot oil over the fish and garnish with the julienned ginger and scallion white.

STEAMED BEEF WITH CRACKED RICE | 粉蒸牛肉

SICHUAN

This steamed beef dish is unique in that the beef slices are coated with cracked rice before cooking, which allows the rice to absorb the juices that seep out of the meat. | SERVES 2 OR MORE, PAIRED WITH A VEGETABLE DISH

MARINADE

2 tablespoons white rice wine

1 tablespoon soy sauce

2 tablespoons Sichuan chile bean paste

1 tablespoon minced garlic

1 tablespoon minced fresh ginger

1 teaspoon sugar

¼ teaspoon Sichuan peppercorn powder

1 pound flank steak, cut against the grain into ⅛-inch-thick slices

¼ cup white rice

1 dried lotus leaf, rehydrated (see page 78) in cold water

Chopped cilantro

Mix the marinade ingredients together in a shallow dish. Add the beef slices, mix well, and let marinate in the refrigerator for 30 minutes.

Meanwhile, toast the rice in a wok over medium heat, stirring continuously to prevent scorching, until it turns slightly brown, about 8 minutes. Let the rice cool completely on a plate, then pulse it in a blender or a food processor until its texture resembles coarse sand.

Line a 10-inch bamboo steamer with the rehydrated lotus leaf. Pour about 3 cups water into a wok and bring it to a boil. Coat the beef slices on all sides with the cracked rice and arrange them in layers on the lotus leaf.

Put the bamboo steamer in the wok, cover the steamer, and steam the beef for about 30 minutes or until it is completely cooked and tender.

Serve the beef in the steamer, garnished with the chopped cilantro.

STEAMED PORK BELLY WITH PICKLED MUSTARD GREENS | 梅菜扣肉

HAKKA

The fermented dried mustard greens in this recipe are known as meigan cai. *With a sweet and salty taste, this dried pickled green is an iconic Hakka ingredient. Paired with pork belly, its flavor blends with the fatty taste of the meat to produce an incredibly aromatic dish.* | SERVES 2 OR MORE, PAIRED WITH A VEGETABLE DISH

12 ounces pork belly

1 tablespoon dark soy sauce

2 cups vegetable oil

4 ounces fermented dried mustard greens (*meigan cai*), cut into small pieces

2 garlic cloves

SAUCE

3 tablespoons *laojiu* cooking wine

1 tablespoon dark soy sauce

1 tablespoon soy sauce

2 teaspoons sugar

1 teaspoon tapioca starch

Put the pork belly in a pot and add enough cold water to cover it completely. Slowly bring the water to a boil and then parcook the pork belly for 20 minutes. Drain the meat, discarding the water, and let it cool just until you can handle it.

Spread the dark soy sauce over the entire pork belly and let it marinate at room temperature for about 15 minutes.

Heat the vegetable oil in a wok over high heat until it is beginning to shimmer, about 350°F. Crisp the skin of the pork belly by lowering it into the oil, skin-side down. Use a spatula to move the pork belly around in the wok so it doesn't stick to the bottom. Fry the skin for about 3 minutes or until it is brown and covered with blisters. Remove the meat from the oil and let it cool.

Remove all the oil from the wok and reserve for future use. Wipe the wok dry and put a wire rack in the wok, add about 5 cups water, and bring it to a boil. (Alternatively, you can use a large pot filled with an inch of water or a traditional steamer.)

Meanwhile, cut the pork belly into 3 by 2-inch pieces that are ¼ inch thick. Arrange the pieces decoratively on the bottom of a 7-inch heatproof bowl. Spread the mustard greens on top of the pork belly and top with the garlic cloves.

Pour the sauce ingredients all over the pork and then put the bowl on the steamer rack. Cover the wok and steam for about 1½ hours, until the meat is tender.

Remove the bowl from the steaming rack and pour all the liquid from the bowl into a saucepan. Flip the pork belly over onto a serving plate.

In a small bowl, mix the tapioca starch with 2 tablespoons water to make a slurry. Bring the sauce to a boil over medium heat, stir in the tapioca slurry, and cook until the sauce has thickened, about 1 minute. Pour the sauce evenly over the pork belly.

STEAMED STICKY RICE WITH SEAFOOD | 海鮮糯米飯
GUANGDONG

*I don't know what it is about sticky rice that always
makes it such a crowd-pleaser. Maybe it's the smooth,
glutinous mouthfeel or perhaps the earthy aroma;
whatever the reason, sticky rice always transforms a
mundane rice dish into a delicacy. This recipe is a classic
Cantonese rice dish with seafood. There is no set rule
for which types of seafood to include as a topping—
select whatever is freshest.* | SERVES 2 AS A ONE-POT
MEAL, 4 AS A SIDE DISH

1 dried lotus leaf, rehydrated (see page 78)
in cold water

2 tablespoons vegetable oil

1 tablespoon minced garlic

1 tablespoon minced fresh ginger

2 cups glutinous rice, soaked in 2 cups water
for at least 4 hours

1 teaspoon salt

¼ teaspoon ground white pepper

TOPPING

2 tablespoons vegetable oil

1 tablespoon minced garlic

1 tablespoon minced fresh ginger

½ ounce dried shiitake mushrooms, rehydrated
(see page 78) and cut into ½-inch-wide pieces

4 ounces fresh or canned bamboo shoots
(drained if canned), cut into ⅛-inch-thick slices

2 tablespoons white rice wine

2 teaspoons soy sauce

1 teaspoon sugar

¼ teaspoon ground white pepper

8 ounces medium shrimp, shelled and deveined

8 ounces bay scallops

8 ounces squid, cleaned and cut into 1-inch squares

2 tablespoons chopped scallions

2 tablespoons chopped cilantro

Line a 10-inch bamboo steamer with the rehydrated
lotus leaf, covering the bottom and sides. Use a pair
of scissors to cut off any excess leaf around the edge
of the steamer.

Heat a wok over high heat until a droplet of water
sizzles and evaporates immediately upon contact.
Swirl the vegetable oil around the bottom and sides
of the wok to coat it evenly. Add the garlic and
ginger to the wok and stir-fry until fragrant, about
30 seconds. Turn the heat off.

Drain the rice thoroughly and add it to the wok.
Add the salt and pepper and mix well. Transfer
the rice to the lined bamboo steamer and spread it
out evenly.

Clean the wok, pour in about 3 cups water, and
bring the water to a boil. Put the bamboo steamer
in the wok, cover the steamer, and steam the rice for
30 minutes or until it is soft. When the rice is cooked,
remove the steamer from the wok and put it on a
large round platter, covered to keep warm.

Discard the water from the wok and dry the
wok completely. Heat the wok over high heat until a
droplet of water sizzles and evaporates immediately
upon contact. Swirl the vegetable oil around the
bottom and sides of the wok to coat it evenly.
Add the garlic and ginger to the wok and stir-fry
until fragrant, about 30 seconds. Add the shiitake
mushrooms and bamboo shoots and stir-fry for
another 30 seconds. Add the wine, soy sauce, sugar,
and pepper and continue to stir-fry for another
30 seconds. Add the shrimp, scallops, and squid,
and stir-fry for 30 seconds or until the seafood is
thoroughly cooked and has changed color.

Uncover the steamer and spread the topping over
the rice. Serve from the steamer, garnished with the
chopped scallions and cilantro.

CHAPTER THIRTEEN

The Making of Hearty Soups

LUOYANG（洛陽）WAS THE CAPITAL OF MANY
ANCIENT CHINESE DYNASTIES DATING BACK
TO THE 17TH CENTURY BCE, AND THE AREA
SURROUNDING LUOYANG IS CONSIDERED TO
BE THE BIRTHPLACE OF CHINESE CULTURE.
But the city did not reach its height of prosperity until much later, during
the Sui（隋）and Tang（唐）Dynasties, around the 6th century. Its population
had by then ballooned to a million residents—an unprecedented size
for that era. Luoyang's international commerce extended all the way to
the Middle East and Europe via the Silk Road, and to East Asia through
canals and the Yangtze River. It was during this period that an unusual
soup-based feast was developed; it became known as the Luoyang
Water Banquet.

Initially created as a celebration banquet for the nobility and for feudal
lords, the feast consists of twenty-four dishes with soupy gravies and
sauces: eight cold ones and sixteen hot ones. The first eight cold dishes
are served together as one course along with wine. This is followed by the
hot dishes served in three courses: four dishes in the first course, eight
dishes during the second course, and a final course of four dishes. The
offerings include many different types of meat and vegetables.

It has been speculated that the Water Banquet owes its existence to the fact that the Luoyang region is relatively arid. The liquid in the meal adds moisture to the body. When Empress Wu Zetian (武则天), the only female ruler of China, came to power during the middle of the Tang Dynasty, she moved the capital from Chang'an to Luoyang and acquired a special fondness for the Water Banquet. It is claimed that she enjoyed the banquet because the moisture in the meal improved and maintained her complexion.

The Water Banquet illustrates the long and enduring role that soup making has played in Chinese culinary culture and regional traditions, especially the preponderance of soup making in the Fujian province and southern China. Peng Yiwan, a culinary expert of Fujian, speculates that, during the Tang Dynasty, officials from the empress's court spread this soup culture as they expanded their administration.

Various techniques have had an impact on a broad range of regional cooking in China, but four main ones can be distinguished. They include clear soup, thickened soup, braised soup, and steamed soup—each with distinct characteristics. Clear soup is a simple broth containing cut-up ingredients. For a thickened soup, bite-size ingredients are cooked in a stock that's then thickened with starch. Braised and steamed soups are slow cooked in a clay pot either directly over low heat or over boiling water.

CLEAR SOUP | 湯

Clear soup is the most typical Chinese soup: clear rich broth combined with bite-size ingredients, served unembellished. Yet this simple method can produce some of the heartiest soups ever known. The key is to use a rich stock base and to select ingredients that create appealing flavor combinations. Although there are many traditional combinations of ingredients in classic soups, it is often the home cook who determines what seasonal or on-hand ingredients will go into the soup of the day.

Although rich savory stock is the flavor booster for making clear soup, using plain boiling water is not unheard of in a Chinese home kitchen. A simple Chinese soup of laver and sliced pork can be made from boiling water in minutes. I remember how at home in Singapore our family cook, Ah Eng, routinely made this soup when my brother and I would return from school at lunchtime. She would boil a pot of water, coat some pork loin strips with a simple velveting mixture, and drop them into the water. A bit of cooking wine, thinly julienned ginger, and dried seaweed went in next. Then a couple of beaten eggs were added to create swirls of fluffy egg ribbons. Finally, she would adjust the seasoning and serve the soup with chopped scallions. Although uncomplicated, it was one of my favorite soups to accompany a simple lunch.

Chinese clear soup can be made at the last minute as a supplement to a meal or as an elaborate, elegant soup for a banquet. The method is simple, yet the finished soup can be made complex by selecting creative combinations of ingredients.

CHICKEN SOUP WITH YOUNG COCONUT | 嫩椰煲雞湯

HAINAN

Coconut is a major crop on Hainan Island. Unfortunately it is rarely used in cooking elsewhere in China. This chicken soup, made with young coconut water and tender meat, is rich and full of tropical flavor. | SERVES 6 OR MORE, AS A SOUP COURSE

8 ounces boneless, skinless chicken breast, cut into ⅛-inch-thick slices

2 whole young coconuts

4 cups chicken stock (see page 88)

6 thin slices fresh ginger

1 tablespoon goji berries

2 teaspoons salt

½ teaspoon ground white pepper

Put the chicken in a pot, add enough water to cover it completely, and bring the water to a boil over medium heat. Parboil the chicken for about 3 minutes, skimming off any scum that forms on the surface. Drain the chicken completely and discard the water.

Using a cleaver, cut off the top of the coconuts to make a hole about 2 inches in diameter—be careful not to spill any of the coconut water that is inside. Drain the coconut water into a container. Skim off any coconut husk or impurities from the coconut water.

Cut each coconut in half to expose the young tender meat. Use a spoon to scoop 1-inch pieces of coconut meat into a bowl.

Pour the chicken stock and the coconut water into a pot and bring to a boil over medium heat. Add the chicken, coconut meat, ginger, goji berries, salt, and pepper to the pot and bring to a boil. Cook for 3 minutes, until all the ingredients are heated through.

EIGHT TREASURES WINTER MELON SOUP | 八寶冬瓜湯

GUANGDONG

This classic soup has long been served at traditional Chinese banquets, often presented in a whole winter melon carved into a tureen shape. Eight different ingredients, not counting the melon, constitute the eight treasures. The selection of these ingredients can be seasonal and the choice is up to the cook. The typical suggestions in this recipe are just a start. | SERVES 6 OR MORE, AS A SOUP COURSE

6 cups Chicken, Pork, and Ham Stock (page 90)

6 ounces winter melon, peeled, seeded, and cut into ½-inch cubes

1 small carrot, cut crosswise into ⅛-inch-thick rounds

¼ cup white rice wine

2 ounces medium shrimp, shelled and deveined

2 ounces sea scallops, cut crosswise into ¼-inch-thick rounds

2 ounces straw mushrooms, halved

2 ounces gingko

2 ounces fresh or canned bamboo shoots (drained if canned), cut into ½-inch squares

2 ounces ham, cut into ½-inch squares

1 ounce dried shiitake mushrooms, rehydrated (see page 78), stemmed, and quartered

1 teaspoon salt

½ teaspoon ground white pepper

Pour the stock into a large pot and bring it to a boil. Add the winter melon and carrot to the pot and boil gently over medium heat for 5 minutes or until they are soft. Add the wine, shrimp, scallops, straw mushrooms, gingko, bamboo shoots, ham, shiitake mushrooms, salt, and pepper and continue to boil for another 3 minutes, until everything is heated through.

EIGHT TREASURES WINTER MELON SOUP

Although the term *geng* (羹) is used nowadays to describe a thickened soup, it was used in ancient China to refer to a dish made by cooking meat in liquid to create a stew (see page 189). Thus *geng* is an ancient concept that has evolved into one of the finest soups known in Chinese cooking, often featuring exotic ingredients such as seafood, fancy mushrooms, and rare vegetables.

A thickened soup turns out best when started with a rich stock made from bones and aromatics. A good soup base will not only enhance the final soup's flavor but also provide body. Solid ingredients are added after being cut into small pieces. If meat or seafood is called for in a recipe, it is always taken off the bone or picked from the shell first. Finally, ribbons of egg are swirled into the mixture before thickening is added to create a silky-smooth soup. It's an elegant achievement of Chinese soup making.

WEST LAKE BEEF SOUP
西湖牛肉羹
ZHEJIANG

Hangzhou is a city in Zhejiang province on the eastern shore of West Lake, a celebrated body of water with a long history of literary and political associations. This soup is thought to have originated in Hangzhou and to have been named after the adjacent lake because the swirling egg and tofu in the soup resemble the eddies on the lake's surface. That explanation may be a legend, but the simple yet savory taste of the soup itself has made it a legendary dish. | SERVES 6 OR MORE, AS A SOUP COURSE

8 ounces ground beef

2 tablespoons tapioca starch

6 cups beef stock (see page 89) or water

4 ounces soft tofu, cut into 1/8-inch dice

3 large dried shiitake mushrooms, rehydrated (see page 78) and cut into 1/8-inch dice

1 tablespoon minced fresh ginger

1 large egg white, lightly beaten

2 teaspoons salt

1/2 teaspoon ground white pepper

3 tablespoons julienned scallion greens

6 cilantro sprigs

Put the beef in a pot and add enough water to completely cover it. Bring the water to a boil and parcook the beef for 2 minutes. Then drain it completely and discard the water.

In a small bowl, mix the tapioca starch with 2 tablespoons water to make a slurry.

Pour the beef stock into the pot and bring it to a boil. Add the beef, tofu, mushrooms, and ginger. Bring to a boil again and swirl the egg white into the soup. Use a ladle to slowly stir the soup one turn to spread the egg white around. Season the soup with the salt and pepper. Bring the soup to a boil over medium heat, stir in the tapioca slurry, and cook until thickened, about 1 minute.

Garnish the soup with the scallions and cilantro.

CRABMEAT AND WHITE ASPARAGUS SOUP | 蘆筍蟹肉羹

GUANGDONG

Popular during the 1960s, this soup always reminds me of mid-20th-century culture. Despite its retro feel, I never tire of it. Canned or jarred white asparagus is traditional, but I see no reason not to use fresh white asparagus when it is in season. | SERVES 6 OR MORE, AS A SOUP COURSE

2 (8-ounce) live crabs

3 tablespoons tapioca starch

6 cups chicken stock (see page 88)

8 ounces white asparagus, cut on the diagonal into ¼-inch-thick slices

1 teaspoon salt

¼ teaspoon ground white pepper

1 large egg white

3 tablespoons thinly sliced scallions

Put a wire rack in a wok, add about 5 cups water, and bring it to a boil.

Kill the crabs by stabbing them in the belly with a knife. Put the crabs on a shallow plate, put the plate on the rack, and cover the wok. Steam the crabs for about 10 minutes or until they have turned bright red and are cooked through. Remove from the rack and let cool.

Pull the body of each crab away from the shell. Scrape the bright orange roe from the shell and break it apart into small pieces. Set the roe aside. Remove the gills from the body and discard them. Crack each crab's body and claws and pick the meat out of the shell using a lobster pick or toothpick. Set the crabmeat aside.

In a small bowl, mix the tapioca starch with ⅓ cup water to make a slurry.

In a medium pot, bring the chicken stock to a boil over medium heat. Add the white asparagus and cook for about 3 minutes, until just tender. Add the crabmeat, crab roe, salt, and pepper and bring to a boil again. Swirl the egg white into the soup. Use a ladle to slowly stir the soup one turn to spread the egg white around. Continue cooking for another minute or until the egg is completely cooked.

Bring the soup to a boil over medium heat, stir in the tapioca slurry, and cook until thickened, about 1 minute.

Serve garnished with the sliced scallions.

When a Soup Is Not a Soup: *Hui* | 燴

The technique for making a thickened soup is known in Chinese as *hui*. *Geng* soup itself is a product of the *hui* technique. Yet the *hui* technique is also often used for making braised dishes with lots of thickened gravy. The word *hui* is used to refer to such a gravy dish as well as the technique that produces the dish. This dual usage of *hui* never fails to confuse many people about the difference between a *hui* dish and a *geng* dish. To be clear, when a dish is made using the *hui* process with bite-size ingredients plus a thick gravy, then it is called a *hui* braised dish. But adding extra stock to the dish and making it a soup turns it into a *geng*.

MOCK SHARK FIN SOUP | 素魚翅羹

GUANGDONG

Shark fin consists mainly of soft collagen and has a chewy, gelatinous texture; not much taste is discernible. To imitate this texture, Japanese yam cake, called konnyaku, *is often used in place of the endangered fins. In Asia it is possible to purchase* konnyaku *that has been extruded into thin strands that look like shark fins. Alternatively, block* konnyaku *can be purchased and then cut into thin strands. Traditionally the soup's flavor comes from the stock and other ingredients, so even with the mock shark fins it will taste very similar to true shark fin soup. This recipe calls for vegetarian stock to make a vegetarian dish, but if Chicken, Pork, and Ham Stock (page 90) is used, the soup will taste even closer to the original.* | SERVES 6 OR MORE, AS A SOUP COURSE

2 cups mung bean sprouts

6 cups vegetarian stock (see page 89)

6 ounces *konnyaku* (Japanese yam cake, preferably containing seaweed powder), cut into thin strands 2 inches long and ¹⁄₁₆ inch thick

4 ounces fresh or canned bamboo shoots (drained if canned), julienned

2 ounces dried kelp, rehydrated (see page 78) and julienned

1 ounce dried wood ear mushroom, rehydrated (see page 78) and julienned

2 teaspoons salt

½ teaspoon ground white pepper

3 tablespoons tapioca starch

1 large egg, lightly beaten

½ cup Chinkiang black vinegar

Bring a saucepan of water to a boil.

Trim both ends of the mung bean sprouts, keeping only the crunchy white part. (Known as "silver sprouts" or *yinya* [銀芽], these sprouts regularly accompany shark fin soup.) Blanch the sprouts in the boiling water for just about a minute. Drain and set aside.

Bring the stock to a boil in a pot over medium heat. Add the *konnyaku*, bamboo shoots, kelp, wood ear mushroom, salt, and pepper. Simmer the soup for about 20 minutes, until all the ingredients are tender.

Meanwhile, mix the tapioca starch with ⅓ cup water in a small bowl to make a slurry.

Swirl the egg into the soup. Use a ladle to slowly stir the soup one turn to spread the egg around. Continue cooking for another minute or until the egg is completely cooked. Bring the soup to a boil over medium heat, stir in the tapioca slurry, and cook until thickened, about 1 minute.

Serve the soup with the sprouts and black vinegar on the side.

HUI BRAISED TOFU WITH BAMBOO PITH MUSHROOMS | 竹笙燴豆腐

GUANGDONG

Bamboo pith mushroom (phallus indusiatus) is a type of wild mushroom found in southern China. It has a spongy stem and a cap with a lacy veil extension, hence their English name, "veiled lady mushroom." The Chinese call it bamboo pith because the texture and tube-shaped stem resemble the inside of a bamboo stem. This mushroom is prized by the Chinese and often served at fancy banquets. It can be found in most Chinatown markets. | SERVES 2 OR MORE, PAIRED WITH A VEGETABLE DISH SUCH AS GARLIC STIR-FRIED GREENS (PAGE 100)

3 ounces dried bamboo pith mushrooms, rehydrated (see page 78)

4 ounces enoki mushrooms

2 tablespoons tapioca starch

2 tablespoons vegetable oil

4 thin slices fresh ginger

2 garlic cloves, thinly sliced

2 cups chicken stock (see page 88), vegetarian stock (see page 89), or water

2 tablespoons oyster sauce or vegetarian stir-fry sauce

¼ cup Shaoxing cooking wine

1 tablespoon soy sauce

1 teaspoon salt

¼ teaspoon ground white pepper

1 small carrot, peeled and cut on the diagonal into ⅛-inch-thick slices

10 ounces soft tofu, cut into 2-inch-long strips cut ¼ inch thick

2 ounces snow peas, ends pinched and discarded

Cut off and discard the cap and root end of the bamboo pith mushrooms, leaving the stem intact. Cut off and discard the root ends of the enoki mushrooms and separate the mushrooms.

In a small bowl, mix the tapioca starch with ⅓ cup water to make a slurry.

Heat a wok over high heat until a droplet of water sizzles and evaporates immediately upon contact. Swirl the vegetable oil around the bottom and sides of the wok to coat it evenly. Add the ginger and garlic to the wok and stir-fry until fragrant, about 30 seconds. Add the stock, oyster sauce, wine, soy sauce, salt, and pepper, mix well, and bring to a boil.

Add the carrot and cook for 3 minutes or until tender. Add the bamboo pith and enoki mushrooms and tofu, and cook for about 2 minutes until all of the ingredients are heated through. Add the snow peas and continue to cook for another 2 minutes, until they are crisp-tender. Stir in the starch slurry and continue to cook until thickened, about 1 minute.

BRAISED SOUP 燉湯

Boiling meat slowly with other ingredients to make a soup is an ancient technique that can be traced back to the Bronze Age, and it remains one of the most beloved methods for cooking tough cuts of meat, perhaps because it creates a delicious broth in the process. The braised soup technique has developed into a highly sophisticated process. Several variations have been developed, based upon two different heat sources: direct heat through a clay pot and steam heat. The Chinese character *dun* (燉) for "braising soup" is also used to refer to white braised dishes (see page 219). The techniques are fundamentally the same; the main difference is that much more liquid is involved in soup making.

With braised soup the ingredient selection is very important. This method generally uses good marbleized meat that can withstand long, slow cooking. Pork shoulder, fresh ham, and ham hock are all excellent choices, as are beef or lamb cuts typically used for stewing and braising. Duck and shellfish also make excellent ingredients for soup braising. What is important is to choose ingredients that can produce a rich, clear broth.

As in all other Chinese braising methods, the first step is to parboil the meat. Parboiling not only seals the meat, but it also curdles the blood and impurities so that they can be easily removed to produce a clear broth.

Once the parboiling is completed, the meat is transferred to either a clay pot or a smaller pot for the braising process. Enough liquid is added to the pot to cover the meat by about an inch. Then aromatics and spices are added and the slow-cooking process begins. Simmering can last for 2 to 3 hours, depending upon the meat. Any accompanying vegetables are added halfway through or just before completion, depending upon the ingredients.

DUCK SOUP WITH PICKLED MUSTARD GREENS | 酸菜鴨肉湯
HAKKA

Cooking with pickled mustard greens is very common in southern China and is part of Hakka cuisine. This duck soup is a classic example. After simmering for hours, the soup becomes infused with a very rich duck flavor and the pickle further enhances its taste. | SERVES 6 OR MORE, AS A SOUP COURSE

½ Long Island duckling (1½ pounds), cut into 12 pieces

6 ounces pickled mustard greens (*suan cai*), cut into 1-inch squares

1 (1-inch-long) piece of fresh ginger, crushed with the flat side of a knife

½ teaspoon salt

¼ teaspoon ground white pepper

Put the duck pieces in a pot and add enough water to cover them completely. Bring the water to a boil over medium heat and parboil the duck for about 20 minutes, continuously skimming off any scum that forms on the surface. Drain the duck completely and discard the water.

Put the duck, pickled mustard greens, ginger, and 8 cups water in the pot and bring the water to a boil. Cover the pot and slowly simmer the soup over low heat for 2 hours, until the soup is infused with flavor. Season with the salt and pepper.

MILKY FISH SOUP WITH DILL | 茴香鯪魚湯
SHANDONG

Dill is common in northern Chinese cooking and this fish soup is an excellent way of showcasing its herbal aroma. Here the dill is used in a large quantity, as if it were a vegetable. | SERVES 4 OR MORE, AS A SOUP COURSE

2 (1-pound) whole croakers, cleaned

2 cups vegetable oil

6 thin slices fresh ginger

5 cups Milky Fish Stock (page 91) or water

½ cup Shaoxing cooking wine

1 teaspoon salt

¼ teaspoon ground white pepper

6 ounces soft tofu, cut into ¾-inch cubes

3 ounces dill, cut into 1½-inch-long pieces including stems

Slash the body of each fish diagonally in three places, spaced ½ inch apart, on both sides.

Heat the vegetable oil in a wok over high heat until it is beginning to shimmer, about 350°F. Fry the fish in the oil for about 3 minutes on each side, until they are lightly browned. Remove the fish and drain them on paper towels.

Remove all but 2 tablespoons of the vegetable oil from the wok. Add the ginger to the wok and stir-fry over high heat until fragrant, about 30 seconds. Add the fish stock, wine, salt, and pepper and bring to a boil. Add the fish, cover the wok, and cook over high heat for about 15 minutes, until the fish is tender. Add the tofu to the wok and continue to cook for 10 minutes, until it is heated through.

Uncover the wok and stir the dill into the soup. Boil for another 30 seconds before serving. Remove the meat from the fish and serve it in individual bowls topped with soup.

Milky Soup | 奶湯

A unique variation of soup making that could be mistaken as a failed soup has a rather interesting name. Chinese "milky soup" is not made from any dairy product, but rather from meat stock that has been vigorously boiled to make it cloudy. Boiling creates an emulsion containing a high level of fat from whatever type of meat is being used, giving the stock a milky appearance.

This is not exactly a special technique: any of the soup-making methods can be used to make milky soup. The difference is in how the temperature is controlled. Whereas braised clear soup requires slow, gentle cooking, braised milky soup uses a high temperature to roil the soup, mixing the fats and broth to form a cloudy emulsion.

HAM AND PORK SHANK SOUP WITH WINTER BAMBOO | 醃篤鮮

SHANGHAI

Winter in Shanghai is never severe, but it is characterized by a prevalent dampness. Shanghai residents are therefore grateful for this soup made with fresh pork shank, ham, and bamboo shoots. Slow cooked until the broth becomes rich and flavorful, it is just the remedy for that winter chill. | SERVES 6 OR MORE, AS A SOUP COURSE

2 pounds Chinese salted pork or cured ham, cut into ½-inch cubes

2 pounds boneless fresh pork shank, cut into ½-inch cubes

1 fresh winter bamboo shoot (about 12 ounces), or 8 ounces canned bamboo shoots, drained

1 (1-inch-long) piece of fresh ginger, crushed with the flat side of a knife

8 cups pork stock (see page 89) or water

1 teaspoon salt

¼ teaspoon ground white pepper

2 scallions, cut into 1-inch pieces

In a bowl, soak the Chinese salted pork or ham in 4 cups water for 3 hours to dissolve some of the salt. Discard the water.

Meanwhile, put the fresh pork shank in a pot, add enough water to cover it completely, and parboil the pork for about 10 minutes, skimming off any scum that forms on the surface. Drain the pork completely and discard the water.

If using a fresh winter bamboo shoot, follow the instructions on how to prep fresh bamboo shoots on page 82. Then cut the bamboo shoot crosswise into ¹⁄₁₆-inch-thick slices. If using canned bamboo shoots, simply cut them into ¹⁄₁₆-inch-thick slices.

Put the pork shank, ham, bamboo shoots, ginger, and pork stock in a large Chinese clay pot or Dutch oven with a cover. Simmer the soup, covered, over very low heat for 3 hours, until it is infused with flavor.

Just before serving, add the salt and pepper and garnish with the scallions.

PIG STOMACH SOUP WITH MANILA CLAMS | 蛤仔豬肚湯
FUJIAN

At first glance the combination of pig stomach and Manila clams in a soup may seem odd. But the slight gaminess of the stomach joined with the fresh ocean taste of the clams is actually quite successful. Shellfish is beloved by the coastal Fujian residents and this soup represents the characteristically simple type of cooking in which they take pride. | SERVES 6 OR MORE, AS A SOUP COURSE

8 ounces pig stomach, cut into 1-inch squares

8 cups pork stock (see page 89) or water

¼ cup *laojiu* cooking wine

8 thin slices fresh ginger

12 ounces Manila clams

1 teaspoon salt

¼ teaspoon ground white pepper

Put the pig stomach pieces in a pot, add enough water to cover them completely, and bring the water to a boil over medium heat. Parboil the stomach for about 20 minutes, continuously skimming off any scum that forms on the surface. Drain the stomach completely and discard the water.

Put the pork stock, stomach, wine, and ginger in the pot and bring to a boil. Gently simmer over medium heat for 1½ hours, until the stomach is tender.

Add the clams, salt, and pepper and continue cooking for 10 minutes, until all the clams have opened (discard any that do not open).

STEAMED SOUP | 隔水燉湯

One summer I was plagued with a lingering dry cough that no medicine could alleviate. An X-ray showed nothing unusual, but the coughing kept me awake all night, and every morning I was exhausted. At the urging of my physician, Dr. Wing On Tsang, an internist who also practices acupuncture and Chinese herbal medicine, I finally found relief after a few weeks of treatment with steamed Asian pear soup infused with *chuanbei* (川貝), or fritillaria bulbs, a Chinese herbal medicine for clearing the lungs. This soup is steamed in a covered tureen to extract and capture the maximum amount of the medicinal element from the *chuanbei*, a technique used by many Chinese cooks to make herbal soups that can help alleviate or prevent all kinds of ailments.

In addition to being an excellent way of infusing herbal medicine into soup, this method is also perfect for slowly breaking down tough ingredients. Meat cuts with membrane and tendon, shellfish such as abalone and conch, and large fowl such as duck and goose are all perfect ingredients for a steamed soup. The only requirement is to cook the soup for a very long time, usually 3 to 4 hours, which is longer than for a regular braised soup.

There are two approaches to steaming soup in a tureen. The traditional one is to use a large pot with the tureen sitting directly in the water. A new alternative way of soup steaming is to put the tureen on a rack in a steam chamber where it does not touch the boiling water. This alternative method actually cooks the soup at the temperature of the steam, which is higher than that of boiling water, thus reducing the cooking time. Even so, at least 3 hours of cooking is needed.

Similar to the braised soup technique, the meat ingredient is first parboiled and then the other ingredients are added to the stock. But instead of the soup being simmered slowly in a clay pot, it is

steamed in a covered tureen. The tureen is sometimes sealed with a strip of paper to ensure that no volatile elements escape during steaming. Not only does this technique retain the beneficial elements of the soup, but it also holds on to their aromas and flavors.

Chinese Steaming Canisters

There are times when it is more convenient to serve individual portions of steamed soup. In this case, Chinese cooks use a small cylindrical porcelain steaming canister, about 4 inches in diameter. It has two covers: the inner cover to seal the food and the outer one to keep the steam away. (The double seal is designed for steaming herbal or medicinal soup, where the active compound is supposed to be concealed within the canister.)

Alternatively, you can use deep ramekins and cover them with aluminum foil.

STEAMED SILKIE CHICKEN SOUP WITH GINSENG | 洋參烏雞湯

GUANGDONG

American ginseng has been highly prized as an energizing health tonic since the very first American trader started exporting it to China in 1784, so it is fitting to use Wisconsin ginseng to make this Silkie chicken (also called black chicken) soup. Wisconsin is the only region still producing ginseng commercially in the United States because overharvesting has ruined the soil in other growing areas such as the Appalachian and Ozark regions. During the autumn harvest season, fresh Wisconsin ginseng is often available in Chinatown ginseng shops. The Silkie, known to the Chinese as black chicken because its skin color is black, is believed to have medicinal value for cleansing the liver and is also cool in energetic temperature. Longan is a fruit similar to lychee and can be found in its dried form in Chinatown markets. | SERVES 6 OR MORE, AS A SOUP COURSE

1 whole Silkie chicken (1½ pounds)

½ cup white rice wine

½ ounce dried ginseng, or 3 ounces fresh ginseng

8 thin slices fresh ginger

1 tablespoon goji berries

6 jujubes

2 tablespoons dried longan

Put the whole chicken in a pot, add enough water to cover it completely, and bring the water to a boil over medium heat. Parboil the chicken for about 20 minutes, skimming off any scum that forms on the surface. Drain the chicken completely and discard the water.

Put the chicken in a tureen and add the wine, ginseng, ginger, goji berries, jujubes, and longan. Cover the tureen and put it in a stockpot that is large enough to completely contain it. Add water to a depth of about 2 inches. Bring the water to a boil and maintain a moderate boil for about 3 hours, until the soup is infused with flavor. Replenish the water every 30 minutes or so to make sure that there is always plenty of boiling water in the pot.

Serve the hot soup directly from the tureen, removing the cover only at the table.

Harvesting Soup from Steam: Steam Pot Soup

During the reign of Emperor Qianlong in the mid-18th century, a special steam pot for making soup was invented by a Yunnan chef. Chef Yang Li (楊瀝), from Jianshui County (建水縣), combined the idea of a hot pot with a clay pot. His steam pot was made of clay and, like a hot pot, had a vent running upward from the bottom of the pot. But unlike a hot pot, in which the vent goes all the way through the pot to let smoke escape, the vent in Yang Li's steam pot emptied into the interior of the pot. When the pot was placed on top of another regular pot that was filled with boiling water, steam passed up through the spout and condensed within the steam pot. Yang Li put chicken and aromatics in the steam pot and let the soup form slowly, creating a wonderfully flavorful chicken soup. Since then other ingredients have been used to make soups in this kitchen implement, but the original recipe is still the most beloved.

STEAM POT CHICKEN SOUP

汽鍋雞

YUNNAN

Four ingredients are all that is needed to make this phenomenally delicious soup. The steam circulating and condensing in this special pot does the miracle work. As the chicken slowly cooks, its essence is extracted into the condensed liquid. | SERVES 6 OR MORE, AS A SOUP COURSE

1½ pounds chicken legs, cut crosswise into 1-inch-thick pieces

1 cup Shaoxing cooking wine

8 thin slices fresh ginger

1½ teaspoons salt

Put the chicken pieces in a saucepan, add enough water to cover them completely, and bring the water to a boil over medium heat. Parboil the chicken for about 10 minutes, skimming off any scum that forms on the surface. Drain the chicken completely and discard the water.

Put the chicken, 1 cup water, the wine, and the ginger in a Yunnan steam pot and cover the pot. Choose a saucepan that is large enough to hold the steam pot on its rim, and fill it halfway with water. Soak two thin kitchen towels with tap water and wring them out. Roll the towels up lengthwise and use them to line the rim of the saucepan. Set the steam pot on top of the towels. The towels will form a seal to prevent the steam from escaping. Bring the water to a boil and keep it gently boiling over medium heat for 3 to 4 hours, until enough liquid has condensed in the steam pot to make a full pot of soup. Check the water level in the saucepan hourly and replenish it as needed.

Serve the hot soup directly from the steam pot.

PORK, PAPAYA, AND CLOUD EAR SOUP | 瘦肉木瓜銀耳湯

GUANGDONG

This is such a favorite savory summer soup that one forgets the reason for its popularity is its cooling benefits for the body. Papaya and white cloud ear are considered yin *ingredients in Chinese herbal medicine. I like to use steam to make this soup instead of directly boiling it because the gentle steam heat will keep the papaya from becoming overcooked and mushy.* | SERVES 6 OR MORE, AS A SOUP COURSE

10 ounces boneless pork loin, cut into 1-inch cubes

½ small ripe papaya (about 8 ounces), peeled, seeded, and cut into 1-inch cubes

6 cups pork stock (see page 89) or water

½ cup white rice wine

6 thin slices fresh ginger

½ ounce white cloud ear mushroom, rehydrated (see page 78) and torn into ½-inch squares

1 tablespoon goji berries

1 teaspoon salt

¼ teaspoon ground white pepper

Put the pork in a pot, add enough water to cover it completely, and bring the water to a boil over medium heat. Parboil the pork for about 10 minutes, skimming off any scum that forms on the surface. Drain the pork completely and discard the water.

Put the pork in a tureen and add the papaya, stock, wine, ginger, cloud ear, goji berries, salt, and pepper. Cover the tureen and place it in a stockpot that is large enough to completely contain the tureen. Add water to a depth of about 2 inches. Bring the water to a boil and maintain a moderate boil for about 3 hours, until the soup is infused with flavor. Replenish the water every 30 minutes or so to make sure that there is always plenty of boiling water in the pot.

Serve the hot soup directly from the tureen, removing the cover only at the table.

PEAR SOUP WITH CHUANBEI | 雪梨川貝湯

HOME-STYLE

Although most often consumed as a remedy, this sweet pear soup happens to be delicious and is safe to enjoy as a regular snack even if you don't have a cough. | SERVES 4, AS A SWEET COURSE

8 ounces rock sugar

4 small Asian pears (about 10 ounces total), peeled, cored, and quartered

½ ounce dried white cloud ear mushroom, rehydrated (see page 78) and torn into ½-inch squares

16 dried *chuanbei* (see page 286)

Combine the rock sugar with 6 cups water in a medium saucepan, bring to a boil, and boil until the sugar is completely dissolved. Then let the syrup cool.

Put four Asian pear quarters in each of four Chinese steaming canisters. Distribute the white cloud ear and *chuanbei* equally among the canisters. Distribute the syrup among the canisters and seal the canisters.

Put a wire steaming rack in a wok or stockpot and arrange the four canisters on the rack. Add water to a depth of about 2 inches. Bring the water to a boil and maintain a moderate boil for 1 hour, until the soup is infused with flavor. Replenish the water every 30 minutes or so to make sure there is always plenty of boiling water in the wok.

Remove the canisters from the steaming rack. The soup can be served piping hot straight from the canisters, or it can be chilled in the refrigerator and serve cold.

CHAPTER FOURTEEN

Playing with Fire

GO TO ANY CHINATOWN IN THE UNITED STATES AND YOU'LL FIND RESTAURANTS WITH LARGE WINDOWS DISPLAYING VARIETIES OF ROASTED DUCK, CHICKEN, AND PORK. Tourists love to take photographs of the ducks and chickens hanging there with their necks and heads still attached. For years these restaurants' owners struggled with local health department regulations, which dictate that hot food must be maintained at 140°F, which can dry out the meat, or kept out for only 2 hours.

Chinese restaurants often simply resigned themselves to the fact that they would have to pay fines for breaking the rules and considered it part of the cost of doing business. However, in 2011, after conducting a study of the Chinese roasting process, the Department of Health in New York City finally changed their regulations to allow roasted meat to hang for up to 4 hours. The study indicated that the hang-roasting process in fact keeps the skin or outside of the meat dry enough to inhibit the growth of harmful bacteria for a longer period of time. The Chinese knew their roasting techniques made a big difference in the taste and texture of the meat, and now they know it also affects storage.

In China, roasting and grilling are almost never done at home. Indeed, there are neither ovens nor grills in most Chinese kitchens. Consequently, Chinese roasting and grilling techniques are generally geared toward commercial applications, which also partly explains why there are so many restaurants and meat shops in Chinatown selling roasted and grilled meat.

Hang roasting, the most traditional roasting technique, calls for meat to be hung on a hook and roasted in a wood-burning open-hearth oven. Although modern restaurants use gas-burning ovens that are large enough to hang the meat, Peking duck restaurants in Beijing continue to use wood-burning ovens. Oven roasting is a modern adaptation of Western roasting and is usually reserved for smaller pieces of meat or dishes cooked in roasting pans.

Grilling can be divided into two types: cooking directly over an open fire and cooking on a hot grilling plate. Open-fire grilling usually involves cooking meat on skewers, on grates, or by spit roasting. All these different ways of grilling are employed throughout China, but cooking on a grilling plate is used particularly in the cold northern region near Mongolia. Thin slices of meat are cooked on the grilling plate and then served with baked bread pockets.

In addition to roasting and grilling, there are two other dry-heat specialty techniques. The first is salt baking, in which the meat cooks while buried in hot salt. Usually the salt is heated in a clay pot on the stovetop, but some dishes are now baked in the oven. The other technique is clay roasting, where the meat is completely wrapped in clay and then roasted over an open fire.

Some of these techniques, such as pan roasting and plate grilling, can be easily adapted for home cooking and produce great results. Most, however, are not very practical at home. Take hang roasting, for example: A home oven is not tall enough for hanging a whole duck, making it impossible to achieve an evenly brown, crisp skin on all sides. Still, there are times when it is simply fun to try to replicate the techniques at home. Follow the suggestions in this chapter as closely as you can and you will begin to appreciate how much effort restaurant kitchens go to in order to produce these sumptuous roasted and grilled foods.

HANG ROASTING 掛爐烤

The oven traditionally used for hang roasting is usually wood-burning and built of brick. It has an open hearth with a large capacity for cooking multiple pieces of meat and fowl. Modern large drum-shaped enclosed gas-burning ovens with hanging rods have pretty much replaced the old-fashioned oven in almost all restaurants, and chefs have successfully produced popular Cantonese barbecued pork, crispy roast chicken, and many other traditional roast meats in them. The only exception is in Beijing, where restaurants specializing in Peking duck still stick to the wood-burning ovens. The aroma from the smoke on the duck skin is simply unsurpassed.

Peking duck is the best-known delicacy to come out of the hanging oven. The dish has a long history in China and probably became prominent during the early Ming Dynasty, when the capital was in Nanjing (南京). But the roasting technique was not perfected until the late Qing Dynasty, after the capital moved north to Beijing. Multiple steps were added to ensure a crispy duck skin and the technique was refined to become an art form.

Reproducing the results achieved in a hanging oven is next to impossible in a home kitchen, but there are certain steps that can be taken to simulate the effect.

PEKING DUCK | 北京烤鴨

BEIJING

The classic Peking roast duck is not seasoned with any spices. The main attraction is the crisp brown skin, and it receives all the attention during the cooking process. Wrapped in a warm thin pancake with cucumber, scallions, and sweet bean paste, Peking duck skin is a delicacy.

To make Peking duck in a home kitchen, many compromises have to be made. Although it is possible to produce a tasty facsimile, in my opinion it is impossible to replicate restaurant-quality Peking duck exactly. So here is my adaptation for preparing Peking duck at home, which assumes that the duck will have been butchered the Western way with the neck cut off and the abdomen cut open. Note that this recipe takes 3 days from start to finish. | SERVES 8 OR MORE, AS AN APPETIZER

1 whole Long Island duckling (about 4 pounds)

SYRUP GLAZE
⅓ cup maltose syrup or honey
1 tablespoon white rice vinegar

4 ounces cucumber, cut into strips 2 inches long and ⅛ inch wide
½ cup julienned scallion whites
¼ cup sweet bean paste

Pancakes (page 300)

Cut off the front two sections of the duck wings, leaving the short stumps. Remove the excess duck fat near the cavity opening. Use a trussing needle and butcher's twine to sew the abdominal cavity closed. Then use a clean bicycle pump to force air through the neck opening into the cavity, pumping enough air to separate the skin from the meat of the entire duck. Pull the flap of skin over the neck hole and truss it as well.

Push the tip of a disposable chopstick through one wing stump and into the breast bones to spread and secure it away from the body. Break off the excess chopstick. Repeat for the other wing.

Bring a small saucepan of water to a bare simmer. (The water temperature should be just under the boiling point.) Put the duck on a rack in a roasting pan and ladle some of the barely simmering water over the duck a few times, then turn the duck over and blanch the other side. Repeat this blanching process until the skin is taut, about six times total. Discard the collected hot water in the roasting pan and return the duck and the rack to the pan.

In a saucepan, mix ½ cup water with the maltose syrup and vinegar and heat this over medium heat until it just comes to a boil. Ladle the syrup evenly over the duck and on both sides. Retrieve the syrup from the roasting pan, cover it, and refrigerate.

Air-dry the duck in the refrigerator, uncovered, for at least 2 days. Depending on the humidity in the environment, you may need to extend the air-drying for a third day. The duck is ready for roasting when the skin has the texture of a dry sausage casing.

Take the duck out of the refrigerator and let it sit at room temperature for about 2 hours.

Preheat the oven to 375°F.

Heat the reserved syrup and ladle it over the duck to coat it on both sides. Use a turkey baster to fill the cavity with water by squeezing the tip through the trussed abdomen cut. Fill it with water until it is just about to flow from the opening.

Set the duck, breast-side up, on a roasting rack in a roasting pan (ideally an adjustable poultry rack so the duck can be supported firmly). Roast the duck for about 15 minutes. Turn the duck one-quarter turn to the right and roast for another 15 minutes. Turn the duck onto the other side and roast for 15 minutes.

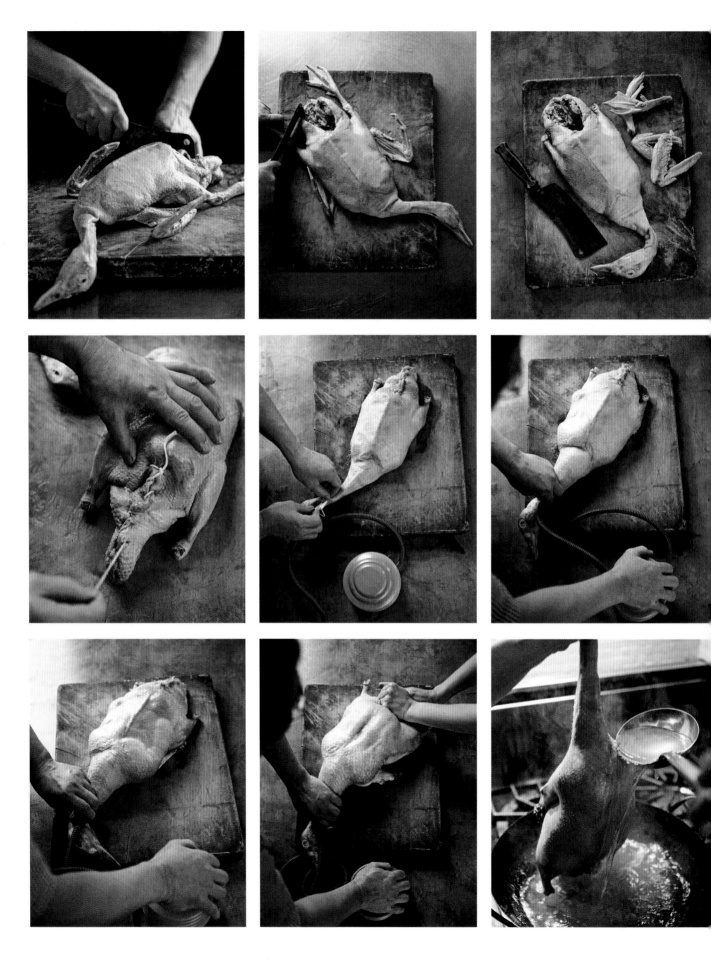

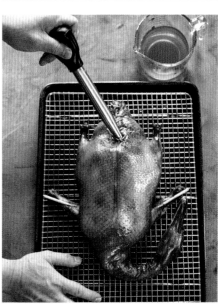

Finally, increase the oven temperature to 425°F and roast the duck, breast-side up, for another 15 minutes to finish. The duck is ready when the skin is dark brown and a meat thermometer inserted into the thigh reads 160°F.

Remove the pan from the oven and let the duck rest for about 10 minutes. Then slice the meat and skin together off the duck, forming pieces about 1½ by 1 inch. Serve the skin and meat with the cucumber, scallions, and sweet bean paste, all wrapped in the pancakes.

NOTE: Traditionally, the skin is the only part served with the pancakes. The meat is shredded and stir-fried, and the carcass is made into a soup with napa cabbage. This is known as "Peking Duck Three Ways."

The Secret of Chinese Roast Duck

One of the secrets to making Chinese roast duck with crisp brown skin on the outside and moist tender meat inside is in the butchering. In the standard Western method, the duck abdomen is cut open and the internal organs are removed from the cavity. The Chinese method, however, keeps the abdomen intact. Instead, only a small slit is cut under the right wing, between the breastbone and the first rib, and the entire internal organ system is removed through the slit. At the end there are only three spots with small openings: under the wing, at the neck, and the anus.

To ensure crisp skin the duck is air-dried for a few days; then syrup is brushed on the skin. When the duck is ready to be roasted, the anal opening is sealed with a wooden stopper and aromatic broth is poured into the cavity through the hole under the wing. When the duck is roasted hanging on a hook, the skin browns and crisps while the broth gently steams the meat inside.

PANCAKES

MAKES 32 PANCAKES

2 cups all-purpose flour
Toasted sesame oil

Put the flour in a large bowl. Bring ¾ cup water to a boil in a small saucepan, then immediately pour the boiling water over the flour. Use a wooden spoon to mix the flour until the dough is cool to the touch. Using your hands, knead the dough on a lightly floured surface until it is smooth. Let it rest for about 20 minutes, covered in plastic wrap.

Divide the dough into 32 equal balls. Press two of the dough balls flat to form disks. Brush some sesame oil on one side of one of the disks, then stack the other disk on top of the oiled disk. Roll the stacked dough out on a flour-dusted surface to form a round pancake about 5 inches in diameter. Repeat this step with the rest of the dough balls to make 16 double-layered disks.

Heat a frying pan over very low heat for 8 minutes. Cook a disk of dough in the dry pan for about 3 minutes on each side, until a slight wisp of steam is detected. Check occasionally to make sure the pancake does not brown at all. When it is cooked, remove it from the pan and then gently separate the two layers into two pancakes. Repeat with the rest of the disks.

Keep the pancakes warm, wrapped in a towel, until ready to serve. They can be steamed to reheat.

CRISPY ROAST DUCK | 烤鴨

SHANDONG

Duck roasting has a long history in Chinese cooking, and many different variations have evolved over time. One step remains universally important, and that is to air-dry the skin thoroughly. This is what produces the crispiest brown skin. Although it also requires 3 days, this recipe is less complicated than that for its famous cousin, Peking duck, and the result is no less satisfying. | SERVES 6 OR MORE, ACCOMPANIED BY TWO OTHER DISHES

1 whole Long Island duckling (about 4 pounds)

1 tablespoon Sichuan peppercorn powder

2 teaspoons salt

2 scallions, cut into 2-inch pieces

1 (1-inch-long) piece of fresh ginger, cut into ½-inch cubes

SYRUP GLAZE

¼ cup maltose syrup or honey

1 teaspoon white rice vinegar

3 scallions, cut into thin julienne

¼ cup sweet bean paste

Cut off the front two sections of the duck wings, leaving the short stumps. Remove the excess fat near the cavity opening. Combine the peppercorn powder and salt and spread it evenly over the duck. Be sure to rub it under the wings as well. Air-dry the duck in the refrigerator, uncovered, for at least 2 days. Depending on the humidity in the environment, you may need to extend the air-drying for a third day. The duck is ready for roasting when the skin has the texture of a dry sausage casing.

Take the duck out of the refrigerator and let it sit at room temperature for about 2 hours.

Combine the scallion pieces, ginger cubes, and ¼ cup water in a blender and puree. Pour the puree into the abdominal cavity of the duck. Use a trussing needle and butcher's twine to sew the cavity closed. Pull the flap of skin over the neck hole and truss it as well. The skin should now form a complete seal so none of the liquid can escape during cooking.

In a small bowl, mix together the maltose syrup, vinegar, and 1 cup water. Use a pastry brush to apply half of this syrup evenly all over the duck skin. Let it air-dry for about 30 minutes. Reserve the remaining syrup.

Preheat the oven to 375°F.

Put the duck, breast-side down, on a rack in a roasting pan (be sure to adjust the duck so the liquid in the cavity does not leak out). Pour 2 cups water into the roasting pan (this will catch the dripping fat and prevent it from burning). Roast the duck for 20 minutes. Turn the duck over and continue roasting, breast-side up, for another 40 minutes. Remove the pan from the oven and brush the remaining syrup evenly all over the duck.

Turn the oven temperature up to 400°F. Return the duck to the oven and further brown the skin for about 10 minutes. The duck is ready when the skin is dark brown and a meat thermometer inserted into the thigh reads 160°F.

Remove the pan from the oven and let the duck rest for about 10 minutes. Remove the wings and legs and cut them into 1-inch-thick pieces. Cut the breast meat off the bones and slice it into ½-inch-thick strips. Arrange the duck pieces decoratively on a platter and serve with the julienned scallions and sweet bean paste on the side.

BARBECUED PORK | 叉燒肉
GUANGDONG

Found everywhere in Chinatown, this pork is the staple of Cantonese restaurants and butchers and is usually roasted hanging in a professional oven. This recipe suggests a way of roasting the pork in a home kitchen. The pork is delicious served by itself or as an ingredient in many different recipes, such as Stir-Fried Lo Mein with Barbecued Pork (see page 114). | SERVES 4 AS AN APPETIZER, 2 AS A MAIN COURSE WHEN PAIRED WITH A VEGETABLE DISH

1 pound pork tenderloin

MARINADE

¼ cup hoisin sauce

1 tablespoon soy sauce

2 tablespoons Shaoxing cooking wine

2 tablespoons sugar

1 teaspoon five-spice powder

Cut the pork tenderloin in half lengthwise, creating two long strips, and put them in a shallow baking dish. Mix all the marinade ingredients together in a bowl and spread the marinade evenly over the pork. Cover and refrigerate for 2 hours.

Preheat the oven to 400°F.

Put the pork on a wire rack set in a roasting pan. Roast, turning the tenderloin over once, for about 20 minutes or until the center of the meat reaches 150°F. Remove the pan from the oven and let the pork rest for 10 minutes. Serve hot or cold.

OVEN ROASTING | 烤箱烤

Although not a traditional Chinese technique, oven roasting is gaining in popularity. The common commercial oven has become an increasingly important piece of cooking equipment in most restaurants in China. These ovens are used for general roasting of modern dishes such as baked stuffed whelk and cumin-flavored roast rack of lamb.

Roasting large pieces of meat is rare in Chinese cooking, but some traditional hang-roasting methods can be adapted to oven roasting. A prime example is crispy roast pork belly. The flat shape of this cut of meat is ideal for roasting in a pan so the skin can be exposed to the ambient heat.

CRISPY ROAST PORK BELLY | 化皮燒肉

GUANGDONG

A perennial favorite at any Chinese barbecue vendor, this roasted pork belly usually is cooked using a whole side of pork with the ribs still intact. At home, we can roast a boneless piece of pork belly in the oven. To crisp the skin successfully, spread a thick layer of coarse sea salt over it. | SERVES 6 OR MORE AS AN APPETIZER, 2 AS A MAIN COURSE WHEN PAIRED WITH A VEGETABLE DISH

2 pounds boneless pork belly

DRY RUB

2 teaspoons salt

1 teaspoon five-spice powder

1 teaspoon sugar

2 tablespoons white rice wine

¼ cup coarse sea salt

3 tablespoons mustard or plum sauce

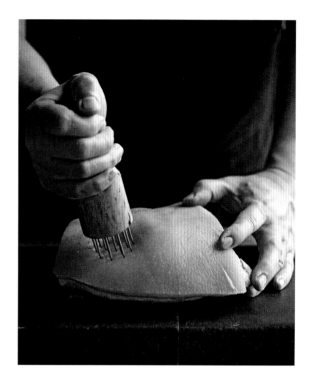

Put the pork belly in a pot, add enough water to cover it completely, and bring the water to a boil over medium heat. Parboil the pork for about 20 minutes, continuously skimming off any scum that forms on the surface. Drain the pork completely and discard the water. Let the pork belly cool until it is cool to the touch.

In a small bowl, combine the dry rub ingredients and mix well.

Prick the skin of the cooled pork belly with a metal skewer until the surface is completely covered with tiny holes. The holes should be very dense, no more than ⅛ inch apart. Pour the wine over the pork belly and rub it all over both sides of the pork. Spread the dry rub evenly all over the meat portion of the belly, but not on the skin. Refrigerate the pork belly, uncovered, skin-side up, for at least 12 hours or overnight.

Preheat the oven to 350°F.

Remove the pork belly from the refrigerator and wrap the meat part with aluminum foil, leaving the skin exposed. Put the pork belly in a roasting pan, skin side up, foil-side down. Spread the coarse sea salt evenly over the skin. Roast the pork for 45 minutes.

Remove the aluminum wrapping and scrape off the salt layer. Fit a rack into the roasting pan and put the pork belly, skin-side up, on the rack. Turn the oven heat up to 425°F and continue to roast the pork belly for another 25 minutes or until the skin is crisp and covered with blisters.

Remove the pan from the oven and let the pork rest for about 10 minutes. Then cut the pork belly into ½-inch-thick slices and arrange them on a plate. (It is easiest to slice the pork belly when it is placed skin-side down on the cutting board.)

Serve with the mustard or plum sauce on the side.

Walk along the main streets of any residential neighborhood in a Chinese city and you'll find vendors grilling small pieces of lamb on metal skewers over a trough of burning charcoal. The smoke and smell wafting from the grill, thick with cumin and chile, is mouthwatering and irresistible. These vendors, Uighurs from the far western Xinjiang region of China, peddle their region's most popular snack food.

Open-fire grilling is found in many parts of China, using a wide array of ingredients and flavors. Grilled octopus can be found in Shanghai, grilled shellfish everywhere in Taiwan, and grilled lemongrass fish is a signature dish of Yunnan province.

For best results, use an outdoor wood or charcoal grill; however, these recipes can also be prepared using the broiler in a home oven.

GRILLED LAMB SKEWERS
WITH CUMIN | 孜然烤羊肉串
XINJIANG

The lamb for this simple grilled dish is not marinated but instead simply sprinkled with spices and seasonings; the charcoal infuses the meat with a smoky flavor. You will need 12 metal skewers for the lamb. | SERVES 4 AS A SNACK, 2 AS A MAIN COURSE WHEN PAIRED WITH A VEGETABLE DISH

12 ounces boneless lamb leg meat, cut into 1-inch cubes

¼ cup vegetable oil

3 tablespoons ground cumin

2 tablespoons Chinese red chile powder

2 teaspoons salt

Prepare a grill by lighting the charcoal and letting it burn down to hot embers. Spread the charcoal to produce medium heat at the grill, so you can hold your hand just above it for 6 to 7 seconds.

Slide 4 lamb cubes onto each metal skewer, leaving a generous space at the tip. Brush all sides of the meat with vegetable oil, and sprinkle all over with the cumin, chile powder, and salt. Grill the lamb for about 1 minute, then give the skewers a turn. Continue grilling and turning every minute until the meat is browned on the outside and slightly pink on the inside, about 10 minutes total.

GRILLED LEMONGRASS TILAPIA | 香茅草烤魚

YUNNAN

People are often surprised to find lemongrass used in Chinese cooking, but Yunnan province's proximity to Vietnam and Myanmar explains its popularity. This grilled fish, a classic Yunnan dish that's only recently being discovered outside the region, has a fresh herbal flavor and smells divine. | SERVES 2 OR MORE, PAIRED WITH A VEGETABLE DISH

FRESH HERB RUB

½ cup thin slices tender lemongrass bulb

1 cup firmly packed mint leaves

1 cup firmly packed Thai basil leaves

1 cup firmly packed cilantro leaves

½ cup thinly sliced scallions

1 (½-inch-long) piece of fresh ginger, thinly sliced

1 teaspoon salt

2 tablespoons lime juice

1 whole tilapia (about 1½ pounds), cleaned

1 stalk lemongrass, cut into 2-inch pieces

SAUCE

3 tablespoons soy sauce

¼ cup Shaoxing cooking wine

2 tablespoons sugar

¼ cup vegetable oil

¼ cup firmly packed mint leaves

¼ cup firmly packed Thai basil leaves

¼ cup firmly packed cilantro leaves

3 Thai bird's-eye red chiles, thinly sliced

Put all the ingredients for the herb rub in a food processor and pulse six to eight times, until coarsely chopped but not pureed.

Cut three or four diagonal slits on each side of the fish's body. Put the lemongrass pieces in the belly of the fish and spread the herb rub evenly over both outer sides of the fish. Put the fish in a shallow dish, cover, and let marinate in the refrigerator for 2 hours.

Prepare a grill by lighting the charcoal and letting it burn down to hot embers. Spread the charcoal to produce medium heat at the grill, so you can hold your hand just above it for 6 to 7 seconds.

Grease a wire grilling basket if you have one. If not, make sure your grill grates are very clean and well oiled. Grill the fish for about 6 minutes on each side, until the meat near the bones flakes off easily when poked with a knife tip.

While the fish is grilling, combine the sauce ingredients in a small saucepan and bring to a boil. Put the vegetable oil in another small saucepan and heat until it is just beginning to smoke, about 395°F.

Once the fish is cooked, put it on a shallow platter, pour the sauce evenly over it, and then drizzle the oil on top. Garnish with the fresh herbs and chiles.

GRILLED PORK BELLY | 五香烤肉

SHANDONG

Grilling meat is popular in northern China, and this is a modern interpretation of grilled pork belly. The five-spice and the charcoal flavors work well with each other. | SERVES 4 OR MORE, ACCOMPANIED BY TWO OTHER DISHES

MARINADE

¼ cup Shaoxing cooking wine

3 tablespoons dark soy sauce

2 tablespoons soy sauce

2 scallions, cut into 2-inch-long pieces

4 garlic cloves, crushed with the flat side of a knife

2 tablespoons sugar

1 teaspoon five-spice powder

2 pounds pork belly, cut into 3 long 1-inch-wide strips

2 tablespoons sugar

In a bowl, combine all the marinade ingredients and mix well. Put the pork belly strips in a shallow baking dish and pour the marinade on top. Turn the meat to coat it, cover, then let marinate in the refrigerator overnight.

The next day, put a wire rack in a wok, add about 5 cups water to the wok, and bring the water to a boil. Put the pork belly in a large shallow bowl (reserve the marinade left in the baking dish) and put the bowl on the rack. Cover the wok and steam the pork for about 45 minutes, until it is tender. Remove the pork from the rack and let it cool. (This step can be done ahead and the meat refrigerated until you are ready to grill it.)

Prepare a grill by lighting the charcoal and letting it burn down to hot embers. Spread the charcoal to produce medium heat at the grill, so you can hold your hand just above it for 6 to 7 seconds.

Grill the pork belly, basting the meat with the leftover marinade and turning it as needed to ensure even browning, until the meat is heated through and covered with a nice brown sear, about 15 minutes. Pay special attention to the skin to make sure it crisps.

Cut the pork strips crosswise into ¼-inch-thick slices. Arrange them decoratively on a plate and serve with the sugar on the side for dipping.

HOT PLATE GRILLING | 炙烤

Predominantly a northern Chinese technique used around Beijing, this cooking method uses a round grilling plate about 2 feet in diameter and about ¼ inch thick, perforated with thin slits or tiny square holes. Charcoal is burned underneath and the smoke enriches the food as it is being cooked on the plate. The round Korean grilling iron is practically the same and can be substituted for the Chinese version. Beef and lamb are the main types of meat cooked this way, often accompanied by garlic, ginger, leeks, and cilantro and served with palm-size baked bread pockets coated with sesame seeds.

When this cooking method was introduced in Taiwan in the 1950s, it became known as Mongolian barbecue. In Taiwan, the round grilling iron is enlarged to about 5 feet in diameter and can accommodate multiple portions of meat cooked by several chefs at the same time. The list of ingredients has greatly expanded and now includes pork, chicken, and a myriad of vegetables.

HOT PLATE GRILLED LAMB
炙烤羊肉

BEIJING

If you have neither a Beijing grilling plate nor a Korean version, you can pan-fry this lamb in a very hot cast-iron pan. You won't get the charcoal grill flavor, but the result will still be delicious. | SERVES 2 OR MORE, PAIRED WITH A VEGETABLE DISH

1 tablespoon soy sauce

2 tablespoons Shaoxing cooking wine

1 teaspoon sugar

12 ounces lamb leg meat, thinly sliced

1 tablespoon vegetable oil

½ ounce fresh ginger (about six ¹⁄₁₆-inch-thick slices)

2 Chinese leeks or 1 regular leek,
cut into ⅛-inch-thick slices

8 cilantro sprigs

1 teaspoon toasted sesame oil

Combine the soy sauce, wine, and sugar in a small bowl.

Put the lamb in a shallow dish, pour the soy sauce mixture over it, and let marinate at room temperature for 10 minutes.

Heat the grilling plate or a cast-iron frying pan to about 450°F. Brush the vegetable oil onto the pan and then immediately add the lamb. Quickly stir the lamb around until the color just turns to brown, about 10 seconds. Add the ginger and leeks and continue to stir for 30 seconds. Then add the cilantro and stir for another 30 seconds or until the lamb is cooked through. Sprinkle with the sesame oil.

SALT BAKING | 鹽焗

Salt baking is a uniquely Hakka cooking technique, traditionally used only for baking chicken. However, this method has been adapted in modern times for cooking fish and shrimp as well. That said, the salt-baked chicken remains famous and sought after. The technique calls for heating salt in a clay pot to a temperature of about 300°F. Then the chicken is buried and baked in the salt. Originally, all this was done on the stovetop, which made it difficult to keep the heat spread evenly throughout the clay pot. A modern adaptation of the technique is to bake the clay pot in an oven, which supplies a more even ambient heat.

The salt coating transmits steady, even heat to the chicken, so it will turn out tender and succulent with a fragrant salt smell. The use of galangal, a variety of ginger from Southeast Asia, illustrates how the Hakka people have incorporated new ingredients into their cooking.

SALT-BAKED CHICKEN | 東江鹽焗雞

HAKKA

This recipe describes the traditional stovetop technique for baking the chicken in hot salt and also gives the instructions for baking it in the oven. The results will be similar, so the choice is yours. | SERVES 6 OR MORE, ACCOMPANIED BY TWO OTHER DISHES

1 (1½- to 2-pound) whole young chicken

DRY RUB
1 tablespoon ground galangal
3 tablespoons kosher salt

2 scallions
4 slices fresh ginger

3 pounds coarse sea salt or kosher salt
6 whole star anise
2 tablespoons Sichuan peppercorns

DIPPING SAUCE
3 tablespoons toasted sesame oil
2 tablespoons grated fresh ginger
1 teaspoon salt

Rinse the chicken and pat it completely dry with a kitchen towel or paper towels. Mix the dry rub ingredients in a small bowl, then spread the rub evenly all over the chicken. Put the chicken on a rack in a roasting pan and refrigerate it overnight, uncovered, to dry the skin.

When you are ready to bake the chicken, put the scallions and ginger inside the chicken's cavity. Wrap the chicken up in parchment paper and secure it tightly with butcher's twine.

In a wok, heat the salt, star anise, and Sichuan peppercorns over high heat until the salt is hot and beginning to smoke, about 300°F. Pour a 1-inch layer of this salt mixture into a large clay pot or a cast-iron Dutch oven. Put the chicken in the pot and then pour the rest of the salt on top of the chicken. Cover the pot and cook over medium heat for about 30 minutes. Turn the heat off and let the chicken sit in the covered pot for another 30 minutes. (Alternatively, use unheated salt to completely cover the parchment-wrapped chicken in a Dutch oven; cover the Dutch oven and bake in a preheated 375°F oven for 1½ hours.) To test for doneness, remove some of the salt on top and tear open the parchment to reveal the thigh; a meat thermometer inserted into the thigh should read 160°F.

In a small bowl, mix together the ingredients for the dipping sauce.

Uncover the pot, remove the salt, and transfer the chicken to a cutting board. Remove the parchment paper and let the chicken cool slightly. Cut up the chicken and arrange the pieces decoratively on a platter. Serve with the dipping sauce.

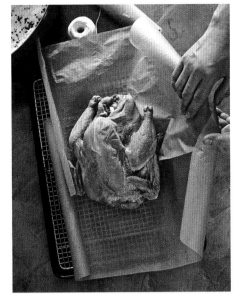
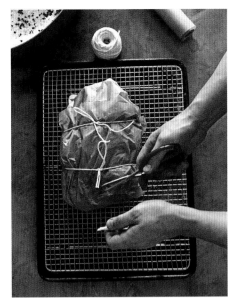

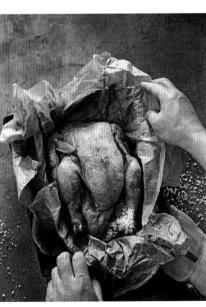

A starving beggar during the Qing dynasty is said to have stolen a chicken and, being hotly pursued by its owner, hastily buried it in the mud near a riverbank to hide it. Later that night he returned and retrieved the chicken with its feathers all covered in mud. He started a fire of twigs and branches to cook the chicken. Not having any utensils, he placed the entire chicken directly into the fire. As the mud dried, a tight clay crust formed around the fowl. When the bird was cooked and the crust was cracked open, the feathers stuck to the clay, exposing juicy, tender meat that emitted an incredible aroma. The roasted chicken was so delicious that the former beggar decided to start selling his creation to the local villagers. Unbeknownst to him, he had just invented one of China's greatest culinary traditions.

This is the legend most often told by the Chinese. To be sure, there are other competing stories, but I like this one best. Now called Beggar's Chicken, this dish originated in the Hangzhou (杭州) area in Zhejiang (浙江) province and can be found in many of its restaurants. Not many home cooks attempt clay roasting, simply because of the laborious process. But if successfully roasted, the cracking of the clay crust and having the dining room instantly filled with an incredible aroma is one of the more dramatic presentations in Chinese cuisine. With this technique, the clay completely seals the chicken as well as the stuffing and spices. Consequently, the meat is kept moist and the spices are infused thoroughly during roasting.

BEGGAR'S CHICKEN │ 叫花子雞

ZHEJIANG

Not quite as simple as the original mud-covered chicken, this preparation requires rather elaborate steps to get to the roasting stage. But don't skip any of them because they ensure that the chicken stays flavorful and moist. The stuffing ingredients can be modified to suit your own taste. Whatever ingredients you choose, the aroma released when the shell is cracked will be intoxicatingly entwined with that of the lotus leaves and star anise. Note that you will need 8 pounds of nontoxic pottery clay for this recipe. │ SERVES 6 OR MORE, ACCOMPANIED BY TWO OTHER DISHES

MARINADE

¼ cup soy sauce

2 tablespoons Shaoxing cooking wine

4 whole star anise

1 tablespoon whole cloves

1 whole chicken (about 4 pounds)

STUFFING

2 tablespoons vegetable oil

1 tablespoon minced fresh ginger

2 tablespoons minced scallions

8 ounces pork tenderloin, cut into ½-inch cubes

8 ounces small shrimp, shelled and deveined

4 ounces Smithfield ham, cut into ½-inch cubes

4 ounces fresh or canned bamboo shoots (drained if canned), cut into ½-inch cubes

½ ounce dried shiitake mushrooms, rehydrated (see page 78) and cut into ½-inch cubes

4 whole star anise

2 tablespoons soy sauce

1 tablespoon Shaoxing cooking wine

½ teaspoon ground white pepper

Enough pork caul fat to wrap around the chicken

3 large dried lotus leaves, rehydrated (see page 78) in cold water

1 tablespoon toasted sesame oil

Combine all the marinade ingredients in a small saucepan and cook over low heat for about 15 minutes, until the spices are infused into the liquid. Let the marinade cool.

Put the chicken in a large bowl and pour the marinade over it. Cover and let marinate in the refrigerator for at least 5 hours or overnight.

To make the stuffing, heat a wok over high heat until a droplet of water sizzles and evaporates immediately upon contact. Swirl the vegetable oil around the bottom and sides of the wok to coat it evenly. Add the ginger and scallions and stir-fry until fragrant, about 30 seconds. Add the pork, shrimp, ham, bamboo shoots, and mushrooms and continue to stir-fry for about 1 minute, until the meat is just about three-quarters done. Add the star anise, soy sauce, wine, and pepper and stir-fry for another minute or until the meat is completely done. Transfer the stuffing to a bowl and let it cool.

Remove the chicken from the marinade and brush off the spices. Stuff the chicken with the stuffing, then tightly wrap the chicken completely in the caul fat. Put the chicken, breast-side up, on a piece of lotus leaf. Fold the leaf up over the sides and wings of the chicken and onto the breast. Flip the wrapped chicken over onto another lotus leaf and repeat the folding. Flip the chicken again and wrap the third leaf around it. The chicken should now be completely covered. Tie the wrapped chicken tightly with butcher's twine. Cover the entire package with a layer of clay about ¼ inch thick.

Preheat the oven or a grill to 400°F. Bake the chicken in the oven or covered grill for 2 hours, at which point the chicken and stuffing will be cooked through.

When you are ready to serve the chicken, crack open the clay and unwrap the lotus leaves. Remove the stuffing, put it in a serving dish, and drizzle the sesame oil over it. Cut the chicken into serving pieces (see page 72) and arrange it on a platter, using the lotus leaves as a base.

CHAPTER FIFTEEN

Enriching with Smoke

FOR CENTURIES BEFORE THE ADVENT OF MODERN HOUSEHOLD TECHNOLOGY, COOKING IN CHINA WAS DONE ON WOOD-BURNING STOVES. Made of brick and mortar, the stove was set against one wall of a home's kitchen. It had openings in the front to allow access for firewood and round openings in the top for positioning woks. The smoke was directed toward the back of the stove and out through a hole at the top of the wall. Meat was often preserved by hanging in the rising smoke.

Although it is still possible to find this type of kitchen setup in rural China, urban dwellers today are more used to slick modern kitchen appliances. Few people are even aware of the fact that smoking food used to be a household endeavor. Smoked food is now produced commercially in factories or in professional restaurant kitchens.

But that doesn't mean you can't smoke food in your home. And if you do, you can avoid the additives and preservatives found in commercial products. Household smokers are available at a very reasonable price, or you can improvise: A wok with a metal steaming rack and a cover readily converts into a practical smoker. The only extra consideration is to make sure the kitchen is very well ventilated, lest you trigger the smoke alarm!

Smoking techniques have been used not only to enhance flavors but also to preserve food. In *On Food and Cooking*, Harold McGee wrote that wood smoke contains many chemicals that slow the growth of microbes, hence extending the storage period of the ingredient. The Chinese have been taking advantage of this property for a long time—consider the meat that used to hang above the stove—and have developed sophisticated smoking techniques as a result.

For cold smoking, wood chips are heated very slowly, and the smoke they produce circulates in a confined area. The temperature remains relatively low, hence the name. This method is used primarily to cure meat such as ham and bacon that will then be cooked before being served.

Hot smoking, on the other hand, is done in a small container over direct heat so the ingredient cooks as it smokes. This approach is more common at home than cold smoking. Two hot smoking techniques are found in the Chinese kitchen: smoking raw ingredients, such as fish, eggs, soy products, and other food that cooks quickly, and smoking parcooked ingredients, including pork, beef, lamb, chicken, duck, squab, and offal. Although hot smoking produces enough heat to cook food, it is a good idea to parcook large pieces of meat before smoking since the smoking time is usually not sufficient to completely cook them through.

Wood chips and tea leaves are the predominant aromatics for both hot and cold smoking. However, dried flowers, dried fruit peels, bamboo leaves, rice husks, spices, and other dried ingredients are also used in parts of China. When a special smoky brown color is desired, sugar is added to the aromatics to coat the outside of the ingredient with a thin layer of caramel.

The recipes that follow offer instructions for using a wok for smoking, but dedicated smokers can of course be used successfully. Follow the manufacturer's instructions and adjust the recipes accordingly.

SMOKING RAW INGREDIENTS | 生燻

When working with ingredients that cook in a short time, smoking them while raw is a way to infuse them with flavor without overcooking them. Generally used for fish, this technique calls for the fish to be marinated in an aromatic mixture first, then smoked over wood chips or tea leaves. To ensure proper cooking, splash a small amount of water on the wood chips to create steam at the beginning of the smoking process. As it evaporates, the steam cooks the fish before the smoke develops and smoking begins.

Small whole fish are ideal for smoking. Larger fish—over 1 pound—should be cut into 3- to 4-inch-long sections before being smoked.

SMOKED YELLOW CROAKER
生燻黃魚

JIANGSU

Yellow croakers are freshwater fish found mainly in lakes and streams in China. They are sometimes available frozen in Chinatown shops in major cities. Good alternatives include brook trout, whitefish, and small carp. | SERVES 4, AS AN APPETIZER

MARINADE

3 tablespoons soy sauce

1 tablespoon white rice wine

1 tablespoon sugar

3 thin slices fresh ginger

1 scallion, cut into 2-inch pieces

2 whole yellow croakers (about 1 pound each)

½ cup apple or maple wood chips

2 tablespoons green tea leaves

3 or 4 large napa cabbage leaves

2 tablespoons sugar

1 tablespoon toasted sesame oil

Combine all the ingredients for the marinade in a medium bowl and put the fish in the bowl. Marinate the fish, covered, in the refrigerator for 6 hours.

Line a wok and its cover with aluminum foil for easy cleaning. Put the wood chips and the tea leaves in the wok and pour ¼ cup water over them. Put a metal steaming rack in the wok and arrange the cabbage leaves on the rack to ensure the fish does not stick to the rack. Set the fish on the cabbage leaves, discard any ginger or scallion pieces that cling to it, and cover the wok.

Turn the heat to medium and let the water start to evaporate to create steam. The steaming will last for 15 to 20 minutes, after which time all of the water will have evaporated and smoke will start to develop. Smoke the fish for 5 minutes; then remove the cover and sprinkle the sugar around the sides of the wok. Replace the cover and continue to smoke the fish for another 10 minutes, until it is cooked through and a brown caramel color.

Remove the fish and transfer it to a plate. Let it cool to room temperature. Pour the sesame oil over the fish before serving.

SMOKING PARCOOKED INGREDIENTS | 熟燻

Smoking can enhance the flavor of just about any kind of food, but most meat ingredients—including pork, beef, lamb, chicken, squab, duck, and eggs—need to be precooked before being smoked because smoking alone will not cook them. The precooking step can be done by steaming, braising, or frying. Braising in an aromatic liquid cooks the meat and infuses flavor. For steaming and frying, the meat should be marinated first, then cooked. In all cases, be sure that the meat is cooked to the desired doneness.

Wood chips, tea leaves, and other fragrant ingredients are used to impart flavor to the meat.

TEA-SMOKED DUCK | 樟茶鴨
SICHUAN

As a signature dish of Sichuan cooking, this duck has a mouthwatering smokiness with an aromatic undertone from the marinade. When perfectly fried, the crisp skin is irresistible. This is an elaborate recipe, so plan ahead. You can serve this duck sandwich-style in steamed buns, which can be purchased in Chinatown markets. | SERVES 6 OR MORE, ACCOMPANIED BY TWO OTHER DISHES

MARINADE

½ cup soy sauce

½ cup Shaoxing cooking wine

¼ cup sugar

1 (2-inch-long) piece of fresh ginger

2 scallions

2 tablespoons salt

3 whole star anise

4 ounces cassia bark

1 tablespoon Sichuan peppercorns

1 tablespoon whole cloves

1 tablespoon fennel seeds

1 (2-inch) square of dried tangerine peel

1 whole duck (4 to 5 pounds)

SMOKING INGREDIENTS

5 ounces green tea leaves

2 (2-inch) squares of dried tangerine peel

GLAZE

¼ cup maltose syrup or honey

1 tablespoon white rice vinegar

4 quarts vegetable oil

¼ cup sweet bean paste

3 scallions, julienned

10 steamed buns (optional)

Put all the ingredients for the marinade in a large saucepan and bring to a boil. Lower the heat and simmer for 20 minutes. Let cool to room temperature.

Put the duck in a large bowl and pour the marinade over it. Cover and let marinate in the refrigerator for at least 8 hours or overnight.

Put a wire rack in a wok, add about 5 cups water, and bring to a boil. Remove the duck from the marinade, scraping off any solid ingredients that cling to it. Transfer the duck to a platter and put the platter on the steamer rack. Cover the wok and steam the duck for about 45 minutes, until the meat is tender. Remove the duck from the wok and let it dry for about an hour at room temperature.

Line a wok and its cover with aluminum foil for easy cleanup, and put the tea leaves and tangerine peel in the wok. Set a steaming rack in the wok, cover the wok, and set it over low heat. Heat the wok until smoke starts to appear. Then put the duck on the steaming rack and cover the wok. Smoke the duck for 15 minutes.

Remove the duck from the wok. Mix the maltose syrup and vinegar in a small bowl and brush the skin of the duck with this syrup. Let it dry at room temperature for 1 hour.

Heat the vegetable oil in a wok over high heat until it is beginning to shimmer, about 350°F. Fry the duck in the hot oil, using a ladle to pour the oil over the duck and turning the duck over every few minutes, for a total of 15 minutes or until the skin is crisp and browned.

Carve the breast meat off the bones and slice it ½ inch thick. Cut the legs and wings in half. Arrange the breast meat on a plate with the leg and wing pieces alongside. Serve the duck accompanied by the sweet bean paste and julienned scallions. If you like, stuff the duck meat, sweet bean paste, and scallions into steamed buns.

SIZZLED CONCH WITH SPICY DRESSING

CHAPTER SIXTEEN

Appetizing Cold Dishes

I ONCE TOOK MY FRIEND MAUREEN TO A SICHUAN RESTAURANT IN THE FLUSHING NEIGHBORHOOD OF NEW YORK CITY. Over the past several decades this area has turned into one of the most vibrant Chinese immigrant quarters in the United States—not the traditional immigrants from the southern provinces of China, but rather people from northern and western parts of the country. The restaurant we visited was operated by an immigrant from Chengdu and offers up truly authentic Sichuan food. Along one side of the dining room, next to the entrance, was a long refrigerated display case. In it a huge array of cold dishes was exhibited: beef tripe in chile oil, spicy pig's ear with cilantro, cucumber in chile sauce, Chinese celery and pressed tofu with *mala* dressing, and a myriad of other vibrantly colored dishes. Maureen, who was originally from Boston and had not been exposed to many authentic Chinese restaurants, was so mesmerized by these cold dishes that when we sat down she ordered at least eight of them.

Very few people outside of China know that a large variety of cold dishes are common to the cuisine. The ingredients in cold dishes are normally marinated, pickled, fermented, or precooked. Precooked cold dishes include flavor-potted food served at room temperature, or aspic dishes served cold. While traditionally raw food, other than garnishes, is almost never served, some modern restaurants are beginning to adopt the Western tradition of serving salad and crudités.

Broadly speaking, Chinese cold dish techniques can be categorized into three loosely defined groups: dressed cold dishes, pickled dishes, and precooked dishes. In dressed cold dishes, cooked ingredients are served with a sauce on top. Pickled dishes can be either cured in a spiced soy sauce brine or fermented. Precooked dishes are more elaborate in preparations and are either flavor-potted (see page 221) or braised in natural gelatin and molded into aspic to make one of the most sophisticated cold dishes one can find.

Similar to the Western dining custom, Chinese cold dishes are offered at the beginning of a meal as appetizers. A few different cold dishes are usually served together in slightly smaller portions than main courses. This assortment of cold dishes can truly increase one's appetite in anticipation of the meal to come.

DRESSED COLD DISHES | 涼拌

The most common Chinese cold dishes are made with cooked ingredients that are dressed with a sauce, which can range from a simple soy sauce, vinegar, and sesame oil vinaigrette to a thick, rich sesame dressing. Main ingredients often include chicken, shrimp, jellyfish, tofu, and eggplant.

Many different ways of precooking the main ingredient are used, but the most common ones are boiling and steaming. These techniques normally retain the natural taste of the ingredient, allowing the dressing or sauce to become the defining flavor. The timing for precooking the main ingredient is very important. Meat should be cooked until it is tender but not to the point of falling apart, whereas vegetables should always be cooked al dente so as to retain a certain crunch. Raw ingredients are becoming very popular in salads and are usually dressed in similar sauces.

BLACK VINEGAR AND GARLIC VINAIGRETTE | 蒜香涼拌汁

This garlicky black vinaigrette is excellent for cold vegetable dishes. A little bit of chile oil can be added to make it spicy. | MAKES ⅓ CUP DRESSING

2 tablespoons soy sauce

1 tablespoon Chinkiang black vinegar

1 tablespoon toasted sesame oil

1 tablespoon minced garlic

1 teaspoon sugar

Combine all the ingredients in a small bowl or jar and mix well. Let the sauce rest for about 20 minutes to allow the vinegar to mellow the garlic's sharp taste before serving.

MALA SPICY VINAIGRETTE
麻辣凉拌汁

Mala is the classic Sichuan flavor of numbing and spicy heat. This dressing is excellent for creating a Sichuan-inspired cold dish. | MAKES ⅓ CUP DRESSING

1 tablespoon whole Sichuan peppercorns

¼ cup vegetable oil

1 tablespoon soy sauce

1 tablespoon Sichuan Spiced Chile Oil (see page 59)

1 tablespoon toasted sesame oil

1 teaspoon Chinkiang black vinegar

1 tablespoon minced garlic

1 tablespoon minced fresh ginger

1 tablespoon minced scallions

1 teaspoon Chinese red chile flakes

½ teaspoon Sichuan peppercorn powder

1 teaspoon sugar

Toast the whole Sichuan peppercorns in a dry wok or frying pan over medium heat, moving them around to prevent them from burning, for about 10 minutes or until fragrant.

Add the vegetable oil to the wok and reduce the heat to low. Simmer for 10 minutes. Strain the oil into a small container and discard the peppercorns.

Add the soy sauce, chile oil, sesame oil, vinegar, garlic, ginger, scallions, dried chiles, Sichuan peppercorn powder, and sugar to the spiced oil and mix well. Let the dressing rest for about 15 minutes before using.

SESAME PASTE DRESSING
芝麻凉拌汁

One of the most common sauces for cold dishes is this sesame paste dressing, which pairs equally well with meat and vegetables. This sauce is excellent for use on raw vegetables such as lettuce or cucumbers as well. | MAKES ⅓ CUP DRESSING

2 tablespoons Chinese toasted sesame paste

1 teaspoon toasted sesame oil

1 teaspoon chile oil (optional)

1 teaspoon white rice vinegar

2 teaspoons minced garlic

½ teaspoon salt

1 teaspoon sugar

Combine the sesame paste and 2 tablespoons water in a small bowl and mix well. Add the sesame oil, chile oil (if using), vinegar, garlic, salt, and sugar and mix well. Let the sauce rest for about 10 minutes before using.

COLD CHICKEN IN SESAME SAUCE | 麻醬雞絲
ZHEJIANG

Hailing from the Yangtze River Delta region, this cold dish is great in the summer. The chicken and cucumber combination creates a contrast in textures, and the sesame paste sauce enlivens the flavor. | SERVES 4 OR MORE, AS AN APPETIZER

½ cup Shaoxing cooking wine

1 (1-inch-long) piece of fresh ginger, crushed with the flat side of a knife

8 ounces boneless, skinless chicken breast

6 ounces cucumber, peeled and cut into strips 2 inches long and ⅛ inch thick

Sesame Paste Dressing (page 329)

1 tablespoon toasted sesame oil

1 teaspoon sesame seeds

1 tablespoon chopped cilantro

Combine 3 cups water with the wine and ginger in a medium saucepan and bring to a boil. Submerge the chicken breast in the boiling water and simmer over medium heat for 5 minutes, until just cooked through. Drain the chicken and let it cool. Shred the chicken with your fingers into thin strands.

Arrange the cucumber strips on a plate and mound the shredded chicken on top. Pour the sesame dressing over the chicken and drizzle with the sesame oil. Sprinkle the sesame seeds and chopped cilantro on top before serving.

EGGPLANT SALAD | 涼拌茄子
SHANGHAI

One of the oldest vegetables recorded in Chinese cuisine, eggplant can be stir-fried, stuffed and steamed, or served cold as a salad, as in this recipe. The garlic creates a nice spicy kick and the vinegar boosts the subtle flavor of the nightshade. | SERVES 4 OR MORE, AS AN APPETIZER

3 Asian eggplants (about 1 pound total)

Black Vinegar and Garlic Vinaigrette (page 327)

1 scallion green, thinly sliced

3 cilantro sprigs, coarsely chopped

1 small fresh red chile, thinly sliced (optional)

Preheat the broiler.

Put the eggplants on a broiling pan and broil for about 8 minutes on each side, until the skin is completely blistered. Let the eggplants cool, then remove the skin. It should separate easily: Simply pull it away from the flesh, starting at the tip and pulling back toward the stem. Try to leave the stem intact. Arrange the eggplants on a flat plate and cut the flesh lengthwise with three long slashes to create long strips.

Just before serving, pour the vinaigrette evenly over the eggplants. Garnish with the sliced scallion green and chopped cilantro, as well as the red chile, if desired, and serve immediately.

EGGPLANT SALAD

CHINESE CELERY AND
PRESSED TOFU SALAD

CHINESE CELERY AND PRESSED TOFU SALAD | 香乾拌芹菜

SICHUAN

Chinese celery and pressed tofu make a winning combination. The crunch from the celery and the firm, chewy quality of the tofu create a study in contrasting textures. Pressed tofu is usually flavored with five-spice or smoked. Either one works well in this recipe. If Chinese celery is not available, use regular celery but be sure to remove the strings before cutting it into strips.

SERVES 4 OR MORE, AS AN APPETIZER

DRESSING

1 tablespoon toasted sesame oil

2 teaspoons white rice vinegar

1 teaspoon Sichuan peppercorn powder

½ teaspoon Chinese red chile flakes

1 teaspoon salt

1 teaspoon sugar

8 ounces pressed tofu, cut into ⅛-inch-thick strips

4 ounces Chinese celery, cut into 2-inch pieces

1 fresh red chile, seeded and cut into strips 2 inches long and 1/16 inch thick

Mix the dressing ingredients together in a medium bowl. Add the tofu, celery, and chile strips and toss together. Refrigerate for at least 10 minutes and up to 2 hours before serving chilled.

SHRIMP SALAD WITH MUSTARD MAYONNAISE | 芥末蝦沙拉

GUANGDONG

Mayonnaise is not an ingredient one would expect to find in a Chinese recipe, but don't be put off by its use here. This is an imitation Western shrimp salad that was popular around the mid-20th century and was often served at Cantonese banquets. It is now out of style but it is still delicious, so it is due for a comeback.

SERVES 4 OR MORE, AS AN APPETIZER

⅓ cup Shaoxing cooking wine

4 thin slices fresh ginger

1 scallion (white, green, or both white and green parts), cut into 2-inch pieces

8 ounces medium shrimp, shelled but not deveined

SALAD DRESSING

1 tablespoon toasted sesame oil

1 tablespoon dried mustard powder

¼ cup mayonnaise

GARNISH

1 tablespoon sesame seeds

Chopped cilantro

In a medium saucepan, combine 2 cups water, the wine, ginger, and scallion and bring to a boil. Simmer for 5 minutes. Add the shrimp and boil for just 2 minutes, until they are turning pink. Do not overcook.

Drain the shrimp thoroughly, discarding the liquid and the aromatics. Let the shrimp cool for about 10 minutes or until cool to the touch. Then cut the shrimp in half lengthwise and devein them. Put the shrimp in the refrigerator, covered, to cool further for about 5 minutes.

In a medium bowl, mix the sesame oil, mustard, and mayonnaise. Stir in the shrimp, cover, and refrigerate until ready to serve or for up to 6 hours.

Arrange the shrimp decoratively on a plate and garnish with the sesame seeds and cilantro.

COLD PIG'S EAR IN CHILE OIL | 紅油豬耳

SICHUAN

Beloved by the Chinese, pig's ear is a perfect example of using texture as the primary quality in a dish. The brittle texture of the cartilage is a complete contrast to the soft skin. The bright red appearance of this Sichuan appetizer may seem alarming, but its flavor is at once spicy and cooling. | SERVES 4 OR MORE, AS AN APPETIZER

2 pig's ears (about 12 ounces total)

COOKING LIQUID

1 (1-inch-long) piece of fresh ginger, cut into 3 slices

2 scallions (white, green, or both white and green parts), cut into 2-inch pieces

3 whole star anise

1 teaspoon Sichuan peppercorns

1 teaspoon salt

SAUCE

1 tablespoon soy sauce

¼ cup Sichuan Spiced Chile Oil (see page 59), including some of the chile flakes

1 teaspoon toasted sesame oil

1 teaspoon Chinkiang black vinegar

1 teaspoon sugar

White sesame seeds, toasted

Cilantro sprigs

Put the pig's ears in a pot, add enough water to cover them completely, and bring the water to a boil over medium heat. Parboil the ears for about 20 minutes, skimming off any scum that forms on the surface. Drain the ears completely and discard the water.

Put the pig's ears and all the ingredients for the cooking liquid in a medium saucepan. Add 4 cups water and bring to a boil. Turn the heat down to low and gently simmer the pig's ears for 45 minutes, until tender. Drain the pig's ears and let them cool.

Cut the pig's ears into 2-inch-long, ⅛-inch-thick strips. Combine all the sauce ingredients in a large bowl and mix well. Toss the pig's ear strips in the sauce, then transfer them to a rimmed plate. Garnish with the sesame seeds and cilantro before serving.

SIZZLED CONCH WITH SPICY DRESSING | 熗螺片

YUNNAN

A variation on precooking ingredients for cold dishes is to quickly cook them in hot oil. This technique is perfect for delicate foods such as shellfish or fish. This recipe is inspired by the flavors of Yunnan and marries garlic, chile, peanuts, and sesame seeds to create a complex taste. | SERVES 4 OR MORE, AS AN APPETIZER

SAUCE

1 tablespoon soy sauce

2 tablespoons vegetable oil

1 tablespoon toasted sesame oil

2 tablespoons Chinkiang black vinegar

1 tablespoon sugar

3 cups vegetable oil

12 ounces conch, thinly sliced

3 tablespoons minced garlic

2 tablespoons ground unsalted peanuts

2 tablespoons Chinese red chile flakes

1 tablespoon sesame seeds, toasted

1 cup chopped cilantro

Combine all the ingredients for the sauce in a small bowl.

Heat the vegetable oil in a wok over high heat until it is beginning to shimmer, about 350°F. Put the conch in the oil, stirring to separate the slices, and cook for about 5 seconds, until the slices curl slightly. Remove the conch from the oil and drain it thoroughly on paper towels, then transfer it to a shallow bowl.

Pour the sauce over the conch and garnish with the garlic, peanuts, chile flakes, sesame seeds, and cilantro.

Marinating or pickling in flavored brine can be accomplished in a few hours, or over a longer period of time that sometimes lasts for a few days. But the basic preparation technique is the same. Mostly used for vegetables, the method calls for making a brine with different spices and then marinating the vegetable.

Another variation of Chinese pickling, known as *jiang* (醬), uses soy sauce as the pickling brine. The soy sauce is often fortified with sugar, giving it a salty and sweet taste. This pickling technique can be used for cucumbers, celtuce stems, and radishes. *Jiang* pickles are most commonly served as a side dish or as an accompaniment to rice porridge.

SWEET-AND-SOUR WATERMELON RADISH | 甜酸蘿蔔絲
BEIJING

Watermelon radishes are native to northern China and are very popular in the region. They are used as a garnish for noodles, cooked in soups, and made into pickles. This sweet-and-sour pickle can easily be made at the last minute. | SERVES 4 OR MORE, AS AN APPETIZER

2 medium watermelon radishes

1 tablespoon white rice vinegar

½ teaspoon salt

1 tablespoon sugar

2 tablespoons chopped scallion greens

Peel the radishes and julienne the pink flesh into matchstick pieces about ⅛ inch thick. Put the radishes in a bowl and stir in the vinegar, salt, and sugar. Marinate in the refrigerator for at least 15 minutes before serving cold, garnished with the scallion greens.

CUCUMBER SALAD
WITH GARLIC | 涼拌黃瓜
HOME-STYLE

This cucumber salad is simple and can be made at the last minute. It can be eaten as is or used as a base for a more complex salad. Add some chile oil and it becomes a spicy salad. Add parboiled carrots, wood ear mushrooms, or peanuts and you have a mixed salad. | SERVES 4 OR MORE, AS AN APPETIZER

1 large hothouse or 3 small Persian cucumbers (8 ounces total)

½ teaspoon salt

1 tablespoon finely minced garlic

1 tablespoon toasted sesame oil

Quarter the cucumbers lengthwise and slice off the center portions to remove the seeds. (For large hothouse cucumbers you may want to further cut the quarters lengthwise into eighths.) Then cut the lengths into 2-inch-long pieces.

Put the cucumbers in a bowl, sprinkle with the salt and garlic, and mix well. Cover and refrigerate for 20 minutes.

When you are ready to serve the salad, drain the juice that the salt has extracted from the cucumber pieces, retaining as much of the garlic as possible, and arrange the cucumbers on a plate. Pour the sesame oil over the cucumbers and serve cold.

CUCUMBER SALAD WITH GARLIC

SPICY LOTUS ROOT SALAD
麻辣拌蓮藕

SICHUAN

The crunchy texture and the mild taste of lotus root makes it a perfect canvas for showcasing Sichuan mala. | SERVES 4 OR MORE, AS AN APPETIZER

1 large section fresh lotus root (about 8 ounces)

1 tablespoon Sichuan peppercorns

2 tablespoons vegetable oil

1 tablespoon Chinese red chile flakes

1 teaspoon white rice vinegar

1 teaspoon sugar

1 tablespoon toasted sesame oil

1 tablespoon minced garlic

1 teaspoon salt

2 tablespoons chopped cilantro

Peel off the outer skin of the lotus root with a vegetable peeler. Cut the lotus root crosswise into ⅛-inch-thick slices. Put the lotus root slices in a medium saucepan and add enough water to cover. Bring the water to a boil, then simmer for about 10 minutes, until the lotus root is soft and crunchy but not mushy. Drain well and transfer to a shallow bowl. Refrigerate until cool.

Toast the peppercorns in a dry wok or frying pan over medium heat, moving them around to prevent burning, for 10 minutes or until fragrant. Turn off the heat, and crush the peppercorns with a large spoon. Add the vegetable oil and red chile flakes to the wok. Stir over low heat for 10 minutes or until the oil turns red. Pour the spice oil from the wok into a medium bowl, and mix it with the vinegar, sugar, sesame oil, garlic, and salt.

Add the lotus root to the sauce and mix well. Marinate in the refrigerator for at least 2 hours and up to 6 hours. Before serving, garnish with the cilantro.

SOY-PICKLED DAIKON RADISH
醬蘿蔔

SHANDONG

Pickling in soy brine is one of China's ancient methods of preserving vegetables. Any firm vegetable can be used for pickling once its moisture is leached out using salt and sugar. Cucumbers and celtuce stems are both excellent options. | SERVES 4 OR MORE, AS AN APPETIZER

1 medium daikon radish (12 ounces)

2 teaspoons salt

1 tablespoon sugar

SOY PICKLING BRINE

3 tablespoons soy sauce

2 teaspoons white rice vinegar

2 tablespoons sugar

Peel the daikon radishes and slice them very thin (for the best results, use a mandoline to slice them). Put the daikon slices in a medium bowl and sprinkle with the salt. Stir the daikon well to make sure the salt is applied evenly and let it marinate for about 30 minutes at room temperature. At this point, the moisture will have bled out of the daikon and collected in the bottom of the bowl. Squeeze as much of the liquid out of the daikon as possible and discard all the liquid.

Sprinkle the sugar over the daikon and mix well. Let the daikon marinate for another 30 minutes at room temperature. As with the salt, a pool of liquid will form at the bottom of the bowl. Once again squeeze out as much of the liquid as possible and discard all the liquid.

Add the ingredients for the soy pickling brine to the daikon and mix well. Transfer the daikon and brine to a storage container, cover, and refrigerate at least overnight or for up to a month.

Serve the pickled radish in a small bowl with some of the soy brine.

FERMENTED PICKLED DISHES | 酸醃

Pickling by fermentation is an ancient method of preserving food that also creates beneficial probiotics. Although the Chinese have long valued the idea of consuming fermented food as a healthful practice, Western scientists substantiated this advantage only over the past century. The real craze over probiotics did not start until just recently.

To start the fermentation process, a spiced salt brine is put together. Then vegetables are added to the brine and left at room temperature to ferment. Known as lacto-fermentation, the process creates acid and lowers the pH level, making it possible to store the pickles for an extended period of time.

The fermentation works best if the ingredients are kept in a special pickling jar that is made with a trough around the mouth. During fermentation a cover is placed over the mouth and water is poured into the trough. As the carbon dioxide gas builds up during fermentation, it pushes through the water at the cover and escapes without letting outside air return inside. This will prevent contamination from other harmful bacteria. However, it is possible to pickle in a tightly sealed clean plastic container. Just remember to open the lid slightly every day to let the gas escape.

SICHUAN FERMENTED PICKLES
四川泡菜

SICHUAN

Pickling using a fermentation process similar to the ones used to make Korean kimchi or European sauerkraut is an excellent way of adding probiotics to food. The spicy and sour taste of this pickle makes it an ideal accompaniment to other more complex Sichuan dishes. | SERVES 8 OR MORE, AS AN ACCOMPANIMENT TO OTHER DISHES

PICKLING BRINE

¼ cup salt

1 cup white rice wine

6 whole star anise

10 dried red chiles

1 teaspoon Sichuan peppercorns

4 bay leaves

1 pound cabbage, cut into 2-inch squares

8 ounces daikon radish, cut into ½-inch-thick strips

8 ounces green radish, cut into ½-inch-thick strips

8 ounces carrots, cut into ½-inch-thick strips

1 (1½-inch-long) piece of fresh ginger, cut into ¼-inch-thick slices

2 fresh red long horn chiles

2 fresh green long horn chiles

Bring a generous 4½ quarts water to a boil in a pot. Thoroughly clean a 1-gallon Chinese pickling jar or a glass container with a lid. To sterilize the jar, pour about 2 cups boiling water into the jar, swirl the hot water around, and then discard the water.

To make the pickling brine, measure 2½ quarts boiling water and pour it into a clean saucepan. Add

(CONTINUES)

the salt and stir to dissolve it, then let the brine cool. Stir the rice wine, star anise, dried chiles, Sichuan peppercorns, and bay leaves into the cooled brine.

Put the cabbage pieces, daikon and green radish strips, carrot strips, ginger slices, and red and green chiles in the pickling jar, pushing them down firmly. Pour the brine into the jar, making sure the liquid completely covers all the vegetables. (If necessary, boil extra water and pour it into the jar so all the vegetables are submerged.) Fill the trough of the pickling jar halfway with water. Cover the jar and let it stand in a cool area of the kitchen for 7 to 10 days. The longer the vegetables are fermented, the more sour they become.

Beginning on the seventh day, periodically remove the cover and sample the vegetables. When the sourness of the vegetables is to your liking, remove them from the jar and store them in a covered clean container in the refrigerator for up to 4 months.

Cut the vegetables into small pieces about ¼ inch thick before serving.

ASPIC 凍

Chinese cooks have long taken advantage of naturally occurring gelatin to make wonderfully elegant aspic dishes. Pig's skin and pig's feet are full of collagen that will dissolve when cooked in a liquid. When cooled, the liquid gels and the cook can suspend all sorts of ingredients in it.

When making the gelatin broth, the Chinese use herbs and spices to enhance the already rich pork broth. To ensure that the liquid remains clear, a very low temperature is used when simmering the broth. (There is no clarification technique using an egg white raft in Chinese cooking.) An alternative method is to put pig's skin in an aromatic broth and then steam the combination for 3 to 4 hours; this can also produce beautifully clear gelatin liquid for making aspic.

In most Chinese aspic recipes the pig's skin or pig's feet used for making the gelatin ultimately become part of the ingredients suspended in the jelly. Sometimes shellfish is also incorporated in a jelly. In those situations, making the liquid with fish stock and pig's skin would infuse great seafood flavors into the finished jelly.

CURED PIG'S FEET IN ASPIC | 水晶淆蹄

JIANGSU

Cured ham hock in aspic may not sound like a great combination at first. But this beautifully pink meat, along with aromatic aspic, is simply as delicious as it is stunning. Originating in the city of Jinjiang, this savory dish is accented perfectly by fragrant black vinegar and thinly julienned ginger. Curing the ham hock takes 2 days, so be aware that it takes 3 days to complete this dish. | SERVES 6 OR MORE, AS AN APPETIZER

4 fresh ham hocks (6 pounds total; ask your butcher to cut the ham hocks lengthwise, splitting the bones in half)

CURING MIX

3 tablespoons salt

2 teaspoons pink salt

BRAISING AROMATICS AND SPICES

1 (1-inch-long) piece of fresh ginger, cut into 3 pieces

2 scallions (white, green, or both white and green parts), cut into 2-inch pieces

4 whole star anise

1 teaspoon Sichuan peppercorns

½ cup Shaoxing cooking wine

½ teaspoon salt

DIPPING SAUCE

2 tablespoons Chinkiang black vinegar

2 tablespoons julienned fresh ginger

Wash and thoroughly dry the ham hocks. In a small bowl, combine the two salts for the curing mix; spread the mixture evenly over the meat side of the ham hocks. Put the hocks in a roasting pan, skin-side down. Refrigerate, covered, for 2 days.

Remove the ham hocks from the refrigerator and rinse them thoroughly. Wrap the braising aromatics and spices in cheesecloth and tie it tightly. Put the ham hocks, skin-side down, in layers in a stockpot and then add 2 quarts water, the wine, and the salt. Put the cheesecloth bag in the pot and bring the liquid to a boil. Immediately turn the heat down to very low and simmer the ham hocks very slowly for 2 hours.

Remove and discard the cheesecloth bag and drain the ham hocks, reserving the braising liquid. When the meat is cool to the touch, remove the bones from the ham hocks. Arrange the ham hock meat, skin-side down, at the bottom of a 9-inch square mold. Pour the braising liquid over the ham hocks and then cover and refrigerate overnight or for up to 4 days.

When you are ready to serve the aspic, unmold it by dipping the mold in a hot water bath for 30 seconds and then flipping it over onto a plate. Cut the aspic into slices about 2 inches long, 1 inch wide, and ⅛ inch thick. Arrange the slices decoratively on a plate. Stir together the black vinegar and julienned ginger and serve on the side.

OLD BEIJING BEAN AND PIG'S SKIN ASPIC | 老北京豆醬

BEIJING

This traditional Beijing aspic is perfect as a summer appetizer, and pork skin not only is excellent for creating gelatin but also is rich in umami. The addition of edamame, pressed tofu, and carrots to the aspic provides extra texture and color. When sliced into cubes and arranged decoratively on a plate, this dish makes a beautiful presentation. | SERVES 6 OR MORE, AS AN APPETIZER

6 ounces pig skin

BRAISING LIQUID

½ cup white rice wine

1 tablespoon dark soy sauce

1 tablespoon soy sauce

1 (2-inch-long) piece of fresh ginger

1 teaspoon salt

BRAISING SPICES

3 whole star anise

1 teaspoon Sichuan peppercorns

½ ounce cassia bark

2 bay leaves

1 small carrot, cut into ½-inch cubes

6 ounces five-spice pressed tofu, cut into ½-inch cubes

⅓ cup shelled edamame

DRESSING

¼ cup Chinkiang black vinegar

2 tablespoons minced garlic

Put the pig's skin in a pot, add enough water to cover it completely, and bring the water to a boil over medium heat. Parboil the skin for about 10 minutes, skimming off any scum that forms on the surface. Drain the skin completely and discard the water.

Return the pig's skin to the saucepan and add all the braising liquid ingredients along with 4 cups water. Wrap the braising spices in cheesecloth and tie it tightly. Put the spice sachet in the saucepan and bring the liquid to a boil, then turn the heat down to very low and simmer the pig's skin, covered, for about 2 hours.

Discard the ginger and the spice sachet. Take the pig's skin out and set it aside on a cutting board. Add the carrot cubes to the braising liquid and cook for about 5 minutes or until they are tender. Add the pressed tofu and the edamame to the braising liquid and continue to cook for 2 minutes. Turn the heat off and set the braising liquid aside to cool slightly.

Cut the pig's skin into 2-inch-long, ⅛-inch-thick strips. Put the strips in a 9 by 4-inch mold. Pour the braising liquid, including the vegetables, into the mold. With a spoon, mix the pork skin strips and the vegetables so they spread evenly throughout the mold. Cover and refrigerate overnight or for up to 4 days.

Before serving, combine the dressing ingredients in a small bowl and let the garlic marinate for about 30 minutes.

When you are ready to serve the aspic, unmold it by dipping the mold in a hot water bath for 30 seconds and then flipping it over onto a plate. Cut the aspic into 1-inch cubes. Stack the blocks decoratively on a plate and pour the vinegar-garlic dressing all over the aspic.

CHAPTER SEVENTEEN

Sweet but Not Dessert

JUST BECAUSE DESSERT IS NOT PART OF THE NORMAL CHINESE DINING CONCEPT DOESN'T MEAN THAT THERE ARE NO SWEET DISHES IN CHINESE COOKING. In actuality Chinese sweet dishes are diverse and delicious—they just aren't necessarily served at the end of a meal. They are more commonly served along with other savory dishes. This is rather perplexing to many Americans. However, the Western notion of dessert is beginning to have an influence, and many upscale restaurants in China are now designating a special dessert section on their menu to accommodate this change in the dining public's attitude.

Many Chinese sweet dishes are made with the same cooking techniques as savory dishes. For example, sweet herbal soups are prepared the same way as savory braised soups. It is also common to make savory dishes using sugar-cooking techniques. A prime example is steamed ham in syrup, where salted ham is sliced and steamed in a sugar syrup flavored with dried osmanthus blossom.

The first of the three main techniques for cooking with sugar is to cook a dish in sugar syrup, thus sweetening the main ingredients. The second is to caramelize the sugar before coating the main ingredients in it, creating a hard, crunchy outside layer. The third, sugar coating, covers the main ingredients with a white sugar crust that is dry but not crunchy. All these techniques are used to make sweet dishes that are served alongside savory dishes.

COOKING IN SYRUP | 蜜汁

I was invited to dine at Peng Yuan restaurant (彭園湘菜館) when I visited Chef Peng Chang-Kuei's family in Taipei. Chef Peng, who was originally from Hunan, was the creator of General Tso's Chicken (see page 173), as well as numerous other modern Hunan dishes. The night I had dinner with the Peng family, I was served one of his celebrated dishes: thin rectangular slices of ham steeped in fragrant sugar syrup, accompanied by crisp rectangles of fried tofu skin, all served in sandwich-style steamed buns. It was simply the most wonderful taste sensation of a ham dish I've ever had: delicate syrup moistening the rich ham paired with the texture duo of crunchy tofu skin and soft buns. Chef Peng named his dish Double Fortune Squares (富貴雙方), referring to the ham and tofu skin in the sandwich. This is the ultimate example of cooking with syrup in Chinese food, attesting to the genius of Chef Peng.

Syrup is used extensively in Chinese cooking. Braising and steaming fresh fruits, root vegetables, and medicinal herbs in syrup is very common. The same cooking techniques described in previous chapters for braising and steaming are all relevant for cooking with syrup. The only difference is that the braising liquid is a simple syrup that's almost always lightly scented with osmanthus blossoms.

The use of the delicate flavor of sugar syrup to blend with a stronger, more pronounced taste is a trick the Chinese customarily use to incorporate medicinal herbs into a remedy. A little bit of sugar does help the medicine go down, just as Mary Poppins says!

STUFFED LOTUS ROOTS IN SYRUP | 桂花糖藕

Shanghai cooking has a reputation of being heavily sweetened, and this dish certainly reinforces that image. It is one of the most common sweet dishes that accompany savory dishes. The lotus root is stuffed with glutinous rice and then stewed in a syrup flavored with osmanthus blossom. The cooked root is cut into thin slices, which are displayed like floral wheels covered with the fragrant syrup. It is incredibly delicious paired with other heavier-flavored Shanghai dishes. | SERVES 4 OR MORE, AS AN APPETIZER

2 medium lotus root sections (1 pound total), peeled

¼ cup glutinous rice, soaked in 2 cups water for about 4 hours

¾ cup sugar

1 tablespoon dried osmanthus blossoms

2 teaspoons tapioca starch

Cut a ½-inch-thick slice from one end of each lotus root section and set the slices aside. Drain the glutinous rice thoroughly and stuff the holes of the lotus roots with the rice, tapping the section as you do so to ensure that the holes are completely filled. Replace the ends of the lotus roots and use three or four strong toothpicks to secure each one. Be sure to insert the toothpicks at an angle to anchor them tightly.

In a medium saucepan, combine 4 cups water, the sugar, and the osmanthus blossoms, and bring the water to a boil. Put the lotus roots in the pan and turn the heat to medium. Gently boil the lotus roots for about 1½ hours.

In a small bowl, mix the tapioca starch with 3 tablespoons water to make a slurry.

Remove the roots from the syrup and set them aside to cool to room temperature. Bring the syrup to a boil again and add the tapioca starch slurry, stirring to thicken the syrup. Cool the syrup as well.

To serve, cut the lotus roots crosswise into wheels. Arrange them decoratively on a plate and pour the syrup all over the slices.

STEAMED HAM IN OSMANTHUS BLOSSOM SAUCE | 蜜汁火腿

HUNAN

This recipe is a simpler version of the Double Fortune Squares (see page 349) created by Chef Peng Chang-Kuei. Air-dried ham from the city of Jinhua in Zhejiang province is recommended for this recipe, but unfortunately, it is not possible to obtain Jinhua ham in the United States. Luckily, dry-cured Virginia ham is very similar in taste and makes a good substitute.

SERVES 4 OR MORE, AS AN APPETIZER

12 ounces dry-cured Virginia ham, thinly sliced and cut into 8 (2 by 3-inch) pieces

¾ cup sugar

2 tablespoons Shaoxing cooking wine

1 tablespoon dried osmanthus blossoms

½ teaspoon tapioca starch

8 sandwich-style steamed buns

Arrange the ham slices decoratively in a 7-inch bowl. Add 1 cup water and ¼ cup sugar to the bowl. Put a wire rack in a wok, add about 5 cups water, and bring the water to a boil. Put the bowl on the steaming rack, cover the wok, and steam the ham for about 1 hour.

Pour off and discard the syrup, leaving the ham in the bowl, and pour 1 cup fresh water and another ¼ cup sugar into the bowl; steam for another hour.

Repeat this process one more time, but do not discard this final batch of syrup. (The purpose of this three-step process is to remove excess salt from the ham and replace it with sugar.)

Drain the syrup into a saucepan and add the wine and osmanthus blossoms. Bring the syrup to a boil and cook for about 3 minutes.

In a small bowl, mix the tapioca starch with 2 tablespoons water to make a slurry.

Strain the syrup into a clean saucepan, discarding the osmanthus blossoms. Return the syrup to the heat, add the tapioca starch slurry, and stir until thickened.

Invert the bowl with the ham over a rimmed serving plate and release the ham onto the plate. Pour the syrup over the ham. Serve with sandwich-style steamed buns.

CARAMEL COATING | 拔絲，琉璃

There are two stages of sugar caramelization that the Chinese have learned to exploit in their cooking. The first one is a common practice similar to the Western technique of caramel coating for nuts and dried fruits. In this case the sugar is heated until it reaches the hard crack stage, then tossed with nuts or dried fruits before cooling. It is a great way to add crunch to ingredients. Candied nuts and dried fruits are commonly served on the side at Chinese banquets.

The other is a curious technique of heating sugar to the soft crack stage and using it to coat fresh fruits or root vegetables with piping-hot pliable caramel. The diner picks up a piece of the caramel-coated fruit, pulling strands of taffy along the way, and plunges it into ice water to instantly cool and harden the caramel before eating it. The cool, hard candy shell juxtaposes nicely with the soft, hot fruit center.

SESAME CANDIED WALNUTS
蜜核桃
HOME-STYLE

The sesame flavor on these candied walnuts is a pleasant twist on simple caramel. You have to work very quickly once the caramel is ready for coating. Make sure all the walnuts are coated and still warm when spreading them out on the baking sheet for cooling. This fast work will pay off with fragrant, crunchy, sweet walnuts.
MAKES 2 CUPS

2 cups walnut halves (8 ounces)
2 tablespoons toasted sesame oil
½ cup sugar
2 tablespoons sesame seeds

Preheat the oven to 350°F.

Spread the walnut halves in a single layer on a rimmed baking sheet and roast them in the oven for about 5 minutes. Make sure they are just lightly browned—do not overcook them. Put the walnuts in a bowl and set them aside.

Line the baking sheet with parchment paper and grease the parchment with 1 tablespoon sesame oil. Keep all the ingredients readily accessible near the stove so you can work quickly when the sugar caramelizes.

Heat the sugar and 1 tablespoon water in a wok over medium heat, stirring the sugar around with a wooden spoon. Keep stirring while the sugar melts and the bubbles turn from large to tiny. When the color of the sugar syrup turns yellowish, add the walnuts. Immediately add the remaining 1 tablespoon sesame oil and the sesame seeds, and stir the walnuts quickly. Remove the walnuts from the wok and spread them out on the parchment paper–lined baking sheet, separating them while they are still hot. Let the walnuts cool completely before removing them from the parchment.

Serve the walnuts in a small bowl as table snack before dinner.

JUJUBE

SUGAR-COATED
CASHEW NUTS

SESAME CANDIED
WALNUTS

PULLED CARAMEL APPLE | 拔絲蘋果

BEIJING

One of the most fascinating sweet dishes in the Chinese cooking repertoire, pulled caramel apples have become a regular dessert offering in modern upscale restaurants. The apple pieces are first deep-fried in batter, then quickly coated with hot caramel. They are served hot, and diners pick up the caramel-coated apple and dip it into ice water to harden the coating. It is fun to eat in addition to being absolutely delicious. In place of apples, other ingredients such as banana, potato, sweet potato, or mountain yam can be substituted. The only adjustment is to coat root vegetables with flour instead of batter. | SERVES 6 OR MORE, AS A SWEET COURSE

2 tablespoons toasted sesame oil

1 teaspoon white sesame seeds, toasted

BATTER

¼ cup all-purpose flour

¼ cup tapioca starch

2 large eggs

2 large Fuji apples, peeled, cored, and cut into ¾-inch-thick pieces

3 cups vegetable oil

1 cup sugar

Grease a serving plate with 1 tablespoon of the sesame oil and set it aside. Fill two small bowls with ice water and set them aside. Keep the toasted sesame seeds and remaining 1 tablespoon sesame oil readily accessible.

Combine the batter ingredients in a medium bowl and mix well. Submerge the apple pieces in the batter, making sure that all the pieces are coated. Heat the vegetable oil in a wok until it is shimmering, about 350°F. Deep-fry the apple by dropping individual pieces into the hot oil and cooking until they are light yellow. Remove the apple pieces from the wok and drain them on paper towels. Reheat the oil to about 395°F and fry the apple pieces again until golden brown. Drain the fried apples on paper towels to absorb any excess oil.

Remove all but 2 tablespoons of the vegetable oil from the wok. Add the sugar and 2 tablespoons water to the wok and turn the heat to medium. Stir the sugar continuously as it melts. The melted sugar will produce large bubbles at the beginning and will turn a yellowish color. When the bubbles become fewer and tiny and the color turns brown, reduce the heat to low. The sugar temperature should have reached about 300°F at this point. Immediately add the apple pieces to the caramel and toss them gently, making sure all the pieces are coated. Do not disturb the apple pieces too much lest the batter coating fall apart. Drizzle the remaining 1 tablespoon sesame oil all over the apple pieces and sprinkle with the sesame seeds.

Put the candied apple pieces on the oiled serving plate. Serve along with the two bowls of ice water for dipping.

SUGAR COATING | 掛霜

Also known as "snow coating" in Chinese, this technique is used for covering nuts and fresh fruits with a layer of white candy coating. Unlike caramel coating, the sugar is not heated to the point of the yellow soft crack stage; instead, it only reaches the firm ball stage or about 250°F. At this stage the sugar will harden to a white-colored soft candy resembling snow.

When the coating is used to coat fruits, the fruit is first coated with a batter and deep-fried. This approach is similar to the pulled caramel technique. The only difference is the type of sugar coating that results at the end. The sugar used for snow coating can be enhanced by adding flavoring agents. Almond extract, milk powder, and desiccated coconut are all excellent when sprinkled into the syrup just before it cools.

SUGAR-COATED CASHEW NUTS
掛霜腰果
HOME-STYLE

Serving a table snack before a dinner is a real treat, and candied cashews make an elegant choice. This recipe calls for desiccated coconut to be added to the coating, which makes it even more flavorful. Consider a collection of nuts including this one the next time you plan a Chinese dinner. | MAKES 2 CUPS

½ **cup granulated sugar**

¼ **cup desiccated coconut**

2 **cups unsalted dry-roasted cashews (about 8 ounces)**

2 **tablespoons confectioners' sugar**

Line a baking sheet with parchment paper and set it aside.

Put the granulated sugar and 3 tablespoons water in a wok and heat it over medium heat. As the sugar melts, large white bubbles will form. As the bubbles turn smaller, the temperature should reach about 250°F. Add the desiccated coconut and the cashews to the syrup and stir to completely cover the nuts with the syrup. Turn the heat off and sprinkle the confectioners' sugar over the cashews.

Remove the cashews from the wok and spread them out on the parchment paper–lined baking sheet. Let the nuts cool completely before serving them in a small bowl as a table snack before dinner.

ACKNOWLEDGMENTS

If I was told ten years ago that I would be writing a cookbook, I would have thought it a pipe dream. Yes, I'd been a very enthusiastic home cook for years, and spent six months interning in Chef Josh Capon's kitchen in Soho, but this was only the beginning of my culinary career. In 2008 my friend Kim Foster encouraged me to write about my cooking and my Chinese cooking blog, *Red Cook*, was born. Through this platform I found loyal supporters and progressively expanded my involvement in the culinary world.

I soon met Andrew Coe and Anne Mendelson, who introduced me to other food writers and historians. Gary Cheong, who has been a good friend and supporter for many years, introduced me to Wendy Chan, Shelley Menaged, and Kelly Ann Hargrove—all of whom furthered my ambition to pass on my knowledge of Chinese cooking to others.

Special thanks have to be given to Grace Young, who shared her deep knowledge of writing cookbooks and book proposals. I would not have been able to submit a proper book proposal without her guidance.

Of course, this book would not have been possible without the support of Steve Troha, my agent, and Rica Allannic, my editor. Thank you Steve for trusting me, and Rica for making this book a reality. Thank you to the entire team at Clarkson Potter, including Aaron Wehner, Doris Cooper, Sara Katz, Joyce Wong, Kim Tyner, Jane Treuhaft, Stephanie Huntwork, Ian Dingman, Michael Nagin, Anna Mintz, Lauren Velasquez, and designer Jan Derevjanik.

I would like to thank Warren Livesley and Russell Mills for being my first line editors. Thank you photographer Jody Horton, food stylist Suzanne Lenzer, and prop stylist Johanna Lowe for bringing a sense of animation to the illustrations. Much appreciation likewise goes to Jody's assistants, Christopher Corona and Sean Johnson, and to Suzanne's assistants, Kate Schmidt and Michaela Hayes. Also, thanks to Hwai-Ping Sheng and Barry Will in Hong Kong for helping me procure many of the props.

Recipe testing is a crucial part of writing a cookbook and I would like to thank my testers who are some of the most dedicated professionals and home cooks: Stephanie Browner, Adam Hickman, Diana Kuan, Margaret Chen, Simon Fan, Bob Fitterman, David Fitterman, and Evan Schwartz.

Thanks, too, to Peter D'Aquino, Dr. Wing On Tsang, and Professor Chi Fai Chau of National Chung Hsing University in Taiwan for helping me understand food therapy and its health benefits.

Finally, I would like to thank all those who helped connect me to the culinary professionals as well as chefs and food experts I consulted with in China and Taiwan: Thank you to: Christopher Kirwan, for introducing me to Chef Alan Yang at the Fairmont Beijing Hotel in Beijing; Sita Yeung, for escorting me to restaurants in Beijing; David Xu and Yuenchi Sze, for connecting me with Benjamin Luo, Yiwan Peng, and Chef Zhanghai Wang in Xiamen. Special thanks go to Yiwan Peng for teaching me the relationship of Fujian cooking and the ancient culinary traditions of the Central Plain. I also give a big hug to James Tang for introducing me to Chef Feng Zhou of the Fuxin Hotel in Qingdao. I learned so much from Chef Zhou regarding Northeastern Chinese cooking. In Chengdu, I thank Tom He, who was introduced to me by Diane Drey, for bringing along professors Shunbin He and Xuebin Qiao from Sichuan Higher Institute of Cuisine to explain the flavor profiles of Sichuan cuisine.

In Taiwan, thanks to Peiling Liu and Sabrina Liu for introducing me to Barbara Chang and Ann Chen. Barbara and Ann accompanied me everywhere in Taipei to visit with Chef YanJi Zeng (or Chef Ah Ji) and Kuo-Chen Tseng. Many thanks as well to Chuck Peng and Zhiling Chen for speaking to me about the life and cooking of Chef Chang-Kuei Peng.

My success depends on all the people who cheer me on and support my work, and I do not presume to have listed them all. My sincere apology and gratitude to anyone I neglected to list here.

BIBLIOGRAPHY

Anusasananan, Linda Lau. *The Hakka Cookbook*. Berkeley, CA: University of California Press, 2012.

Bailey, Alton Edward. *Bailey's Industrial Oil & Fat Products*. Hoboken, NJ: John Wiley & Sons, 2005.

Chang, Kwang-Chih. "Ancient China." In *Food in Chinese Culture*, by Kwang-Chih Chang. New Haven, CT: Yale University Press, 1977.

Chen, Mengyin. *Shi Jing (Dining Chronical)*. Hong Kong: The Commercial Press (H. K.) Ltd., 2009.

Chen, Wei. *The Complete Book of Roasted and Spiced Food*. Shanghai: World Publishing Company, 2004.

Chen, Yunpiao. "The Atar and the Table: Field Studies on the Dietary Culture of Chaoshan Inhabitants." In *Changing Chinese Foodways in Asia*, by Chee-beng Tan and David Y. H. Wu, 22. Hong Kong: The Chinese University Press, 2001.

China Cuisine Association; Japan Association of Chinese Cuisine. *Chinese Cooking Techniques*. Edited by Jian Shi and DongMei Zhao. Hong Kong: Wan Li Book Co., Ltd., 2006.

Coe, Andrew. *Chop Suey*. New York: Oxford University Press, 2009.

Kingham, Neil. *A User's Guide to Chinese Medicine*. CreateSpace Independent Publishing Platform, 2013.

Kuo, Irene. *The Key to Chinese Cooking*. New York: Alfred A. Knopf, 1977.

Kuwen Collection. *Mastering Basic Knife Techniques*. Beijing: China Textile Publishing House, 2012.

Lan, Ling. *Shandong Jujia Yinshi Xisu (Food and Drink Customs of Shandong)*. Jinan: Jinan Publishing House, 2012.

Lee, Jennifer 8. *The Fortune Cookie Chronicles*. New York: Twelve, 2008.

Lei, Dong. *Encyclopedia of Cooking and Seasoning*. Beijing: Beijing Science and Technology Press, 2013.

Naxon, Lenore. "My Dad, the Inventor of the Crock Pot," in *Beyond Bubbie*, April 8, 2013 (accessed March 1, 2014). http://www.beyondbubbie.com/my-dad-the-inventor-of-the-crock-pot

Peng, Yiwan. *Minnan Yinshi (Southern Min Cuisine)*. Xiamen, Fujian: Lujiang Publishing House.

Qiu, Pangtong. *Chinese Noodles History*. Qingdao: Qingdao Publishing House, 2010.

Southwest Frontier Minority Research Center, Yunnan University. "Yunnan Culinary Culture." *Social Science Front* (Jilin Academy of Social Sciences) 3 (2007).

Yang Chao, Buwei. *How to Cook and Eat in Chinese*, 3rd ed. New York: Vintage Books, 1972.

Young, Grace. *Stir-Frying to the Sky's Edge*. New York: Simon & Schuster, 2010.

———. *The Wisdom of the Chinese Kitchen*. New York: Simon & Schuster Editions, 1999.

Yu, Ying-Shih. "Han." In *Food in Chinese Culture*, by K. C. Chang. New Haven, CT: Yale University Press, 1977.

INDEX

Note: Page references in *italics* indicate recipe photographs.